*Di Guoyong*

*on*

*Xingyiquan*

*Volume II*
*Forms and Ideas*

Available from **tgl books**

Jiang Rongqiao's Baguazhang

Yan Dehua's Bagua Applications

Li Tianji's The Skill of Xingyiquan

Di Guoyong on Xingyiquan: Volume I, Foundations

Di Guoyong on Xingyiquan: Volume II, Forms and Ideas

Di Guoyong on Xingyiquan: Volume III, Weapons

A Shadow on Fallen Blossoms

Falk's Dictionary of Chinese Martial Arts

Beijing Bittersweet

Shadowboxing in Shanghai

www.thewushucentre.ca

# Di Guoyong
# on
# Xingyiquan

## Volume II
## Forms and Ideas

Third Edition of Form and Theory
The 2020 Set Edition

邸国勇
形意拳械精解
2020年修订版

translated and edited
by Andrea Mary Falk
霍安娣翻译，主板

Translation copyright © 2007 by Andrea Mary Falk

Third edition copyright © 2021 Andrea Mary Falk

The 2020 Set Edition

ISBN 978-1-989468-16-6

All Rights Reserved

---

Library and Archives Canada Cataloguing in Publication of first editions

Di, Guoyong. Di Guoyong on Xingyiquan / translated and edited by Andrea Falk. Translation of Xingyiquanxie Jingjie.

Complete contents: v. 1. Five element foundation -- v. 2. Theory and forms -- v. 3. Weapons and partner routines. ISBN 0-9687517-6-8 (v. 1) ISBN 0-9687517-7-6 (v. 2) ISBN 0-9687517-8-4 (v. 3)

1. Hand-to-hand fighting, Oriental. I. Falk, Andrea, 1954- II. Title.

GV1112.D51813 2005   796.815'5   C2005-904173-0

---

Volume II of a three volume set. Volume I Foundations. Volume II Forms and Ideas. Volume III Weapons.

Translated and edited by Andrea Falk 2006 to 2007 in Beijing, China, and in Victoria and Morin Heights, Canada.

With thanks for the assistance of Di Guoyong, Beijing.

Third Edition edited by Andrea Falk, 2021 in Québec, Canada.

The techniques described in this book are performed by experienced martial artists. The author, translator, and publishers are not responsible for any injury that may occur while trying out these techniques. Please do not apply these techniques on anyone without their consent and cooperation.

# TABLE OF CONTENTS

Translator's Preface to Volume II .....................................................vii
Translator's Preface to the Second Edition.........................................vii
Editor's Preface to the to 2020 Set Edition .......................................viii

## CHAPTER ONE: BAREHAND FORMS

The Eight Moves .................................................................1
The Twelve Great Punches ...............................................18
The Xingyi Composite Form ..............................................40
The Mixture of Moves .......................................................73

## CHAPTER TWO: THE EIGHT SKILLS

Introduction to the Eight Skills .........................................97
The Skill of Spreading ......................................................98
The Skill of Intercepting .................................................109
The Skill of Wrapping ....................................................114
The Skill of Bridging ......................................................120
The Skill of Scooping .....................................................131
The Skill of Butting ........................................................138
The Skill of Passing ........................................................146
The Skill of Guiding .......................................................153
The Eight Skills Connected Form ...................................164

## CHAPTER THREE: PARTNER FORM

Introduction to Protect the Body ....................................187
Names of the movements ...............................................189
Descriptions of the movements .....................................190

## CHAPTER FOUR: DISCUSSIONS ON THEORY AND TEACHING

Breathing for Power .......................................................217
The Five Elements in Xingyiquan..................................218
The Six Models for the Body in Xingyiquan .................227

The Three Levels of Xingyiquan .................................................. 230
Teaching Methodology
    A Discussion of Power ........................................... 234
    Teaching Progressions ........................................... 235
    Teaching Suggestions ........................................... 236
    Part and Whole method ........................................... 238
    Use of Imagery ........................................... 241

## APPENDIX

Glossary
    Pinyin order
    Section 1: Basic parts of the body ........................................... 245
    Section 2: Xingyi terminology ........................................... 246
    Section 3: Xingyi movement names ........................................... 251
    Section 4: Further terms to define movements ........................................... 255
    Section 5: Xingyi people referred to in the books ........................................... 255
    English order
    Section 6: Basic parts of the body ........................................... 256
    Section 7: Xingyi terminology ........................................... 257
    Section 8: Xingyi movement names ........................................... 261
    Section 9: Further terms to define movements ........................................... 265

Pronunciation of pinyin ........................................... 267

About the translator ........................................... 270

## TRANSLATOR'S PREFACE TO THE SECOND VOLUME

Volume two of Di Guoyong's three volume translated set contains almost all of the further empty hand techniques and forms from his original two volume set in Chinese. I hope that it is a helpful reference material to students and teachers of Xingyiquan.

I am glad to finally get Volume two done, and thank you for your patience. It took a bit longer to complete than planned because of a delay in getting the photos and the amount of work involved in getting over six hundred photos print ready. For this I apologize. I hope that you do not mind the photos in sweatsuit intermingled with those in the proper uniform. Aside from having no real choice, I feel they give a touch of the reality of playing in the parking lot with Di Guoyong. I felt that these additional photos, mostly for views from the front, improved the book enough to make up for the differences in the photo styles.

I have added more words to the glossary from Volume one and added a movement name list. I have also put it in English order so that it can be used as a companion to the glossary in Volume one.

I would like to thank:

The author, Di Guoyong, for his knowledge of and enthusiasm for Xingyiquan, for his patient teaching, and for his help with the translation and easy agreement to my editing.

My parents, William Andre and Mary Elliott Falk, for their painstaking proofreading yet again.

And, always, Xia Bohua and Men Huifeng, for teaching me Xingyiquan way back when.

I have tried hard to get everything right, but if you find any mistakes they are mine alone.

Andrea Falk 霍安娣
Morin Heights, QC, Canada
April 2007

## TRANSLATOR'S PREFACE TO THE SECOND EDITION

As I suddenly ran out of books in the first edition of Volume II, I thought to fix a few errors and reduce the font size to make the font the same as the other volumes. Little did I think that the old files would be a disastor. The sheer volume of work involved in fixing up and editing the file meant that I also took the time to adjust the translation. There are not so many changes that you need to buy this second edition if you already have the first, but I feel it is an improvement.

Since reducing the font size reduced the page count, I was able to include *Zashichui*, the Mixture of Moves Form. Di Guoyong was quite disappointed that I had not translated it orginally, so I am most happy to oblige him in this second edition. The reasons that I had not originally put *Zashichui* in the book were book size issues and that I had not learned it directly from him.

People have asked about the extra photos, taken in training clothes, whether they were to make up for mistakes or what. They are fill in photos that we took to clarify the actions from another angle, or to add in-between moves. I have the original rolls of film, and there are no mistakes in any of the postures of the hundreds and hundreds of photos taken for the three volume set. The photos are always a joy to look at and work with, even reformating them yet again for this edition.

Andrea Falk 霍安娣

Québec, Canada

May 2019

## EDITOR'S PREFACE TO THE 2020 SET EDITION

All three books needed to be redone to enable print-to-order sales, but the original files of the books were lost. As I set up the books again, I went through them to standardise the formatting to make them a more cohesive set. The main changes I made were to move things around. This was in order to even out the sizes of the books as much as possible, because the printer had problems making books of widely different thickness come out with the same look. I tried to do the readjustment in accordance with learning and teaching progressions. I moved the twelve animals to Volume I, to include them as basic techniques to Xingyiquan. I put all the theoretical and teaching discussions, the Protect the Body partner form, and the glossaries to Volume II, making it the next level – learning empty hand forms, more applications, and more thinking about things. Volume III is now specific to the weapons.

I corrected some typographical errors, adjusted some translation, and made some editorial changes while I was doing this work. I had to work on the photos yet again, and one yet again impressed with Di Guoyong's perfection and ease in all the movements and postures. If you already have the books, the original translation was solid, you do not need to buy the new set. This is the final edition of the set, and I really hope there are no remaining errors.

Andrea Falk 霍安娣

Morin-Heights, QC, Canada

January 2021

CHAPTER ONE

# BAREHAND FORMS

# THE EIGHT MOVES

## 八势

### INTRODUCTION TO THE EIGHT MOVES, *BA SHI*

The Eight Moves is another short traditional form, usually learned after the Five Elements Connected. Similar to the Five Elements Connected, there are seventeen movements in one direction, and then the movements repeat on the way back. It contains the five elements, the sparrow-hawk, chicken and horse from the twelve animals, and some additional moves such as *dragon and tiger play together*, *white crane flashes its wings*, and *wheel around and pound*.

Why is it called The Eight Moves? You could say because it adds three animals to the five elements. But if you look at it from a structural point of view, in terms of power flow, there are eight key combinations. The first is *sparrow hawk folds its wings* and *sparrow hawk enters the woods*; the second is the *single horse*; the third is the *retreating crosscut, golden rooster drinks water*, and *golden rooster pecks a grain of rice*; the fourth is *retreat and restrain* and *aligned stance pounding punch*; the fifth is *left crosscut, dragon and tiger play together*, and *aligned stance punch*; the sixth is *withdraw elbow cover, aligned stance pounding punch*, and *white crane flashes its wings*; the seventh is *wheel around and pound*; and the eighth is *sparrow hawk pierces the sky* and *sparrow hawk wheels over*. The name makes sense in terms of the overall construction, the flow of power, and the applications contained in the form.

The footwork of The Eight Moves has a distinctive characteristic. When you use a withdrawing step to change the stance, the weight shift must be quick. *Retreat and restrain*, in particular, shifts back to the left foot so that the right foot is able to step forward quickly. Also, when withdrawing the foot for the elbow cover after *aligned stance left punch,* as soon as the left foot withdraws, the weight shifts to the left leg so that the right foot can step forward quickly and easily. The shifting between the feet helps you to initiate an attack.

The rhythm of the form is focussed on the power launch of the eight key combinations. At each point of power launch, first store power and then launch it. Power must be full, stable, and complete. Pay attention to the bodywork, always

## THE EIGHT MOVES, *BA SHI*

storing power before launching: pre-load back to launch forward, pre-load right to launch left. The power launch should be hard and ferocious, and the spirit should be powerful.

## NAMES OF THE MOVEMENTS

1. Opening Move (left *santishi*)
2. Sparrow Hawk Folds Its Wings
3. Sparrow Hawk Enters The Woods
4. Reverse Stance Right Horse
5. Retreating Left Crosscut
6. Right Splitting Strike
7. Golden Rooster Drinks Water
8. Golden Rooster Pecks A Grain Of Rice
9. Retreat And Restrain
10. Right Aligned Stance Cannon, or Pounding Punch
11. Advance Left Crosscut
12. Dragon And Tiger Play Together
13. Left Aligned Stance Drive, or Crushing punch
14. Right Aligned Stance Cannon, or Pounding Punch
15. White Crane Flashes Its Wings
16. Wheel Around And Pound
17. Sparrow Hawk Pierces The Sky
18. Sparrow Hawk Wheels Over

(the following moves are a repetition back in the returning direction)

19. Sparrow Hawk Folds Its Wings
20. Sparrow Hawk Enters The Woods
21. Reverse Stance Right Horse
22. Retreating Left Crosscut
23. Right Splitting Strike
24. Golden Rooster Drinks Water
25. Golden Rooster Pecks A Grain Of Rice
26. Retreat And Restrain
27. Right Aligned Stance Cannon, or Pounding Punch
28. Advance Left Crosscut
29. Dragon And Tiger Play Together
30. Left Aligned Stance Drive, or Crushing Punch
31. Right Aligned Stance Cannon, or Pounding Punch
32. White Crane Flashes Its Wings
33. Wheel Around And Pound

## CHAPTER ONE: BAREHAND FORMS

34. Sparrow Hawk Pierces The Sky
35. Sparrow Hawk Wheels Over

(the following moves are the closing section)

36. Sparrow Hawk Folds Its Wings
37. Sparrow Hawk Enters the Woods
38. Turn Around With A Left Elbow Strike
39. Right Aligned Stance Crosscut
40. Three Basins Touch The Ground
41. Retreat With A Left Splitting Strike
42. Closing Move

**Description of the Movements**

1. **Opening Move (left *santishi*)**  qǐ shì  起势

Start with *santishi*. Move into *santishi* as usual. (image 1.1)

See also Volume I, Chapter Two, for more detailed text and images on *santishi*.

2. **Sparrow Hawk Folds Its Wings**

yàozǐ shùshēn  鹞子束身

ACTION: Shift forward onto the left leg and take a long step forward with the right foot, landing firmly with the knee slightly bent and the foot grabbing the ground. Bring the left foot to the right ankle without touching down. Clench both fists, pulling the left fist back to the belly and punching the right fist forward and down. The right fist finishes outside the left fist at belly height, fist surface down. Press the head up and look at the right fist. (image 1.2)

**Pointers**

- The right foot and fist arrive simultaneously.
- Take a long step forward, land firmly, and bring the left foot up quickly.
- Keep the elbows protecting the ribs and keep the fists protecting the midline, like a sparrow hawk tucking in its wings and body.

4    THE EIGHT MOVES, *BA SHI*

3.   **Sparrow Hawk Enters The Woods**    yàozǐ rùlín    鹞子入林

ACTION: Advance the left foot a long step and follow in a half-step with the right foot to take a *santi* stance. Bend the right elbow to drill the fist up to eye height, fist heart in. Turn the trunk ninety degrees rightward. Punch the left fist out past the sternum, finishing at solar plexus height with the arm slightly bent and the fist eye up. Bring the right fist to the right temple, turning the fist heart forward as the body turns rightward, keeping the elbow down. Press the head up and look past the left fist. (image 1.3)

**Pointers**

- o   The left punch should arrive simultaneously with the left foot.
- o   Release the shoulders and drop the elbows, reaching forward into the left shoulder. Turn the waist and send the fist forward from the shoulder.
- o   Be especially careful to keep the right elbow down.

4.   **Reverse Stance Right Horse**    àobù yòu mǎxíng    拗步右马形

ACTION: Advance the left foot a half-step and follow in the right foot, rubbing into the ground just behind the left heel. Bring the right fist from the head to strike forward to chest height with the wrist slightly hooked in and the fist heart down. Hook the left fist and press down, then pull back to in front of the right shoulder. Both arms are slightly bent. Press the head up and look past the right fist. (image 1.4)

**Pointers**

- o   The right punch arrives simultaneously as the right foot rubs into the ground, so that the power is united.
- o   First draw a small circle with the right fist and then punch forward, first pulling it back to send it forward. The right elbow is slightly higher than the shoulder and the arm is rounded. Be sure to reach forward with the shoulder, open the upper back and close the chest to issue power.

5.   **Retreating Left Crosscut**    tuìbù zuǒ héngquán    退步左横拳

ACTION 1: Withdraw the right foot a half-step and cut the right elbow in, rotating the fist heart up. Lower the left fist to the chest, turning the fist heart down. Look past the right fist. (image 1.5)

CHAPTER ONE: BAREHAND FORMS 5

ACTION 2: Bring the left foot past the right foot then back to the left rear, landing with a thump and shifting the weight evenly between the feet. Slide the left fist along under the right arm to drill forward to a crosscut strike at shoulder height, fist heart turning up. Tuck the right fist over and press down, pulling back to the waist. Press the head up and look past the left fist. (image 1.6)

**Pointers**
- o   The right fist should complete the elbow cover as the right foot withdraws. The left fist should complete the crosscut as the left foot lands.
- o   Be sure to first do a small pre-load forward with the body, to give power to the backward movement.

6.   **Right Splitting Strike**   yòu pīquán   右劈拳

ACTION: Advance the right foot a half-step straight forward and follow in with the left foot a half-step. Bring the right fist to the sternum, along the left arm, and then unclench the hand and split forward to chest height. Unclench the left hand and pull it back to the belly. Press the head up and look forward. (image 1.7)

**Pointers**
- o   The right hand should complete the split as the right foot lands. Reach the right shoulder forward, keeping it released and the elbow down. Exhale and settle the *qi* to the *dantian* to put power into the strike.

7.   **Golden Rooster Drinks Water**   jīnjī zhuó shuǐ   金鸡啄水

ACTION 1: Withdraw the right foot to in front of the left foot, lifting the knee with the foot hooked up at the belly of the calf. Stand firmly on the left leg, keeping the knee bent. Clench the right hand and bring the fist back to the belly, then drill it up by the sternum and mouth to eyebrow height. Clench the left hand and lift it to the chest. Look at the right fist. (image 1.8)

## 6 THE EIGHT MOVES, *BA SHI*

ACTION 2: Land the right foot with a thump and lift the left foot at the right ankle. Bend the right leg to lower the body. Drill the left fist up along the right arm, then unclench it and split forward and down to chest height. Unclench the right hand and pull it down to the right hip, palm down. Press the head up and look forward. (image 1.9)

**Pointers**

- Coordinate the hands with the action of the right foot. Complete both the pull back and the drill up with the right hand as the right foot withdraws. Split down with the left hand as the right foot lands with a thump.
- The right foot should thump with a settled, powerful feeling. The lower back should be firm, with the buttocks tucked in, and the head pressed up. Release the tension in the shoulders to reach forward, and settle the elbows. The whole body must be stable.

### 8. Golden Rooster Pecks A Grain Of Rice    jīnjī shí mǐ    金鸡食米

ACTION: Advance the left foot a long step and follow in the right foot with a rubbing step to land with a thump just at the left heel. Clench the right fist to punch forward to chest height. Set the left hand on the right wrist. Press the head up and look past the right fist. (image 1.10)

**Pointers**

- The left foot must take a long step forward. The right punch hits as the right foot lands.

### 9. Retreat And Restrain    tuìbù lēiquán    退步勒拳

ACTION 1: Retreat the right foot a half-step. Place the left palm over the right fist and circle the hands, keeping them connected. Circle and turn the right fist over, first turning underneath the left hand and finishing above it, fist heart up. The left hand finishes palm up. Look at the right fist. (image 1.11)

CHAPTER ONE: BAREHAND FORMS 7

ACTION 2: Withdraw the left foot to land beside the right foot, immediately shifting onto the left leg. Pull the hands back forcefully into the belly. Press the head up and look forward. (image 1.12)

**Pointers**

- Strike the belly with some force with the joined hands, hitting as the left foot thumps. Settle the *qi* to the *dantian*.
- Be sure to drag the foot back to thump, do not lift it to stamp. Sit into the buttocks, draw in the hips, pull the leg, and thump with the foot.

**10.　Right Aligned Stance Cannon, or Pounding Punch**

yòu shùnbù pàoquán　　　右顺步炮拳

ACTION: Take a long step forward with the right foot and follow in a half-step with the left foot. Clench the left fist and drill it up by the sternum to the mouth, then drill it forward and up to nose height. Lift the right fist to the chest, then, as the right foot steps forward and the body turns leftward, punch it forward to chest height, fist eye up. Turn the left fist and pull it back so the fist eye faces the left temple. Keep the left elbow down. Look past the right fist. (image 1.13)

**Pointers**

- The right punch arrives as the right foot lands. Be sure to reach the right shoulder forward.
- Drill and turn the left fist, do not block directly up. Use the turn of the body and the right shoulder to deflect with the left arm.

**11.　Advance Left Crosscut**　jìnbù zuǒ héngquán　　　进步左横拳

ACTION: Advance the right foot a half-step and follow in a half-step with the left foot, keeping most weight on the left leg. Lower the left fist to the chest then slide it forward under the right forearm, drilling and turning the fist heart up to complete a crosscut strike. Tuck, press down, and pull the right fist back to the belly. The left fist finishes at shoulder height with the left shoulder reaching forward. Press the head up and look past the left fist. (image 1.14)

# THE EIGHT MOVES, BA SHI

**Pointers**

- Use body technique to get power into the crosscut. First pull slightly back, then send the fist down and forward. Pay attention in every technique to use the principle of pre-loading the body prior to launching force.
- The left crosscut should arrive as the right foot lands, and the legs should have a scissoring power between them. Tuck in the left knee, stabbing it down into the stance. Twist the waist and reach forward into the shoulder, tucking in the buttocks and pressing the head up. This creates a lengthening feeling, with power stretching up and down.

1.14

## 12. Dragon And Tiger Play Together    lóng hǔ xiāngjiāo    龙虎相交

ACTION: Advance the right foot a half-step and settle solidly onto the right leg. Then lift the left knee and kick forcefully forward with the heel to waist height. Punch the right fist straight forward to chest height with the fist eye up and the arm slightly bent. Pull the left fist back to the left side. Keep the right knee slightly bent. Press the head up and look forward. (image 1.15)

1.15

**Pointers**

- Be sure to punch and kick quickly, and at exactly the same time. Stand firmly on the right leg. The kicking knee extends fully with the foot pulled back to drive into the heel.
- Keep the trunk straight, be careful not to lean backwards, forwards or sideways.
- Pull the left fist back as the right fist punches, so that the action and force is complete and together.

## 13. Left Aligned Stance Drive, or Crushing Punch

zuǒ shùnbù bēngquán          左顺步崩拳

ACTION: After completing the kick, land the left foot forward and follow in a half-step with the right foot, putting most weight on the right leg. Punch straight forward with the left fist to chest height, arm slightly bent and fist eye up. Pull the right fist back to the belly. Press the head up and look forward. (image 1.16)

CHAPTER ONE: BAREHAND FORMS 9

1.16

**Pointers**

- Three actions are done as one: punch with the left fist, pull the right fist back, and land the left foot. Be sure to coordinate the left and right, up and down, and forward and backward forces.

**14.  Right Aligned Stance Cannon, or Pounding Punch**

yòu shùnbù pàoquán        右顺步炮拳

ACTION 1: Withdraw the left foot to inside the right foot and land it, shifting immediately onto the left leg. Bend the left arm and do an elbow over in front of the chest turning the torso slightly rightward, then drill the left fist up to nose height. Do not move the right fist yet. (image 1.17)

ACTION 2: Take a long step forward with the right foot and follow in a half-step with the left foot. Turn the torso leftward and extend the right shoulder forward to punch the right fist forward with the fist eye up. Rotate the left fist and bring it back to the left temple, fist eye facing the temple and elbow hanging down. Press the head up and look past the right fist. (image 1.18)

1.17

1.18

**Pointers**

- First tuck the left elbow in and then drill up with the left fist, combining the actions smoothly.
- Do the elbow cover as the left foot withdraws. Punch the right fist as the right foot steps forward.
- Be sure to shift immediately onto the left leg after the left foot withdraws. This is the only way that you can step the right foot forward smoothly and quickly.

## 10 THE EIGHT MOVES, *BA SHI*

**15.     White Crane Flashes Its Wings**   báihè liàngchì    白鹤亮翅

ACTION 1: Withdraw the left foot a half-step and sit into a horse stance. Lower the fists in front of the body to cross in front of the belly, then brace out. Then drill up to head height with the fist hearts in. Look at the right fist. (images 1.19, 1.20)

ACTION 2: Without moving the feet, rotate the fists so the fist hearts are out, and circle them to brace out to the sides, arms slightly bent. Look at the right fist. (image 1.21)

ACTION 3: Shift back to the left leg and withdraw the right foot to land with a thump beside the left foot. Bring the fists back to the belly, pulling in forcefully to strike the belly. Press the head up, settle the *qi* to the *dantian*, and look forward. (image 1.22)

### Pointers

- Sit down as the hands lower and then drill up. After the fists drill up to head height, rotate them to brace out to the sides. When circling them down, keep a wrapping power in the arms. When they pull back to the belly, keep a holding power.
- The weight shifts first left, then right, and then left again. Pull the fists in to hit the belly as the right foot lands. Settle the *qi* to the *dantian* to help launch power forcefully.
- The right foot should land with a thump, not a stamp. This is a raking and settling type of power that unites the whole body.

CHAPTER ONE: BAREHAND FORMS    11

**16.    Wheel Around And Pound**    fānshēn pào    翻身炮

ACTION: Push off with both legs and turn one-eighty degrees rightward around in the air. Separate the feet in the air and land in a half-horse stance or a *santi* stance with the left foot forward. Drill the right fist up and bring it to the right temple as the body turns, fist eye in and elbow set down. Punch straight forward to chest height with the left fist, fist eye up. Keep the left arm slightly bent. Press the head up and look past the left fist. (images 1.23, 1.24)

1.23    1.24

**Pointers**

- Push off and land equally with both legs at the same time. There must be no timing difference between them. Land with an opening power between the feet, pressing forward and back. That is, the rear foot presses forward and the lead foot presses back.
- Complete the pounding punch simultaneously with the landing.

**17.    Sparrow Hawk Pierces The Sky**    yàozǐ zuān tiān    鹞子钻天

ACTION 1: Advance the left foot a half-step and follow in the right foot to the left ankle without touching down. Turn the left fist over to tuck in and press down with the fist heart down and the elbow slightly bent. Lower the right fist to the right side. Look at the left fist. (image 1.25)

ACTION 2: Take a long step forward with the right foot and follow in a half-step with the left foot. Drill the right fist up and forward to nose height, ulnar edge rotated up. Pull the left fist back to the belly. Press the head up and look forward. (image 1.26)

1.25    1.26

## 12    THE EIGHT MOVES, *BA SHI*

**Pointers**

- Land the right drilling punch as the right foot lands. Exhale to put power into the punch.

### 18.    Sparrow Hawk Wheels Over    yàozǐ fānshēn    鷂子翻身

ACTION 1: Pivot the feet in place, turning around one-eighty leftward to face back along the line of the form. Rotate the thumb side of the right fist in and lift the elbow then, as the body turns, bring the fist forward and press down with the fist heart down. Drill the left fist up through the right arm to nose height, fist heart in. At this point the weight is on the left leg and the right fist is pressing down in front of the belly. Look at the left fist. (images 1.27, 1.28)

1.27

1.28

ACTION 2: Lift the right fist with the forearm crossways, passing outside the left arm, to block up above the head. Press the left fist down and settle the elbow, pulling back to in front of the chest. Shift back onto the right leg. Pull the right fist back to in front of the right shoulder. Lift the left elbow and rotate the thumb side in so that the fist eye is on the body, and slide it along the left ribs to stab down at the hip. Look at the left fist. (image 1.29)

ACTION 3: Squat down on the right leg and extend the left leg, to sit into a pouncing stance. Slide the left fist forward along the outside of the left leg, gradually turning the fist eye up. Pull the right fist back to beside the waist. Move the trunk forward as the left fist extends. Look at the left fist. (image 1.30)

1.29

1.30

## Pointers

- The leftward, rightward, and leftward rotation of the trunk must come from the waist, keeping the whole body together. The right fist covers and presses down as the left fist drills up. The right elbow blocks up as the left elbow settles and pulls in. The right fist pulls back as the left elbow lifts and the left fist lowers to stab forward.
- Be sure to use the shoulders, rolling one closed and opening the other. Transfer power from the waist to the shoulders, from the shoulders to the elbows, and from the elbows to the hands.
- The whole movement is done without a pause, as one coordinated action that moves upward and downward, leftward and rightward. Keep the spirit focussed and the power soft but not slack. The power in this move is hidden, not hard.

**19.　Sparrow Hawk Folds Its Wings**　yàozî shùshēn　鷂子束身

ACTION: Extend the left fist forward and shift forward onto the left leg, keeping the knee bent. Take a long step forward with the right foot and land with stability. Bring the left foot to the right ankle without touching down, pressing the legs together. Lift the right fist to the sternum then punch forward and down to groin height. Pull the left fist back to the belly. The arms are crossed, the right fist outside the left arm. The right fist eye is forward and the left fist heart is in. Press the head up and look forward. (image 1.31)

- The following moves, 20 through 37, are a repetition of the moves 3 through 19, and then move 3 again.
- In this way, all the moves repeat going back in the returning direction. The first section of the form goes out, and the second section comes back.
- Move 35 turns around again. Moves 36 and 37 repeat moves 2 and 3, in the original direction of the form.
- Moves 38 to 42 are the closing combination.

14    THE EIGHT MOVES, *BA SHI*

**20.    Sparrow Hawk Enters The Woods**

This movement is the same as movement 3, going back in the returning direction. (image 1.32)

1.32

| | | |
|---|---|---|
| 21. | Reverse Stance Right Horse | see move 4 |
| 22. | Retreating Left Crosscut | see move 5 |
| 23. | Right Splitting Strike | see move 6 |
| 24. | Golden Rooster Drinks Water | see move 7 |
| 25. | Golden Rooster Pecks A Grain Of Rice | see move 8 |
| 26 | Retreat And Restrain | see move 9 |
| 27. | Right Aligned Stance Cannon | see move 10 |
| 28. | Advance Left Crosscut | see move 11 |
| 29. | Dragon And Tiger Play Together | see move 12 |
| 30. | Left Aligned Stance Drive | see move 13 |
| 31. | Right Aligned Stance Cannon | see move 14 |
| 32. | White Crane Flashes Its Wings | see move 15 |
| 33. | Wheel Around And Pound | see move 16 |
| 34. | Sparrow Hawk Pierces The Sky | see move 17 |
| 35. | Sparrow Hawk Wheels Over | see move 18 |

36.    **Sparrow Hawk Folds Its Wings**  see move 2, going once again in the original direction.

CHAPTER ONE: BAREHAND FORMS    15

### 37.   Sparrow Hawk Enters the Woods

This is the same as move 3, going once again in the same direction as at the beginning. (image 1.33)

### 38.   Turn Around With A Left Elbow Strike

huíshēn zuǒ dǐngzhǒu    回身左顶肘

ACTION: Retreat the left foot back and turn the body around one-eighty degrees to the left, pivoting on both feet. Pull the left fist back, bend the elbow to butt to the rear at shoulder height. The left fist finishes in front of the left shoulder, fist heart down. Lower the right fist in front of the left chest, fist heart down. Press the head up and look at the left elbow. Keep the body weight evenly between the feet. (image 1.34)

**Pointers**

- Butt with the left elbow as the left foot lands and the body turns around. The point of focus is the tip of the elbow. Relax and reach forward with the shoulder.

### 39.   Right Aligned Stance Crosscut

yòu shùnbù héngquán    右顺步横拳

ACTION: Take a long step forward with the right foot and follow in a bit with the left foot. Do a crosscut with the right fist, hitting forward from under the left elbow, finishing fist heart up at shoulder height. Pull the left fist back to the belly. Press the head up and look at the right fist. (image 1.35)

# 16　THE EIGHT MOVES, BA SHI

**Pointers**

- Complete the right crosscut as the right foot lands. First withdraw the trunk a bit, then strike. Settle the right shoulder down with a wrapping power. Twist and drill the right fist to complete a crosscut punch.

## 40.　Three Basins Touch The Ground　sānpán luòdì　三盘落地

ACTION: Bring the right fist leftward to cover with the elbow, unclenching the hand and circling it to outside the left shoulder. Follow the movement of the right hand with the eyes. Step the left foot behind the right foot, landing with the ball of the foot and turning the right foot across to take a scissors stance with the weight evenly distributed between the legs. Unclench the hands and brace out to both sides with the arms rounded and the palms down at hip height, thumb webs in. Release tension in the shoulders, press the head up, and look at the left hand. (images 1.36, 1.37)

1.36　　　1.37

**Pointers**

- Gather power as the right elbow circles and covers, wrapping in the elbows and closing the chest. Launch power equally to both sides as the left foot steps back and the arms brace out.

## 41.　Retreat With A Left Splitting Strike

tuìbù zuǒ pīquán　退步左劈拳

ACTION 1: Retreat the right foot a step and shift onto the right leg, withdrawing the left foot to in front of the right foot. Clench both fists and drill the right fist up by the sternum and forward to nose height, ulnar edge twisted up. Pull the left fist back to the belly. Look at the right fist. (image 1.38)

1.38

ACTION 2: Advance the left foot a half-step without moving the right foot, to take a *santi* stance. Bring the left fist up to the sternum then out along the right arm, unclenching and splitting forward to chest height. Unclench the right hand and pull it back to the belly, palm down. Press the head up and look past the left hand. (image 1.39)

**Pointers**
- Drill the right fist forward as the right foot retreats. Split the left hand forward as the left foot advances.

**42.** **Closing Move**     shōu shì     收势

- The closing is the same as usual from *santishi*.

# THE TWELVE GREAT PUNCHES

## 十二洪捶

### INTRODUCTION TO THE TWELVE GREAT PUNCHES, *SHI'ER HONG CHUI*

The Twelve Great Punches is another traditional Xingyiquan form, and most branches of Xingyiquan have a version of it. Short but varied, with characteristic Xingyiquan movements, it is widely popular. It is a typical traditional form, containing the five elements and four of the twelve animals – sparrow hawk, tiger, snake, and chicken. And as is also typical, there is a repetition of movements out and back, with an additional repetition of movements combined with a closing combination. A characteristic of this form is that it starts with four *aligned stance crosscuts* to four directions, repeats them at the turn around, and then repeats them again at the end – for a total of twelve *aligned stance crosscuts*. This is why the form is often called the Twelve Crossing Punches[1] instead of the Twelve Great Punches.

### NAMES OF THE MOVEMENTS

1. Opening Move
2. Left Drive, or Crushing Fist
3. Right Aligned Stance Crosscut
4. Turn Around With A Right Aligned Stance Crosscut
5. Turn Around With A Right Elbow Strike
6. Left Aligned Stance Crosscut
7. Turn Around With A Left Aligned Stance Crosscut
8. Turn Around, Withdraw With A Drive, or Crushing Punch
9. Advance With A Right Drive, or Crushing Punch
10. Retreat With A Left Drive, or Crushing Punch
11. Right Aligned Stance Drive, or Crushing Punch
12. White Crane Flashes Its Wings
13. Left Cannon, or Pounding Punch

---

[1] Translator's note: The sounds are similar enough for oral transmission to have confused the two. Twelve crossing punches form is shí èr héng chuí 十二横捶. Twelve great punches form is shí èr hóng chuí 十二洪捶.

## CHAPTER ONE: BAREHAND FORMS 19

14. Retreat And Restrain
15. Sparrow Hawk Enters The Woods
16. Step Forward, Tiger Carries
17. Step Forward, Tiger Braces
18. White Snake Spits Its Tongue
19. White Snake Coils Its Body
20. White Snake Slithers Through The Grass
21. Thump, Golden Rooster Blocks Up
22. Golden Rooster Heralds The Dawn
23. Step Forward, Right Drill
24. Sparrow Hawk Wheels Over
25. Sparrow Hawk Folds Its Wings
26. Sparrow Hawk Enters The Woods
27. Right Aligned Stance Crosscut

(the following moves are repetition back in the returning direction)

28. Turn Around With A Right Aligned Stance Crosscut
29. Turn Around With A Right Elbow Strike
30. Left Aligned Stance Crosscut
31. Turn Around With A Left Aligned Stance Crosscut
32. Turn Around, Withdraw With A Drive, or Crushing Punch
33. Advance With A Right Drive, or Crushing Punch
34. Retreat With A Left Drive, or Crushing Punch
35. Right Aligned Stance Drive, or Crushing Punch
36. White Crane Flashes Its Wings
37. Left Cannon, or Pounding Punch
38. Retreat And Restrain
39. Sparrow Hawk Enters The Woods
40. Step Forward, Tiger Carries
41. Step Forward, Tiger Braces
42. White Snake Spits Its Tongue
43. White Snake Coils Its Body
44. White Snake Slithers Through The Grass
45. Thump, Golden Rooster Blocks Up
46. Golden Rooster Heralds The Dawn
47. Step Forward, Right Drill
48. Sparrow Hawk Wheels Over
49. Sparrow Hawk Folds Its Wings
50. Sparrow Hawk Enters The Woods
51. Right Aligned Stance Crosscut

(the following moves are the closing section)

52. Turn Around With A Right Aligned Stance Crosscut
53. Turn Around With A Right Elbow Strike
54. Left Aligned Stance Crosscut
55. Turn Around With A Left Aligned Stance Crosscut
56. Turn Around, Withdraw With A Drive, or Crushing Punch
57. Advance With A Right Drive, or Crushing Punch

## 20    TWELVE GREAT PUNCHES, *SHI'ER HONG CHUI*

58.  Retreat With A Left Drive, or Crushing Punch
59.  Closing Move

**Description of the Movements**

1.     **Opening Move**        qǐ shì              起势

ACTION 1: Stand to attention with the feet together, facing ninety degrees to the line on which you will travel. Press the head up, keep the shoulders settled down, and let the arms hang naturally at the sides with the fingers together. Look straight ahead. Without moving the feet, gradually lift the hands at the sides to shoulder height, palms up and arms naturally bent. Look at the right hand. (image 1.40)

ACTION 2: Bend the elbows so that the hands point to each other in front of the face, palms down. Lower the hands to shoulder height and turn the palms out, thumbs down, pushing forward at shoulder height. Sit down. Brace the arms out rounded, press the head up and look past the hands. (image 1.41, photo taken from the front)

1.40

1.41
FRONT

**Pointers**

  o   Turn the palms and push forward as you sit down. This action is soft and coordinated.

  o   Keep the arms rounded as you push forward, settling the chest, releasing the shoulders, tautening the upper back slightly, pressing the head up, and focussing your attention.

2.     **Left Drive, or Crushing Fist**    zuǒ bēngquán    左崩拳

ACTION 1: Clench the hands and lower them to the waist, with the fist eyes up and fist hearts on the belly. Keep the elbows tight to the ribs. Turn the trunk slightly to the right and look forward. (image 1.42)

ACTION 2: Advance the left foot and follow in the right foot a half-step into a stance shorter than a *santi* stance. Punch the left fist forward to chest height with the fist eye up and the arm

1.42

1.43

## CHAPTER ONE: BAREHAND FORMS

slightly bent. Keep the right fist at the waist. Press the head up and look at the left fist. (image 1.43)

**Pointers**

- When you lower the hands, circle the right hand in an arc.
- The left punch arrives as the left foot lands.
- Bring the right fist in to the waist as the left fist punches. Use the power of the lower back to send the left shoulder forward. Be sure to use body technique to set up the punch. Pre-load back to launch power forward into the punch.

**3. Right Aligned Stance Crosscut**

yòu shùnbù héngquán    右顺步横拳

ACTION 1: Advance the left foot a half-step forward and follow in the right foot to inside the left ankle. Rotate the left fist heart up, tucking in the elbow slightly. Rotate the right fist heart down and thread it from the right side towards the left side. Look at the left fist. (image 1.44)

ACTION 2: Step the right foot a long diagonal step to the forward right and follow in the left foot a half-step, keeping most weight on the left leg. Slide the right fist along under the left arm to do a crosscut forward, turning the fist heart up at shoulder height. Rotate the left fist and pull it back to the belly, fist heart down. Press the head up and look past the right fist. (image 1.45)

1.44

1.45

**Pointers**

- Hit with the right crosscut as the right foot lands, coordinating the upper and lower segments of the body. Hit as the foot lands, breathing out to launch a fully integrated power.
- Twist both fists to perform the crosscut. The left fist rotates the thumb side inward to tuck in and the right fist rotates the little finger side inward to drill out. The hands work together with equal and opposite power.

## 22 TWELVE GREAT PUNCHES, *SHI'ER HONG CHUI*

### 4. Turn Around With A Right Aligned Stance Crosscut

huíshēn yòu shùnbù héngquán　　回身右顺步横拳

ACTION 1: Hook-in step the right foot in front of the left toes, turning the body one-eighty degrees around to the left and shifting onto the right leg. Bend the right elbow and bring the fist to the waist, fist heart down. Stab the left fist to the rear, fist eye down. Look at the left fist. (image 1.46)

ACTION 2: Advance the left foot a half-step forward, shift the weight to the left leg and bring the right foot in to the left foot without touching down. As the body turns around, rotate the left arm to twist the fist heart up at shoulder height. (image 1.47)

ACTION 3: Take a long step forward with the right foot and follow in the left foot a half-step, to sit into a *santi* stance. Slide the right fist forward under the left arm then perform a crosscut, twisting the fist heart up at shoulder height. Tuck the left fist in, twisting the fist heart down, and pull it back to the belly. Press the head up and look at the right fist. (image 1.48)

**Pointers**

- Complete the *turn around crosscut* as one continuous action, with no break in the movement or power flow.
- The key to the movement is the turn, and the order of the actions for a smooth turn is: bend the right elbow and stab out the left fist as you hook-in the right foot; then turn around to the left, twisting the left arm and taking a half step with the left foot; only after that is completed should you step forward with the right foot and complete the right crosscut. Be sure to twist both fists by rotating the arms and the shoulders so that the power of the whole body is integrated.

# CHAPTER ONE: BAREHAND FORMS

**5.    Turn Around With A Right Elbow Strike**

huíshēn yòu dǐngzhǒu    回身右顶肘

ACTION: Step the right foot behind and pivot the left foot in place, turning the body ninety degrees around to the right, to finish in a half horse stance with most weight on the left leg. Rotate the thumb side of the right fist in, to tuck in at the chest with the fist heart down, and butt to the right with the elbow at shoulder height. Bring the left fist out under the right elbow to finish at the right ribs with the fist heart down. Press the head up and look past the right elbow. (image 1.49)

**Pointers**
- Complete three actions as one unified movement: retreat the right foot, turn the body around to the right, and butt to the rear with the right elbow. Hit with the elbow as the right foot lands.
- The left fist is hidden under the right elbow. This is a hidden strike and also protects the right ribs. An alternate name for this movement is *See the Punch Under the Elbow*.

**6.    Left Aligned Stance Crosscut**   zuǒ shùnbù héngquán   左顺步横拳

ACTION 1: Take a long step diagonally to the forward left with the left foot and follow in a half-step with the right foot. Rotate the left fist and hit forward with a crosscut, fist heart turning up at shoulder height, arm slightly bent. Pull the right fist back to the belly, turning the fist heart down. Release tension in the shoulders, settle the elbows down, press the head up, and look at the left fist. (image 1.50)

**Pointers**
- Hit simultaneously with the foot and fist, completing the left crosscut as the left foot lands.
- Get power into the crosscut by turning from the lower back and reaching the shoulder forward, urging from the waist to the shoulder, from the shoulder to the elbow, and from the elbow to the fist. Rotate each segment as it moves forward, twisting and drilling into the crosscut.

## 7. Turn Around With A Left Aligned Stance Crosscut

huíshēn zuǒ shùnbù héngquán      回身左顺步横拳

ACTION 1: Hook-in the left foot and pivot the right foot to turn the body around one-eighty degrees to the right, shifting onto the left leg. Bend the left elbow to bring the fist into the chest, then the waist, fist heart down. Bend the right elbow to stab the fist out to the rear, fist eye down. Shift onto the right leg and bring the left foot beside the right foot without touching down. As the body turns around, rotate the right arm so that the fist heart is up, at shoulder height. Look at the right fist. (images 1.51, 1.52)

ACTION 2: Take a long step forward with the left foot and follow in a half-step with the right foot, putting most weight on the right leg. Slide the left fist forward under the right arm to hit with a crosscut to shoulder height, ulnar edge twisted up to turn the fist heart up. Rotate and tuck the right fist down, pulling back to the belly, fist heart down and elbow tucking into the ribs. Press the head up and look at the left fist. (image 1.53)

**Pointers**

o   This is the same as movement 4, only on the opposite side.

## 8. Turn Around, Withdraw With A Drive, or Crushing Punch

zhuànshēn chèbù bēngquán      转身撤步崩拳

ACTION 1: Hook-in the left foot slightly to the right. Bend the left elbow and lift it, bringing the left fist to in front of the chest, then lowering it to the waist, twisting the fist heart up. Stab the right fist out from the right ribs towards the rear to chest height, rotating the thumb side inward to twist the fist heart up. At this point the weight is on the left leg. Look at the right fist. (image 1.54)

CHAPTER ONE: BAREHAND FORMS    25

ACTION 2: Turn the body around ninety degrees to the right to face the right fist. Retreat the right foot behind the body and shift onto the right leg. Rotate the little finger side of the right fist in to turn the fist heart up and bend the elbow slightly, keeping the fist at chest height. Withdraw the left foot a half-step to in front of the right foot. Look at the right fist. (image 1.55)

ACTION 3: Advance the left foot a half-step and follow in the right foot slightly, with most weight on the right leg. Punch the left fist forward to chest height, elbow slightly bent and fist eye up. Pull the right fist back to the belly. Press the head up and look at the left fist. (image 1.56)

**Pointers**

- Complete the whole movement as one action.
- Use the shoulders to coordinate and put power into the equal and opposite movement of the fists as the left fist comes in and the right fist stabs out. Tuck the right shoulder in to roll the arm in to stab to the rear. After the body has turned around, rotate the right fist, opening the right shoulder and settling into it to put power into the rotation of the arm. Both shoulders must stay settled and released so that the whole body power is integrated.
- Punch with the left fist as the left foot lands.

9.   **Advance With A Right Drive, or Crushing Punch**

jìnbù yòu bēngquán       进步右崩拳

ACTION: Advance the left foot and follow in the right foot to behind the left heel, landing with a thump and putting the weight on the right leg. Punch the right fist forward to chest height with the elbow slightly bent and the fist eye up. Pull the left fist back to the belly with the fist heart in. Press the head up and look at the right fist. (image 1.57)

**Pointers**

- Three actions must happen simultaneously with integrated power: the right fist

# 26    TWELVE GREAT PUNCHES, *SHI'ER HONG CHUI*

punches, the left fist pulls back, and the right foot lands.
- The right foot follow-in step is done by rolling in the hips and closing in the knees. This brings the foot in. The foot must rake in with power, which makes a heavy thumping sound. Breathe out to put power into the move.

### 10. Retreat With A Left Drive, or Crushing Punch

tuìbù zuǒ bēngquán    退步左崩拳

ACTION: First retreat the right foot a half-step and shift back. Then retreat the left foot a step and place the whole foot on the ground, putting most weight on the left leg, withdrawing the right foot slightly and turning it out. Turn the trunk slightly rightward, press the thighs together, and bend the knees to sit into a scissors stance. Pull the right fist back to the right side, fist heart up. Punch the left fist forward to chest height, fist eye up. Press the head up and look at the left fist. (image 1.58)

1.58

**Pointers**
- The left foot should land with a thump, raking into the ground as it retreats. Achieve the thump by coordinating the power: shift the weight back, lean the body to the rear, hit suddenly with the leg, and grasp the ground with the foot.
- Three actions happen together: land the left foot, punch the left fist, and pull back the right fist. Put the power of the lower back and shoulder into the punch.

### 11. Right Aligned Stance Drive, or Crushing Punch

yòu shùnbù bēngquán    右顺步崩拳

ACTION: Advance the right foot and follow in the left foot a half-step, putting most weight on the left leg. Pull the left fist back to the belly, fist heart in. Punch the right fist forward to solar plexus height, elbow slightly bent and fist eye up. Press the head up and look at the right fist. (image 1.59)

1.59

**Pointers**
- Punch as the right foot lands, with exact timing. Put power into the punch by using the waist and shoulder and exhaling.

# CHAPTER ONE: BAREHAND FORMS

**12.  White Crane Flashes Its Wings**  báihè liàngchì  白鹤亮翅

ACTION 1: Withdraw the left foot a half-step and sit into a horse stance. Bend the right elbow and rotate the thumb side of the fist out to circle across past the face to do an elbow cover leftward. Then lower the fists in front of the body to cross in front of the belly, and then brace out just above the knees, fist eyes down. Keep the arms rounded and look at the right fist. (image 1.60)

ACTION 2: Shift towards the left leg. Drill both fists up to eyebrow height, crossing the wrists with the fist hearts in. The left fist is inside the right. Look at the right fist. (image 1.61)

ACTION 3: Rotate the fists so the fist hearts are out, and circle them to brace out to the sides, arms slightly bent. Shift back to the left leg and withdraw the right foot to land with a thump just beside the left foot. Circle the fists down to the belly. Press the head up, settle the *qi* to the *dantian*, and look forward. (images 1.62 and 1.63)

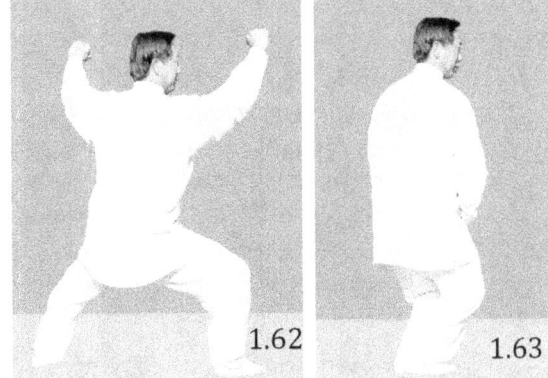

**Pointers**

- The whole movement must be continuous without a break, but with a certain rhythm. Move slowly and then speed up when launching power. The movement must not use brute force, nor should it be rushed. The whole body should be coordinated, not slack, and the power should be integrated.
- Close the shoulders and chest as the right elbow covers across. Open the chest and abdomen when the arms brace out to the sides. When the fists rise and cross, use a drilling power. When they rotate and circle above

## TWELVE GREAT PUNCHES, *SHI'ER HONG CHUI*

the head, use a bracing power. When they circle down, use a wrapping power in the arms. When they pull back to the belly, use a holding power.
- The right foot should press into the ground as it withdraws. It should land with a thump. This is a settling type of power that unites the whole body, so be sure to strike the belly with the fists and settle the *qi* to the *dantian*.
- Pay attention to the weight shifts. Shift left as the fists drill up. Shift right as the fists brace up. Shift left again as the fists pull in to hit the belly.

### 13. Left Cannon, or Pounding Punch    zuǒ pàoquán    左炮拳

ACTION: Take a long step diagonally to the forward right with the right foot and follow in a half-step with the left foot, putting most weight on the left leg. Drill the right fist up past the sternum to nose height, about twenty centimetres from the left side of the head, twisting the ulnar edge up. Bring the left fist to the sternum, then, as the right foot steps, punch forward to solar plexus height. The left punch finishes with the elbow slightly bent and rolled in, and the fist eye up. Take the right fist rightward with the turn of the body, rotating the fist eye to face the right temple. Keep the right elbow down, press the head up, and look at the left fist. (image 1.64)

### Pointers

- Punch as the right foot lands. The feet and hands must work together, arriving at the same time.
- Use power from the lower back and shoulders for the punch. Get the waist behind the shoulder, the shoulder behind the elbow, and the elbow behind the fist. Keep the left elbow tucked in to the ribs.
- Take the right fist across with the body, rotating as it goes, so that it drills and turns, deflecting rather than blocking. Keep the elbow down; it must not be lifted.

### 14. Retreat And Restrain    tuìbù lēiquán    退步勒拳

ACTION 1: Retreat the left foot a half-step and shift back, turning slightly leftward. Roll the right elbow leftward, bringing the fist down to just below shoulder height. Unclench the left hand and place it on the right wrist. Circle the right fist down and in, then up and forward, keeping the left hand on the wrist. Finish the circle with the right fist heart in, arms slightly bent. Look at the right fist. (image 1.65)

ACTION 2: Withdraw the right foot to land with a thump beside the left foot, bending the right leg and lifting the left foot beside the right ankle. Pull the hands back into the belly, pressing the elbows into the ribs. Settle the shoulders, press the head up, exhale, and look forward. (image 1.66)

1.65  1.66

**Pointers**

- Strike the belly as the right foot thumps, hitting with the right fist. Breath out and settle the *qi* to the *dantian* to assist the power launch.
- When circling the right fist, pay attention to keeping the shoulders settled and the upper back stretched taut, especially when the hands are up. Extend the fist forward to pre-load for the backward grappling/binding action.

15. **Sparrow Hawk Enters The Woods**   yàozǐ rùlín   鷂子入林

ACTION: Take a long step forward with the left foot and follow in a half-step with the right foot, keeping most weight on the right leg. Clench the right fist and drill it up by the sternum to nose height then rotate it so that the fist eye faces the temple as the body turns rightward. Keep the right elbow down. Punch the left fist forward to solar plexus height, elbow slightly bent, fist eye up. Look at the left fist. (image 1.67)

1.67

**Pointers**

- The left punch arrives as the left foot lands.
- Be sure to keep the left elbow tucked in during the punch. The punch must follow a straight line.
- Use the turn of the body and the shoulder to get power into the punch. The body turns sideways, like a sparrow hawk flying in between two trees.
- Drill and turn the right fist to deflect, do not block directly up. Be sure to keep the elbow down.

# TWELVE GREAT PUNCHES, *SHI'ER HONG CHUI*

**16.    Step Forward, Tiger Carries**    shàngbù hǔtuō    上步虎托

ACTION 1: Advance the left foot a half-step, then advance the right foot to beside the left ankle. Lower the right fist then unclench both hands and slide the right hand forward under the left arm. When it arrives to cross with the left hand, drill both hands up to head height, then circle them to the sides and lower them to the sides, palms forward, fingers down. Look forward. (images 1.68 and 1.69)

ACTION 2: Take a long step forward with the right foot and follow in a half-step with the left foot, keeping most weight on the left leg to take a *santi* stance. Push forward and down from the waist with both palms, palms forward, fingers angled down, palms about five centimetres apart at belly height. Press the head up and look past the hands. (image 1.70)

1.68

1.69

1.70

**Pointers**

- *Tiger carries* is a technique from the tiger model. The hands must arrive as the right foot lands. They push something away with a forward and downward force.
- Keep the arms rounded and bracing out when circling the hands. Use a wrapping power when bringing in the hands.
- Tuck the elbows in to the ribs just before doing the 'carry', to send the hands forward. Settle the shoulders down and close the elbows in, settling down into the buttocks and bracing the upper back rearwards. Coordinate these actions with a breath out and a settling of *qi* into the *dantian* to launch power. Complete the whole movement as one action without a pause.

CHAPTER ONE: BAREHAND FORMS    31

**17.    Step Forward, Tiger Braces**    shàngbù hǔchēng    上步虎撑

ACTION 1: Advance the right foot a half-step and follow in the left foot without touching down. Cross the wrists, left above the right, palms up. Slice forward and up, and when the hands arrive at nose height, turn the hands over and bend the elbows, so that the hands arrive at chest height, palms out. Look forward. (image 1.71)

ACTION 2: Take a long step forward with the left foot and follow in the right foot a half-step. Extend the arms to brace forward with both palms to chest height. Keep the elbows slightly bent, fingers pointing to each other, and thumbs down. Press the head up and look past the hands. (image 1.72)

1.71    1.72

**Pointers**

- The hands must brace forward as the left foot lands, combining the powers together.
- Empty the chest, open the upper back, and extend the shoulders forward when slicing up with the hands. Straighten the lower back and lift the elbows when turning the palms over. Bow the lower back, shrink in the body, sit back, and extend the arms when bracing forward with the hands. All these actions help to gain maximum power for the brace.

**18.    White Snake Spits Its Tongue**    báishé tùxìn    白蛇吐信

ACTION: Advance the left foot a half-step and then take a step forward with the right foot without moving the left, and keeping the weight on the left leg. Swing the left hand forward while turning the wrist, to hook in and press down. Pull the right hand back to the waist then rotate it and thread it from inside the left hand up to eye level with the palm up. Hook in and press down with the left hand under the right elbow, palm down. Look past the right hand. (image 1.73)

**Pointers**

- Thread the right hand through as the right foot steps forward, as one integrated action. Do not overextend the right arm.

1.73

## 19. White Snake Coils Its Body    báishé chánshēn    白蛇缠身

ACTION 1: Step the left foot forward, turning it out and settling the weight between the legs. Swing the left hand up outside the right arm, then circle it forward and down back to the left hip. Circle the right hand back and up to above the head, palm up and thumb web forward. Brace out slightly with the right arm. Lengthen the body. Look forward. (image 1.74)

ACTION 2: Turn the waist leftward and squat down into a resting stance, lifting the right heel. Stab the right hand directly down outside the left hip, palm out. Thread the left hand in front of the right shoulder, palm up. Tuck the elbows into each other, left forearm outside the right. Look past the left hand. (image 1.75)

### Pointers

- Three actions must be done as one: squat and turn the trunk, stab the right hand down, and thread the left hand up. When circling the arms, they should remain rounded and coordinated with the action of the trunk.
- The downward stabbing hand should have a twisting, wrapping power. The upward threading hand should have a drilling, turning, holding power.
- The body first opens up and then closes in. The resting stance should be stable. Close in the shoulders, tighten the abdomen, bend the waist, close the chest and stretch the upper back taut.

## 20. White Snake Slithers Through The Grass

báishé bō cǎo    白蛇拨草

ACTION: Take a large step forward with the right foot, following in with the left foot a half-step, keeping the weight on the left leg in a *santi* stance. Scoop the right hand forward and up to waist height with the arm bent, the thumb web up, and the fingers forward. Pull the left hand back to the left hip, palm down. Sit the torso down, release the shoulders and settle the elbows. Look at the right hand. (image 1.76)

**Pointers**

- The right arm must scoop forward as the right foot lands. Be sure to settle the trunk down and tuck the buttocks in, rising slightly with the lower back. The shoulders act together, one up and one down. Keep the right elbow settled down. You need to work carefully to find this type of power application.

- *Snake spits its tongue*, *snake coils its body*, and *snake slithers through the grass* are completed as one movement. Be careful about the changing direction of the eyes and point of focus. *Snake spits its tongue* should be quick, *snake coils its body* should bring the body in very tight and small, and *snake slithers through the grass* should be fierce.

**21. Thump, Golden Rooster Blocks Up**

zhènjiǎo jīnjī shàngjià      震脚金鸡上架

ACTION 1: Shift onto the left leg and withdraw the right foot to inside the left ankle without touching down. Bring the right hand down the left side, then swing the arm forward and up, and finally chop forward and down to the right hip, palm down. Pull the left hand back, then swing it up to in front of the head, thumb web forward. The palms face obliquely up. Look at the left hand (image 1.77)

ACTION 2: Land the right foot with a thump, squatting and lifting the left foot to the right ankle without touching down. Press the knees together. Twist and stab the left hand down outside the right hip with the fingers down and palm out. Thread the right hand forward and to in front of the left shoulder. Turn the body to bring the left shoulder forward. Press the head up and look past the left shoulder. (image 1.78)

1.77

1.78

**Pointers**

- Three actions happen as one: stamp the right foot, stab the left hand down, and thread the right hand up.

- The arms first draw a circle, working together. Be sure to keep the arms rounded, bracing out.

- Turn the body when the left hand stabs down. The hand leads, the elbow follows, and the shoulder urges on the action. Close in the chest and shoulders. The arms and elbows cross with a holding power in front of the chest, and serve to protect the chest and ribs.

# 34 TWELVE GREAT PUNCHES, *SHI'ER HONG CHUI*

## 22. Golden Rooster Heralds The Dawn     jīnjī bàoxiào     金鸡报晓

ACTION: Take a long step forward with the left foot and follow in a half-step with the right foot. Scoop the left hand forward and up with the arm bent, the wrist cocked so that the fingers point up and the palm faces forward. Pull the right hand down to the belly, palm down. Press the head up and look past the left hand. (image 1.79)

1.79

### Pointers

- Hit with the left arm as the left foot lands.
- Before the scoop, press the left elbow tightly to the left ribs and bring the left hand from the left hip to the front, settling down the left shoulder. Then lengthen the trunk, open the chest, reach with the shoulder, extend the arm, and settle the elbow down to put a scooping, digging power into the arm. Exhale to add power. In this way you combine the whole body as one unit, so that upper and lower, inner and outer work together in the strike.

## 23. Step Forward, Right Drill     shàngbù yòu zuānquán     上步右钻拳

ACTION 1: Advance the left foot a half-step and follow in the right foot to beside the left ankle. Clench the left hand and rotate it, cocking the wrist to hook in at shoulder height with the fist heart down. Bend the elbow just below shoulder level to press down with the forearm across the body. Press the head up and look at the left fist. (image 1.80)

ACTION 2: Take a long step forward with the right foot and follow in the left foot a half-step. Clench the right hand and drill the fist forward and out, from inside the left wrist, to nose height with the ulnar edge up. Pull the left fist down to the belly, fist heart down. Press the head up and look past the right fist. (image 1.81)

1.80

1.81

### Pointers

- Press down with the left forearm as the left foot advances. Drill forward with the right fist as the right foot steps forward. Always coordinate the hands with the feet.

CHAPTER ONE: BAREHAND FORMS    35

- o  When drilling, sit down into the stance, lengthen the lower back, push forward into the shoulder, and send the elbow forward to the fist. Be sure always to use the whole body behind the punch.
- o  Use equal and opposite force into the fists, one up and one down.

**24.    Sparrow Hawk Wheels Over**    yàozǐ fānshēn    鹞子翻身

ACTION 1: Pivot on both feet to turn around one-eighty to the left to face back in the way from which you came. Lift the right elbow and bring the right arm past the right ear, crossing the forearm over the head as you turn around to the left. As the body gets turned around, press the right forearm past the head to cover forward and down to chest height with the fist heart down. Drill the left fist from inside the right fist, up and forward to nose height, fist heart in. Shift the weight forward onto the left leg. Look past the left fist. (images 1.82, 1.83)

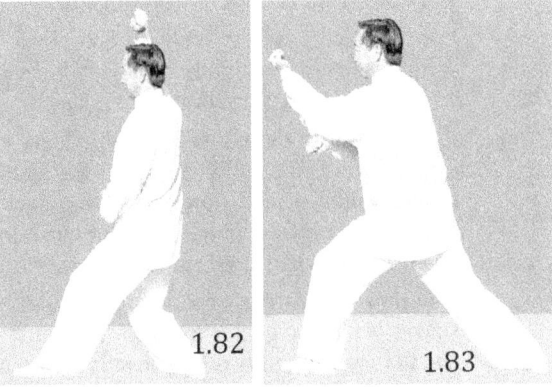

ACTION 2: Do not shift the weight yet. Slide the right fist outside the left forearm to block across the body with the forearm, lifting it above the head, fist heart out. Bend the left elbow to bring the fist back to the chest. Then turn the body rightward and shift back to the right leg. Pull the right fist back as the body turns, and circle it down to the right shoulder. Rotate the left fist and lift the elbow so that the fist eye is in, and slide it out along the left ribs to the left hip. Look at the left fist. (image 1.84)

ACTION 3: Turn the right foot out, bend the right knee to squat fully down, and extend the left leg out, foot hooked in, to take a drop stance. Shift forward and thread the left fist along the left leg, rotating the fist so the fist eye faces up as it reaches forward. Shift forward with the movement of the fist, leading forward with the head. The left fist finishes about ten centimetres ahead of the foot. Pull the right fist back,

## TWELVE GREAT PUNCHES, *SHI'ER HONG CHUI*

rolling it down to the waist, fist eye up. Look at the left fist. (image 1.85)

**Pointers**

- The movement must be completed without a break in the action, as one coordinated whole. The power comes from lengthening the body, which is a soft, hidden power that is very lively.
- Coordinate the hands together: the right fist covers and presses down as the left fist drills out; the right fist blocks up as the left fist pulls back. This movement is quick and takes a lot of coordination to get the upward and downward actions to work together.
- Use the centre of the body to coordinate the backward and forward weight shifts. Turn slightly rightward when shifting back. Coordinate the weight shift with the actions of the hands.
- Pay attention to the action of the shoulders. Close the left shoulder in and roll it inward when sliding the left fist along the ribs and leg. Draw the right shoulder back to draw the torso back when pulling the right fist back. Twist and roll in the shoulder when lowering the right fist. Rotate and use the shoulder to lead the elbow when rotating the left fist.
- You may also do the wheel around without dropping fully into the drop stance, if you are unable to do so. You must use the same power, though, and the same coordination. The only difference is the height of the stance.

**25.    Sparrow Hawk Folds Its Wings**   yàozǐ shùshēn    鹞子束身

ACTION: Extend the left fist along the left leg and shift forward onto the left leg, bending the knee and rising. Then take a long step forward with the right foot and quickly bring the left foot up to the right ankle. Keep the legs together and stand firmly. Lower the left fist to groin height and turn the fist heart in. Punch the right fist forward and down, fist eye forward at belly height. The right fist is outside the the left fist. Keep the arms tight to the ribs. Press the head up and look past the right punch. (image 1.86)

1.86

**Pointers**

- Coordinate the right foot's forward step with the right fist's punch. Be careful to keep the elbows pressing into the ribs and to keep the shoulders closed in. Lead forward into the right shoulder a bit, extending the shoulder and sinking the elbow. Contain the chest and keep the abdomen solid.

CHAPTER ONE: BAREHAND FORMS    37

26.    **Sparrow Hawk Enters The Woods**    yàozǐ rùlín    鹞子入林

ACTION: Take a long step forward with the left foot and follow in a half-step with the right foot. Bend the right elbow to drill the fist up to nose height. Lift the left fist to the sternum, then punch it forward at nose height, elbow slightly bent and fist eye up. Rotate the right forearm and drop the elbow, pulling the right fist back to face the right temple. Press the head up and look past the left fist. (image 1.87)

1.87

**Pointers**
  o    Punch with the left fist as the left foot lands. Turn the waist and extend into the shoulder, coordinating with the step to launch power. Pay particular attention to sinking the right elbow.

27.    **Right Aligned Stance Crosscut**    yòu shùnbù héngquán    右顺步横拳

ACTION 1: Advance the left foot a half-step and follow in the right foot to the left ankle without touching down. Rotate the left fist heart up and lower the right fist to stab through from the left armpit, fist heart down. Close the shoulders in, contain the chest and tauten the upper back. Look at the left fist. (image 1.88)

ACTION 2: Step the right foot diagonally to the forward right and follow in the left foot a half-step, keeping most weight on the left leg. Punch the right fist out to shoulder height in a crosscut, fist heart up. Tuck the left fist down and pull it back to the belly, fist heart down. Press the head up and look past the right fist. (image 1.89)

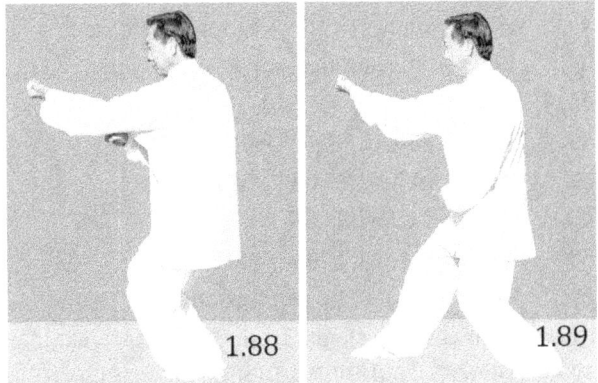
1.88    1.89

**Pointers**
  o    Movement 27 is the same as movement 3.

## TWELVE GREAT PUNCHES, *SHI'ER HONG CHUI*

- The following moves, 28 through 51, are the same as movements 4 through 27, repeating them on the way back. The first section of the form goes out, and the second section of the form comes back to the starting place, where there is another turn around. There is then another repeat, of moves 4 through 10, for a closing combination.

| | | |
|---|---|---|
| 28. | Turn Around With a Right Aligned Stance Crosscut | see move 4 |
| 29. | Turn Around With a Right Elbow Strike | see move 5 |
| 30. | Left Aligned Stance Crosscut | see move 6 |
| 31. | Turn Around With a Left Aligned Stance Crosscut | see move 7 |
| 32. | Turn Around, Withdraw With a Drive, | see move 8 |
| 33. | Advance With a Right Drive | see move 9 |
| 34. | Retreat With a Left Drive | see move 10 |
| 35. | Right Aligned Stance Drive | see move 11 |
| 36. | White Crane Flashes Its Wings | see move 12 |
| 37. | Left Cannon, or Pounding Punch | see move 13 |
| 38. | Retreat and Restrain | see move 14 |
| 39. | Sparrow Hawk Enters the Woods | see move 15 |
| 40. | Step Forward, Tiger Carries | see move 16 |
| 41. | Step Forward, Tiger Braces | see move 17 |
| 42. | White Snake Spits Its Tongue | see move 18 |
| 43. | White Snake Coils Its Body | see move 19 |
| 44. | White Snake Slithers Through the Grass | see move 20 |
| 45. | Thump, Golden Rooster Blocks Up | see move 21 |
| 46. | Golden Rooster Heralds the Dawn | see move 22 |
| 47. | Step Forward, Right Drill | see move 23 |
| 48. | Sparrow Hawk Wheels Over | see move 24 |
| 49. | Sparrow Hawk Folds Its Wings | see move 25 |
| 50. | Sparrow Hawk Enters the Woods | see move 26 |
| 51. | Right Aligned Stance Crosscut | see move 27 |

(the following moves are the closing section)

| | | |
|---|---|---|
| 52. | Turn Around With a Right Aligned Stance Crosscut | see move 4 |
| 53. | Turn Around With a Right Elbow Strike | see move 5 |
| 54. | Left Aligned Stance Crosscut | see move 6 |
| 55. | Turn Around With a Left Aligned Stance Crosscut | see move 7 |
| 56. | Turn Around, Withdraw With a Drive | see move 8 |
| 57. | Advance With a Right Drive | see move 9 |
| 58. | Retreat With a Left Drive | see move 10 |

# CHAPTER ONE: BAREHAND FORMS

**59.     Closing Move**          shòu shì          收势

ACTION 1: Advance the left foot without moving the right foot to sit into a *santi* stance. Turn over and tuck in the left fist then pull it back to the belly, fist heart in. Do not move the right fist. Press the head up and look forward. (image 1.90)

ACTION 2: Bring the right foot up to the left foot, bringing the knees together while keeping them bent. Unclench the hands and circle them up at the sides, palms up. (images 1.91, 1.92)

ACTION 3: Once the hands get to shoulder height, bring the hands to the front, palms down and thumbs in. Press the head up and look forward. Press the hands down in front of the belly and stand up to attention, letting the hands hang down to the sides. Look forward. (image 1.93)

**Pointers**
- Pull the left fist in as the left foot steps forward.
- Press the hands down as you stand up.
- The whole movement is continuous and stable, with full spirit and attention, as strong as a mountain.

# THE XINGYI COMPOSITE FORM

# 形意综合拳

## Introduction To The Xingyi Composite Form, *Xingyi Zonghe Quan*

This form is composed based on the five elements and the twelve animal models, with some of the eight skills – fifty one movements in four sections. The animal models are represented by tiger, horse, chicken, swallow, monkey, snake, and sparrow hawk, while intercept and pass from the eight skills show up in short combinations. There are also a couple of moves from the traditional Mixture of Moves form – *wind sways the lotus leaves* and *push the shutter to gaze at the moon* – and a move from the Five Elements Connected – *white crane flashes its wings*. This makes for an interesting, varied, and aesthetically pleasing performance form. There are also some good combative combinations such as *stroke hook to ear*, *double intercept and punch*, and *passing pull and drill*, which increase the form's practicality. This is an excellent form that shows well Xingyiquan's style and characteristics.

It has a pleasing and balanced choreography, interesting and varied techniques, well connected combinations, and smooth transitions and changes in power application.

## Names Of The Movements

1. Opening Move (left *santishi*)
2. Left Splitting Punch
3. Advance With a Right Drive, or Crushing Punch
4. Retreat With a Left Drive, or Crushing Punch
5. Right Aligned Stance Drive, or Crushing Punch
6. Stroke, Hook to Ear
7. White Ape Presents Fruit
8. Retreat and Ride the Tiger
9. Left Bear
10. Right Crosscut
11. Step Forward, Eagle Grasps
12. Turn Around With a Tiger Carry
13. Double Interception

# CHAPTER ONE: BAREHAND FORMS 41

14. Right Aligned Stance Drive, or Crushing Punch
15. White Crane Flashes Its Wings
16. Left Cannon, or Pounding Punch
17. Lead Left and Plant a Punch Right
18. Right Stroke and Drag Back
19. Reverse Stance Drilling Punch
20. Lead Right and Plant a Punch Left
21. Left Stroke and Drag Back
22. Reverse Stance Drilling Punch
23. Sparrow Hawk Pierces The Sky
24. Sparrow Hawk Wheels Over
25. Sparrow Hawk Folds Its Wings
26. Sparrow Hawk Enters the Woods
27. Double Horse
28. Retreating Left Crosscut
29. Right Splitting Punch
30. Golden Rooster Drinks Water
31. Golden Rooster Pecks a Grain Of Rice
32. Tiger Pounces
33. Tiger Carries
34. Double Interception
35. Right Aligned Stance Drive, or Crushing Punch
36. Wind Sways The Lotus Leaves
37. Turn Around With a Snake Coiling Its Body
38. White Snake Slithers Through the Grass
39. Monkey Scratches Its Mark
40. Monkey Drops Back On Its Haunches
41. Monkey Pulls At Its Leash
42. Golden Rooster Stands On One Leg
43. Golden Rooster Thrusts a Foot
44. Swallow Skims the Water
45. Step Forward and Slice to the Groin
46. Step Forward and Plant In a Punch
47. Right Drilling Punch
48. Advance With a Tamping Hand
49. Push The Shutter To Gaze at the Moon
50. Left Splitting Punch
51. Closing Move

# THE XINGYI COMPOSITE FORM, *XINGYI ZONGHE QUAN*

**Description of the Movements**

1. **Opening Move**     qǐ shì     起势

ACTION: Stand to attention. Gradually lift the hands at the sides to shoulder height, palms up. Bend the elbows so that the hands point to each other in front of the face, palms down. Then press the hands down to the belly, bending the legs to sit with the knees together. Press the head up. Look at the right hand when lifting, then look forward. (images 1.94, 1.95, 1.96)

1.94

1.95

1.96

2. **Left Splitting Punch (*santishi*)**     zuǒ pīquán     左劈拳

ACTION 1: Turn the torso ninety degrees leftward. Clench the right fist and drill it up by the sternum, mouth, then forward to nose height, twisting the ulnar edge of the forearm up. Look past the right fist. (image 1.97)

ACTION 2: Advance the left foot without moving the right foot, settling into a *santi* stance biased toward the right leg. Bring the left fist up by the sternum and drill forward by sliding along the right forearm, then un-clench it and split forward and down to chest height. Pull the right hand back to the belly, palm down. Press the head up and look at the left hand. (image 1.98)

1.97

1.98

**Pointers**

- Land with the left foot and left hand at the same time. Be sure to move both hands along the midline of the body.

## 3. Advance With a Right Drive, or Crushing Punch

jìnbù yòu bēngquán      进步右崩拳

ACTION: Advance the left foot a step and follow in the right foot to just at the left heel, keeping most weight on the right leg. Clench both hands, and punch the right fist straight forward with the elbow slightly bent and the fist eye up. Pull the left fist back to the belly. Reach the right shoulder slightly forward. Press the head up and look past the right fist. (image 1.99)

1.99

**Pointers**

- The right fist lands as the right foot comes in. The right foot should shovel in with a thump, not lift up to stamp. The foot action is like raking forward.
- After the left foot lands, when the right foot is following in, pretend that there is a rope pulling the right foot back. Pull forcefully with the right leg as if trying to break the rope.

## 4. Retreat With a Left Drive, or Crushing Punch

tuìbù zuǒ bēngquán      退步左崩拳

ACTION: Withdraw the right foot a half-step and shift weight to the right leg. Turn the right fist heart up. Retreat the left foot a step backwards and shift your weight mostly onto the left leg. Withdraw the right foot slightly, turning it crossways so that the thighs press tightly together. Pull the right fist back to the waist. Punch the left fist directly forward at chest height, fist eye up. Reach the left shoulder forward into the punch. Press the head up and look past the left fist. (image 1.100)

1.100

**Pointers**

- Three actions must happen at once with a complete, integrated power: punch the left fist; land the left foot; pull back the right fist.
- Reach the left shoulder forward and pull the right shoulder back, using both shoulders to put power into the punch.

44  THE XINGYI COMPOSITE FORM, *XINGYI ZONGHE QUAN*

## 5. Right Aligned Stance Drive, or Crushing Punch

yòu shùnbù bēngquán   右顺步崩拳

ACTION 1: Advance the right foot a half-step forward and follow in a half-step with the left, keeping most weight on the left leg to take a *santi* stance. Drive the right fist to punch directly forward to chest height with the elbow slightly bent, the fist eye up and fist surface forward. Pull the left fist back to the belly. Reach the right shoulder forward. Press the head up and look past the right fist. (image 1.101)

1.101

### Pointers

- Land the right punch timed exactly as the right foot lands.
- The punch is driven forward from the legs, but also from the shoulders. Push forward and pull back with the shoulders.

## 6. Stroke, Hook to Ear   lǔshǒu guàn ér   捋手贯耳

ACTION 1: Advance the right foot forward and follow in the left foot to inside the right ankle. Unclench the left hand and slide it forward under the right arm with the back of the hand on the right arm, fingers up, and thumb web stretched. Pull the right fist back to in front of the right shoulder. Look past the left hand. (image 1.102)

ACTION 2: Take a long step forward with the left foot and follow in a half-step with the right foot, keeping most weight on the right leg. Do a sweeping hook punch with the right fist to hook forward to ear height with the arm slightly bent, finishing with the elbow above the shoulders, fist eye down. Extend the left hand to accept the right fist into the palm. Look at the right fist. (image 1.103)

1.102

1.103

### Pointers

- Swing the right fist rightward and then forward in a hooking punch, in one action. The punch lands as the left foot lands.
- The left hand slides forward to catch the opponent and control him so that you can step forward and punch his ear.

CHAPTER ONE: BAREHAND FORMS        45

7.      **White Ape Presents Fruit**        báiyuán xiàn guǒ        白猿献果

ACTION 1: Advance the left foot a half-step with the toes hooked in and follow in the right foot to beside the left ankle without touching down. Turn the torso ninety degrees rightward. Keep the right fist in the left palm and rotate it with a circular action, so that both palms turn up and the right fist finishes nestled in the left palm. Then unclench the right hand and pull the hands back and down to the belly, hitting with some force. Breathe out, press the head up, and keep the elbows snug to the ribs. (image 1.104)

ACTION 2: Step the right foot forward and follow in a half-step with the left foot, keeping most weight on the left leg. Strike forward and up to mouth height with the heels of the hands together, stretching the fingers forward and up. Look past the hands. (image 1.105)

1.104    1.105

**Pointers**

- This is a carrying action with both hands, and it must land as the right foot lands. Keep the elbows as close together as you can and keep the shoulders settled down.
- When the hands pull back to the belly, hit the belly equally with both, settling the *qi* to the *dantian*.
- Be sure to make the change of direction.

8.      **Retreat and Ride the Tiger**        tuìbù kuà hǔ        退步跨虎

ACTION 1: Retreat the left foot a half-step and withdraw the right foot to beside the left foot, keeping most weight on the left leg. Cross the hands and lower them in front of the body, left inside the right. Turn the right palm to face in and the left palm to face out. (image 1.106)

ACTION 2: Retreat the right foot a long step to the right and withdraw the left foot slightly to sit into a horse stance with the weight biased a bit towards the right leg. Pull the right hand back above and to the right of the head, bracing out with the elbow. Bring the left hand past the chest then brace

1.106    1.107

with a rounded arm down to the left, palm down, thumb web inwards. Look at the left hand. This stance is quite low, the right thigh should be parallel to the ground. (image 1.107)

**Pointers**

- The hands should exert equal and opposite forces, the right hand upward and back and the left hand forward and down.
- Pay attention to the weight shift. Be sure to complete the hand actions as the foot lands. The whole body should be balanced, with power applied evenly in all directions. The movement should be fierce, with full and focussed spirit.

9.  **Left Bear**        zuǒ xióngxíng        左熊形

ACTION 1: Advance the left foot a half-step and follow in with the right foot, turning the torso left. Clench the left fist and bring it back to the waist, first lifting it and then blocking across to the left as it comes in. Bring the right forearm across over the head, fist heart down, to cover and press down in front. Look to the forward left. (image 1.108)

ACTION 2: Take a long step forward with the right foot and follow in a half-step with left foot, touching the ball of the foot down with the heel raised. Shift forward onto the right leg. Continue to cover and press down with the right fist all the way to the belly, fist heart in. Drill the left fist out past the sternum, forward and up to nose height, ulnar edge turned up. Butt forward with the head, tuck the chin in, and look past the left fist. (image 1.109)

**Pointers**

- Block and trap with the left fist as the body turns leftward and the left foot advances.
- Drill the left fist up and cover down with the right fist as the right foot steps forward.
- The bear model contains a head butt, so be sure to tuck in the chin and shift the body forward.

CHAPTER ONE: BAREHAND FORMS    47

**10.    Right Crosscut**          yòu héngquán          右横拳

ACTION 1: Advance the right foot a half-step and follow in with the left foot a half-step to beside the right foot without touching down. Lower the left hand, extending it out at shoulder height with the fist heart up. Lift the right fist to the chest, fist heart down. Look past the left fist. (image 1.110)

ACTION 2: Take a long step to the forward left with the left foot and follow in a half-step with the right foot, keeping most weight on the right leg. Turn the left fist over and tuck it in, pulling back to the belly, fist heart down. Slide the right fist under the left forearm, fist heart still facing down, and punch forward while turning the forearm so that the fist heart faces up by the time it reaches its full extent at shoulder height. Press the head up and look forward. (image 1.111)

**Pointers**

- Hit with the right fist as the left foot lands.
- Turn the waist and extend the shoulder forward into the crosscut hit. Press the head up, sit the buttocks down, and apply a scissoring power between the legs. Tuck the right knee in and stab it down, closing the hips and knees. The fists and arms act as if twisting a rope, using the fully connected body.

**11.    Step Forward, Eagle Grasps**    shàngbù yīngzhuō    上步鹰捉

ACTION 1: Advance the left foot a half-step and lift the right foot inside the left ankle. Drill the right fist up to head height. Lift the left fist to the right elbow, fist heart up. Release the shoulders and close the elbows. (image 1.112)

ACTION 2: Take a long step forward with the right foot and follow in the left foot a half-step. Drill the left fist out along the right forearm until the fists cross, then unclench the hands and turn the palms down. Pull the right hand back to the belly and split the left hand forward and down to waist height. Press the head up and look down at the left hand. (image 1.113)

48  THE XINGYI COMPOSITE FORM, *XINGYI ZONGHE QUAN*

**Pointers**

- For the correct angle in the final position: draw a line between the two feet, then draw a perpendicular line out from the middle of that line, and place the hand there. The hand will be in front of the left side of the body.
- The left hand splits down as the right hand pulls and the right foot lands.
- Be sure to tuck the buttocks in, press the head up, keep the trunk vertical, and settle the shoulders and elbows. Curve the fingers into eagle claw form.

1.113

**12.    Turn Around With a Tiger Carry**    zhuànshēn hǔtuō  转身虎托

ACTION 1: Take a half-step with the right foot, hooked out, then hook-in step the left foot in front of the right toes and shift onto the left leg, turning the body around rightward one-eighty degrees to face back in the way you came. Bring the hands up as the body turns, swinging the left hand and lifting the right hand to cross in front of the body, left hand above the right. Circle the hands up and out to either side, then in to the sides, palms forward and fingers down. Press the head up and look forward. (images 1.114, 1.115)

ACTION 2: Step the right foot diagonally to the forward right and follow in the left foot a half-step. Push the hands forward and down to belly height. Finish with the hands fist-width apart, palms forward, and fingers down. Press the head up and look past the hands. (image 3.116)

1.114

1.115

1.116

**Pointers**

- Take well turned hook-out and hook-in steps to turn the body around quickly. Round the lower back when circling the hands. Hit with the hands as the right foot lands.

CHAPTER ONE: BAREHAND FORMS    49

o   When doing the carrying action downwards, press the head up, settle the shoulders, set the lower back, and tuck in the buttocks. Coordinate these actions with an exhalation to assist in launching power.

13.    **Double Interception**    shuāng jiéshǒu    双截手

ACTION 1: Without moving the feet, clench the hands and take them across to the left with a blocking transverse interception. The right forearm is vertical, fist heart in at nose height in front of the left fist. The left fist is in front of the face. Look forward. (image 1.117)

ACTION 2: Withdraw the right foot a half-step and touch the toes down. Intercept across to the right with both forearms. The left arm is in front with the fist heart in and forearm vertical. The right fist is at the left elbow. Look forward. (image 1.118)

1.117    1.118

**Pointers**

o   Use the waist to draw the arms left and right to intercept. Transfer power from the waist to the shoulders, from the shoulders to the elbows, and from the elbows to the hands. Be sure to rotate the fists as the arms cut across. When intercepting leftward, the right fist rotates externally [thumb turning away from the palm] and the left fist rotates internally [thumb turning into the palm]. When intercepting rightward, the left fist rotates externally and the right fist rotates internally.

o   Withdraw the right foot slightly when intercepting rightward. The left and right interceptions must be done smoothly and continuously without a break in the action or power.

14.    **Right Aligned Stance Drive**

yòu shùnbù bēngquán    右顺步崩拳

ACTION: Advance the right foot and follow in the left foot slightly. Lower the right fist to the side then punch straight forward to chest height with the elbow slightly bent and the fist eye up. Pull the left fist back to the belly. Press the head up and look at the right fist. (image 1.119)

1.119

50   THE XINGYI COMPOSITE FORM, *XINGYI ZONGHE QUAN*

**Pointers**

- The pointers are the same as movement 5 described above.

**15.   White Crane Flashes Its Wings**   báihè liàngchì   白鹤亮翅

ACTION 1: Withdraw the left foot a half step, sitting into a horse stance. Lower the right fist to cross the forearms in front of the belly, then brace out to the sides over the knees. Without moving the feet, drill the fists up to head height with the fist hearts facing in and the wrists crossed, left inside the right. (images 1.120, 1.121)

1.120

1.121

ACTION 2: Rotate the forearms to turn the fist hearts out and open the arms to brace out to the left and right, keeping the arms slightly bent. Pull the right foot back beside the left foot, landing with a thump. While doing this, bring the fists in together at the belly. Press the head up, settle the *qi* to the *dantian*, and look forward. (images 1.122, 1.123)

1.122

1.123

**Pointers**

- The actions of *white crane flashes it wings* involve an upward drill, a turning outer brace, a dropping wrap, and a withdrawing embrace at the belly. Be sure to feel the power of each: drill, rotate, brace, wrap, and embrace. The whole body must be co-ordinated, quick but not rushed, and the power smoothly integrated without any slackness.
- Pay particular attention to the leftward and rightward shifting of the body. When the fists drill up, the weight should shift more towards the left leg. When the arms brace out, weight should shift more towards the right leg. When the arms wrap, weight should shift more to the left leg.
- The fists should hit the belly timed exactly as the right foot lands, settling the *qi* to the *dantian* to assist in exerting power. When the right foot

CHAPTER ONE: BAREHAND FORMS    51

withdraws it must rub along the ground. Land with a thump, do not to lift the foot to stamp.

16.    **Left Cannon, or Pounding Punch**    zuǒ pàoquán    左炮拳

ACTION: Take a long step to the forward right with the right foot and follow-in a half-step with the left. Drill the right fist up by the sternum to nose height. Lift the left fist to the sternum then punch forward as the right foot advances. Punch the left fist to solar plexus height with the arm slightly bent, elbow tucked in, and fist eye up. Rotate the right fist internally (thumb side turning towards the palm) at the right temple, elbow down. Look past the left punch. (image 1.124)

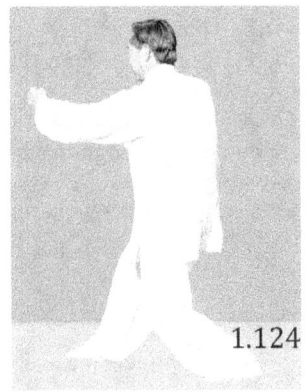
1.124

**Pointers**

o   The left punch and the right foot landing are timed together, so that hand and foot hit as a unit.

o   Turn your waist to put your shoulder into the punch, so that the lower back pushes the shoulder to send the elbow and thus the left fist out.

o   Be sure to keep the right elbow down – don't lift it. Keep the right fist at the right temple.

o   Be sure to turn the body to achieve the punch.

17.    **Lead Left and Plant a Punch Right**    zuǒ lǐng yòu zāi    左领右栽

ACTION: Step the left foot forward without moving the right foot, dodging the torso to the left and shifting onto the left leg. Internally rotate the left fist (thumb side turns towards the palm) and pull it up across the body as the body turns left, doing a drawing, leading action, to finish with an upward block above the head. Punch the right hand straight down to groin height, fist eye in, fist surface down, and arm slightly bent. Lower the torso. Look forward. (image 1.125)

1.125

**Pointers**

o   Complete the action of both hands as the left foot lands.

o   The left hand's action is completed as the body dodges to the left, so that it leads across to the left. Bring the right shoulder forward, close in the right knee and roll in the right hip to plant the right fist straight down.

## 18. Right Stroke And Drag Back  yòu lǚ dài  右捋带

ACTION: Step the right foot forward, hooked out, lifting the left heel in place. Unclench the hands and bring the right hand forward and up to slice up to the shoulder with the palm forward and the thumb web down. Turn the left palm up with the fingers forward, and extend it forward and up to lift up at shoulder height. Finish with the left hand forward and the right hand back and higher. Turn the body slightly rightward. Look past the left hand. (image 1.126)

**Pointers**

o   Complete the action of the hands as the right foot lands.

o   The hands should first extend forward, and then follow the rightward turning of the body to draw across to the right. Bend the left elbow. The right hand finishes in front of the head. Be sure to use the waist to draw the hands across.

## 19. Reverse Stance Drilling Punch  àobù zuān dǎ  拗步钻打

ACTION: Take a long step forward with the left foot and follow in a half-step with the right foot. Tuck the left hand in and turn it palm down to press down, then clench it and hook to the left, bringing it up by the left shoulder with the fist eye down, bending the elbow above the shoulder. Lower the right hand to the waist and clench it, then drill forward and up to nose height, ulnar edge twisted up. Press the head up and look forward. (image 1.127)

**Pointers**

o   Land the right punch as the left foot lands.

o   The left hand draws a circle, first pressing down, then hooking to the left, then drawing up. Use the waist to draw the hands with a heavy power, and use a shaking power at the end. Put power from the lower back into the right drilling punch. Coordinate the shoulders so that the power from the waist moves smoothly through them.

## CHAPTER ONE: BAREHAND FORMS    53

**20.**    **Lead Right and Plant a Punch Left**    yòu lǐng zuǒ zāi    右领左栽

- This movement is the same as movement 17, just transposing right and left. (image 1.128)

**21.**    **Left Stroke and Drag Back**    zuǒ lǔ dài    左捋带

- This is the same as movement 18, just transposing right and left. (image 1.129)

**22.**    **Reverse Stance Drilling Punch**    àobù zuān dǎ    拗步钻打

- This is the same as movement 19, just transposing right and left. (image 1.130)

## 23. Sparrow Hawk Pierces the Sky   yàozǐ zuān tiān   鹞子钻天

ACTION: Rotate the left fist, cock it, and press down with the fist heart down, tucking the forearm across the body. Lower the right fist to the right waist. Advance the right foot a half-step and follow in the left foot a half-step. Drill the right fist forward and up from the sternum, finishing at nose height with ulnar edge up. Pull the left fist back to the belly. Press the head up and look forward. (image 1.131)

### Pointers

- Land the right punch as the right foot lands. The fist is at nose height and the elbow is tucked into the chest, which gives the arm a bend of about one-twenty degrees.

1.131

## 24. Sparrow Hawk Wheels Over   yàozǐ fānshēn   鹞子翻身

ACTION 1: Pivot on the feet to turn around one-eighty degrees to the left to face back in the way from which you came. Lift the right elbow and bring the right arm past the right ear, crossing the forearm over the head as you turn around to the left. Press the right forearm past the head to cover forward and down with the fist heart down. Shift the weight onto the left foot, and complete the right fist cover down to the chest. Drill the left fist up and forward to nose height, fist heart in. Look at the left fist. (images 1.132, 1.133)

1.132

1.133

ACTION 2: Bring the right forearm across the body, lifting it up to block above the head. Settle the left elbow to bring the fist back to the chest. Shift back to the right leg. Pull the right fist back in front of the right shoulder as the body turns. Lift the left elbow and slide the fist along the left ribs to stab down at the hip with the fist eye down. Look at the left fist. (image 1.134)

1.134

ACTION 3: Bend the right knee to squat fully down with most weight on the right leg, and extend the left leg out into a drop stance. Slide the left fist forward along the left leg and pull the right fist back down to the waist. Once the left fist passes the left foot, turn the fist eye up. Look at the left fist. Move the body forward as the left fist moves forward. (image 1.135)

1.135

**Pointers**

- *Sparrow hawk wheels over* emphasizes body technique. It trains the power use in the trunk and the ability to use the waist as the fulcrum, transferring smoothly through the shoulders and arms. The action is soft and smooth without being slack. It should show a hidden power, so should not be done with hard power.
- Be sure to shift the body back and forth, and to lead with the head, drawing the action from the waist. After the right fist has covered and the left fist has drilled out, raise the right fist with the arm across the body, and then draw it back. Use the elbow to draw the fist back. Use a wrapping, twisting power to bring the right fist in to the waist, circling it with a settled power in the shoulder.
- Lift the elbow to hug the left fist to the ribs. Be sure to first lift the elbow and then close the shoulder to stab the fist down. Once the left fist has gone past the left foot, lead forward into the head and shift forward. At this point, gradually rotate and settle the left shoulder and settle and bend the elbow to turn the fist over. This action hides a scooping technique.

**25.    Sparrow Hawk Folds Its Wings**    yàozǐ shùshēn    鹞子束身

ACTION: Shift forward onto the left leg, bending the knee and rising. Take a large step forward with the right foot and quickly bring the left foot up to the right ankle without touching down. Bring the left fist back towards the belly. Bring the right fist by the sternum to punch forward and down, fist eye forward at groin height, crossing over outside the left fist. Finish with the left fist inside, fist heart in and the right fist outside, fist eye forward. Press the head up and look at the right fist. (image 1.136)

1.136

**Pointers**

- Land the right punch as the right foot lands. You must stand firmly on the right leg.

## 56 THE XINGYI COMPOSITE FORM, *XINGYI ZONGHE QUAN*

- Close the shoulders in and hug the elbows to the ribs, closing in the chest and abdomen and tucking in the buttocks. Reach the right shoulder forward slightly into the punch.

**26.  Sparrow Hawk Enters the Woods**  yàozǐ rùlín  鹞子入林

ACTION: Take a large step forward with the left foot and follow in a half-step with the right foot. Drill the right fist up to nose height. As the foot steps forward, rotate the right forearm and drop the elbow, pulling the right fist back to the temple with the fist heart in. Lift the left fist past the sternum then punch it forward at chest height, fist eye up, elbow bent. Press the head up and look at the left fist. (image 1.137)

**Pointers**
- Punch the left fist as the left foot lands, so that hands and feet work together.
- Be sure not to block directly up with the right arm. It must drill and then rotate with the elbow held down.
- Use the forward step, the rotation of the body, and the extention of the shoulder to put power into the punch. Keep the shoulders settled down, and turn the body almost sideways to the line.

**27.  Double Horse**  shuāng mǎxíng  双马形

ACTION 1: Step the right foot forward and lift the left foot to the right ankle. Turn the right fist over so that the fist heart faces up and roll in the forearm, pounding down with the knuckles forward. After the right fist crosses the left arm, pound down with both fists, fist hearts up. Press the head up and look forward. Raise the fists from the hips to in front of the shoulders by bending the elbows and turning the fists so that the fist hearts face down and the fist surfaces face forward with the wrists slightly cocked and the elbows out at shoulder height. (images 1.138, 1.139)

# CHAPTER ONE: BAREHAND FORMS

ACTION 2: Take a large step forward with the left foot and follow in a half-step with the right foot. Strike forward to chest height, keeping the arms slightly bent, the fists about a fist width apart. Press the head up and look forward. (image 1.140)

1.140

**Pointers**

- Settle the shoulders and elbows to pound down with the fists. Use the shoulders and elbows to draw the fists back. Press the head up and lengthen the lower back, straightening the chest a bit, to give a feeling of shoving with the chest.
- Strike forward with the fists as the left foot lands, using whole body power.
- Close the chest, urge the shoulders forward, extend the arms, and round the lower back to do the double strike. Rounding the lower back tucks in the abdomen to push the lower back to the rear, so that the back urges the shoulders forward. The power then transfers from the shoulders to the elbows and from the elbow to the fists, consequetively and segmentally increasing in force to the fist surface.

**28.   Retreating Left Crosscut**   tuìbù zuǒ héngquán   退步左横拳

ACTION 1: Withdraw the right foot a half-step and cut the right forearm in with an elbow cover, rotating the fist heart up. Lower the left fist to the belly, turning the fist heart down. Look past the right fist. (image 1.141)

ACTION 2: Bring the left foot past the right foot then back to the left rear, landing with a thump and shifting the weight back more onto the left leg. Slide the left fist along under the right arm to drill forward to shoulder height, fist heart turning up. Tuck the right fist over and press down, pulling back to the belly. Press the head up and look past the left fist. (image 1.142)

1.141

1.142

**Pointers**

- Turn over the right fist with the elbow cover as the right foot withdraws. Perform a small body movement at this time, pre-loading forward in preparation for the backward movement.

## 58  THE XINGYI COMPOSITE FORM, *XINGYI ZONGHE QUAN*

- Land the left punch as the left foot lands.

**29.   Right Splitting Punch**   yòu pīquán   右劈拳

ACTION: Advance the right foot a half-step straight forward and follow in with the left foot a half-step. Bring the right fist to the sternum, along the left arm, and then unclench the hand and split forward to chest height. Unclench the left hand and pull it back to the belly. Press the head up and look past the right hand. (image 1.143)

1.143

### Pointers

- The right hand should complete the split as the right foot lands. Reach the right shoulder forward, keeping it released and the elbow down. Press the head up to lift the trunk slightly. Exhale and settle the *qi* to the *dantian* to put power into the strike.

**30.   Golden Rooster Drinks Water**   jīnjī zhuó shuǐ   金鸡啄水

ACTION 1: Withdraw the right foot to in front of the left foot, lifting the knee with the foot hooked up at the belly of the calf. Stand firmly on the left leg, keeping the knee bent. Clench the right hand and bring the fist back to the belly, then drill it up by the sternum and mouth and forward to nose height, ulnar edge twisted up. Clench the left hand and lift it to the the right elbow. Look at the right fist. (image 1.144)

ACTION 2: Land the right foot with a thump and lift the left foot at the right ankle. Bend the right leg to lower the body. Drill the left fist up along the right arm to head height, then unclench it and split forward and down to chest height. Unclench the right hand and pull it down to the right hip, palm down. Press the head up and look forward. (image 1.145)

1.144

1.145

### Pointers

- Complete both the pull back and the drill up with the right hand as the right foot withdraws. Split down with the left hand as the right foot lands with a thump.

CHAPTER ONE: BAREHAND FORMS    59

- o  Reach the shoulder forward and settle the elbow for the left split. The right foot should thump with a settled, powerful feeling – settle the whole foot on the ground, bend the knee, straighten the lower back, tuck in the buttocks, and press up the head. The foot should make a firm, solid sound as it lands.

**31.    Golden Rooster Pecks a Grain of Rice**    jīnjī shí mǐ    金鸡食米

ACTION: Advance the left foot a long step and follow in the right foot with a raking action to thump just at the left heel. Clench the right fist to punch forward to chest height. Set the left hand on the right wrist. Press the head up and look past the right fist. (image 1.146)

**Pointers**

- o  The left foot's step must be both long and quick. The right punch hits as the right foot lands. Reach the shoulder forward into the punch.

**32.    Tiger Pounces**    hǔ pū    虎扑

ACTION 1: Retreat the right foot and withdraw the left foot a half-step, shifting onto the right leg. Unclench both hands to reach forward, then clench both hands and pull back to in front of the chest. Look forward. (image 1.147)

ACTION 2: Advance the left foot and follow in with the right foot a half-step. Drill the fists up past the chest to the jaw. As the left foot lands, extend the arms to pounce to chest height. Unclench the hands and turn them over so that the palms face forward as they pounce. Keep the arms slightly bent, palms about a fist-width apart. Reach the shoulders, drop the elbows, press the head up and look forward. (image 1.148)

# THE XINGYI COMPOSITE FORM, *XINGYI ZONGHE QUAN*

**Pointers**

o   One main characteristic of Xingyiquan's footwork is, 'when the lead foot advances then the rear foot must follow in, when the rear foot retreats then the lead foot must withdraw.' The right foot must retreat and the left foot withdraw as the hands reach forward and pull back.

o   The hands must complete the pounce as the left foot lands. Practise the use of the lower back and shoulders to put power into the pounce.

**33.    Tiger Carries**          hǔ tuō                        虎托

ACTION 1: Advance the left foot a half-step, hooked in, then advance the right foot to beside the left ankle. Cross the hands, then circle them to the sides, and then wrap them in to the sides of the waist, palms forward, fingers down. Press the head up and look to the forward right. (image 1.149)

ACTION 2: Take a long step to the forward right with the right foot and follow in a half-step with the left foot. Push forward from the waist with both palms, fingers angled down, palms about a fist-length apart at belly height. Urge the shoulders forward, settle the waist down, press the head up, and look past the hands. (image 1.150)

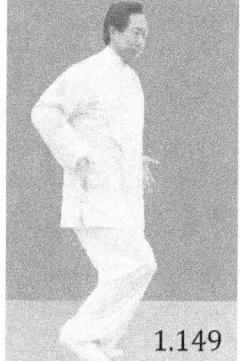

1.149          1.150

**Pointers**

o   Circle the hands out and then in to the sides as the left foot advances. Brace out to the sides with the arms rounded, the chest closed in and the upper back opened taut, bending the waist and shrinking the torso.

o   When bringing the hands in, they should have a wrapping, drawing power. Press the head up, lengthen the lower back, settle the shoulders, and tuck in the elbows.

o   When the hands push forward in the carrying action, they must land as the right foot lands. Tuck the elbows tightly into the ribs to send the hands forward. Settle the shoulders, tuck in the bottocks and close the elbows together. The torso should drop slightly. Coordinate these actions with a breath out.

## 34. Double Interception    shuāng jiéshǒu    双截手

This movement is the same as movement 13. (images 1.151, 1.152)

## 35. Right Aligned Stance Drive    yòu shùnbù bēngquán    右顺步崩拳

This is the same as movement 14. (image 1.153)

## 36. Wind Sways The Lotus Leaves    fēng bǎi héyè    风摆荷叶

ACTION 1: Turn the body leftward and take a half-step to the left with the left foot. Lower the right hand, then unclench and circle both hands down, to the left, and then up. Look at the right hand. (image 1.154)

ACTION 2: Take a front crossover step with the right foot across the left foot further towards the left side, into a cross stance with the weight between the feet. Circle the hands up, rightward and back, turning the trunk around to the right. Finish with the right hand at shoulder height and the left hand in front of the right shoulder, both palms facing the rear right. Look at the right hand. (image 1.155)

62  THE XINGYI COMPOSITE FORM, *XINGYI ZONGHE QUAN*

1.155

- Perform two or three *wind sways the lotus leaves* without a pause between them.

**Pointers**

  o  The hands draw a vertical circle in front of the body, so the body needs to turn. The hands arrive to the rear as the right foot lands in the cross step.

  o  The waist must turn around to face the rear. Settle the shoulders and elbows down so that the final movement of the 'swing' has power – do not just circle the the arms loosely.

**37.  Turn Around With a Snake Coiling Its Body**

   zhuànshēn shé chánshēn       转身蛇缠身

ACTION 1: Lower both hands to slice them leftward and upward. Pivot on the feet to turn the body around leftward one-eighty degrees. Swing the left hand leftward from above the head to chop down to the left hip. Lift the right hand to the right of the head. Follow the movement of the left hand with the eyes. (image 1.156)

ACTION 2: Continue to turn the body leftward another ninety degrees and sit down into a resting stance. Bend the right elbow to bring the right hand down past the face to stab outside the left hip, palm out. Thread the left hand up from the left hip to the right shoulder in a circling motion, palm up. Look past the left hand. (image 1.157)

1.156

1.157

CHAPTER ONE: BAREHAND FORMS    63

**Pointers**

- o  The hands perform the circling chop and the threading stab as you turn and sit into the resting stance. The whole movement must be done in one action with no pausing.
- o  The body should rise when the hands do the circling chop. When the hands perform the threading stab they should externally rotate (thumb side turns away from the palm). In the resting stance the body should be tucked in tightly.

**38.    White Snake Slithers Through the Grass**    báishé bō cǎo    白蛇拨草

ACTION: Take a long step forward with the right foot and follow in a half-step with the left foot, keeping in a low stance with most weight on the left leg. Slice the right hand forward and up from the left hip to waist height with the elbow bent, fingers forward and thumb up. Pull the left hand palm down and back to the left hip. Sit down into the buttocks. Look at the right hand. (image 1.158)

1.158

**Pointers**

- o  Complete the right arm slice as the right foot lands. To launch power into the right arm, sit into the buttocks, tuck in the hips, lengthen the lower back, settle the shoulders, and drop the elbows. Use both shoulders to get power.

**39.    Monkey Scratches Its Mark**    yuánhóu guà yìn    猿猴挂印

ACTION 1: Turn the body slightly to the left and withdraw the right foot to beside the left foot. Lower the right hand, clenching it and drawing it in to the belly. Then step the right foot a half-step to the forward right, circling it around and hooking the foot out, turning the body rightward. Drill the right fist up to in front of the jaw, turning it so the fist heart faces in, to hook and knock away in an outward blocking action at shoulder height. Look at the right hand. (image 1.159)

ACTION 2: Shift forward to the right leg and step the left foot in front of the right toes, hooking it in to take a character eight [八] stance. Continue to turn around to the right. Lift the left hand to the right elbow and continue to rotate the right fist. Look at the right hand. (image 1.160)

1.159

64   THE XINGYI COMPOSITE FORM, *XINGYI ZONGHE QUAN*

**Pointers**

- The right foot must draw a circle when it withdraws and then steps out again, so that it both does a hook-out step and lands hooked out. After the right fist drills up it may unclench as the body turns around, turning into a hooking grab. The hook-out and hook-in steps bring the body around a full one-eighty degrees.
- The whole movement must be coordinated between the footwork, the body work, and the hands.

40.   **Monkey Drops Back On Its Haunches**   tuìbù hóu dūn   退步猴蹲

ACTION 1: Shift onto the left foot, and retreat the right foot a long step behind. Slide the left hand forward on top of the right arm to eye height and pull the right hand back to the left side of the belly. Both palms face down. Look at the left hand. (image 1.161)

ACTION 2: Withdraw the left foot to in front of the right foot and touch the ball of the foot down, shifting onto the right foot. Squat down until the thigh is parallel to the ground. Bring the left hand back to the left hip. Lift the right hand in front of the right shoulder then reach it out in front of the left shoulder, palm down. Look past the left shoulder. The torso should turn rightward when squatting, to bring the left shoulder forward. (image 1.162)

**Pointers**

- When the right foot retreats you may also push off with the left leg to jump back onto the right leg, landing firmly. When the left foot withdraws it must come in quickly and touch down lightly.
- The left hand thread forward as the right foot withdraws. The squatting position should be low.

## CHAPTER ONE: BAREHAND FORMS

**41.    Monkey Pulls At Its Leash**    yuánhóu dáo shéng    猿猴捯绳

ACTION 1: Rise, drawing a vertical circle in front of the body with both hands. Extend the right hand while pulling back the left hand. Then lift the left hand while pulling the right hand back. The hands each draw one circle. Look forward. (images 1.163, 1.164)

ACTION 2: Advance the left foot a half-step and follow in the left foot. Slide the left hand out from the right shoulder in a splitting palm to chest height, palm forward. Pull the left hand back to the belly. Press the head up and look past the left hand. (image 1.165)

### Pointers

- The hand action must be quick and lively. The left hand splits as the left foot advances, hitting sharply together.

**42.    Golden Rooster Stands On One Leg**    jīnjī dúlì    金鸡独立

ACTION 1: Advance the left foot a half-step without moving the right foot. Shift forward so that most of your weight in on the left leg, bending the left knee and lifting the right heel. Lift the right hand to the sternum and thread it forward under the left arm with the palm down. Withdraw the left hand, pulling it back to the chest with the palm down. Urge the right shoulder forward, bend the elbow, and drop the wrist so that the palm is forward and fingers are pointing up at shoulder height. Press the head up and look at the right hand. (image 1.166)

ACTION 2: Take a long step forward with the right foot and quickly follow in the left foot to place it by the right ankle without touching down. Keep the knees together and stand firmly on the right leg with the knee bent. Thread the left hand forward under the right arm and cock the wrist with the fingers at shoulder height. Bring the right hand back to in front of the chest. Reach into the left shoulder. Press the head up and look forward. (image 1.167)

- Perform *golden rooster stands on one leg* twice.

**Pointers**

o   The step must be long and land with stability. The follow-in step must be quick. When the hands thread forward, first lift the wrists and then sit them down with a settling of the shoulder, to settle into the palms.

**43.   Golden Rooster Thrusts a Foot**     jīnjī dēngjiǎo     金鸡蹬脚

ACTION 1: Advance the left foot a half-step and shift forward onto the left leg. Thread the right hand out under the left arm, extending it to the left wrist. Once the wrists cross, turn the palms forward and circle them around each other, comng back to the chest with the wrists together, palms up. Look forward. (image 1.168)

ACTION 2: Lift the right knee and then the foot, to thrust kick to chest height with the ankle dorsi-flexed. Bend the left leg slightly to keep balance. Keep the wrists together and apply a carrying power forward and up to jaw height. Look forward. (image 1.169)

**Pointers**

o   Bend the arms while circling the hands. Stretch the upper back taut and close the chest.

## CHAPTER ONE: BAREHAND FORMS   67

- o   Carry with the hands at the same time as you kick. When carrying, lenthen the lower back, release the shoulders, extend the arms, and close the elbows together.
- o   Keep the hip tucked in when kicking. Do not release the hip forward.

**44.   Swallow Skims the Water**     yànzǐ chāo shuǐ     燕子抄水

ACTION 1: Do not land the right foot after the kick, just bend the knee and bring the foot in to the left ankle. Turn the torso ninety degrees to the right and thread the hands up with the wrists still together. Press the head up and look at the hands. (image 1.170)

ACTION 2: Land the right foot, turned out, and bend the right knee to a full squat, extending the left foot to the left to take a left drop stance. Keep the weight on the right leg, but keep the left foot solid on the ground. Slide both hands down along the body, turning the backs of the palms to touch the body. When they arrive at the waist, rotate the palms up and extend them to either side. Thread the left hand forward along the outside of the left leg, until it is in front of the left foot. Extend the right hand back, palm up. Look at the left hand. (image 1.171)

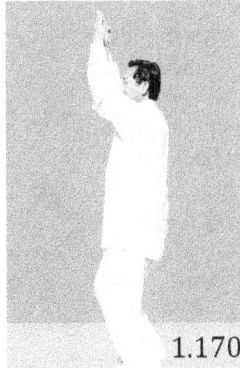
1.170

1.171

**Pointers**
- o   Thread the hands up as the left foot pushes off the ground.
- o   Stab the hands down as you drop into the drop stance. The whole movement must be smooth and coordinated.

**45.   Step Forward and Slice To the Groin**

shàngbù liāoyīnzhǎng     上步撩阴掌

ACTION: Continue to thread the left hand forward and shift forward, bending the left knee to support with the left leg, rising slightly. Take a long step forward with the right foot, turning the foot out crossways and crossing the legs to sit into a resting stance. Slice the right hand forward to strike forcefully with the palm forward at waist height. Tuck the left hand onto the right wrist. Lean the body slightly so that the right shoulder is down and the left shoulder is higher. Look at the right hand. (image 1.172, and from the other side)

68  THE XINGYI COMPOSITE FORM, *XINGYI ZONGHE QUAN*

1.172

1.172 OTHER SIDE

**Pointers**

- Slice up with the right hand as the right foot lands. Turn the waist, roll the body under, and reach with the arm, keeping it bent, to slice up. Squeeze the thighs together.

**46. Step Forward and Plant In a Punch**   shàngbù zāidǎ   上步栽打

ACTION: Take a large step forward with the left foot and follow in with the right foot. Clench both fists and slide the left fist along under the right arm to punch forward and down with the fist heart down, at belly height. Pull the right fist back to the belly with the fist heart up. Press the head up and look at left punch. (image 1.173)

**Pointers**

- Punch with the left fist as the left foot lands, so that the power is integrated.
- To get power into the left punch, be sure to press up into the head, roll the elbow in and pull back forcefully with the right fist. The fists must have equal and opposite power. Be sure to launch power from both shoulders.

**47. Right Drilling Punch**   yòu zuānquán   右钻拳

ACTION 1: First withdraw the left foot a half-step and pull the left fist back to the belly. Then advance the left foot a half-step and drill the left up past the sternum then forward to nose height. Look at the left fist. (image 1.174)

CHAPTER ONE: BAREHAND FORMS   69

ACTION 2: Take a large step forward with the right foot and follow in a half step with the left foot. Tuck the left forearm to press down across the body. Drill the right hand forward and up to nose height, twisting the ulnar edge up, and pull the left fist back to the belly. Press the head up and look forward. (image 1.175)

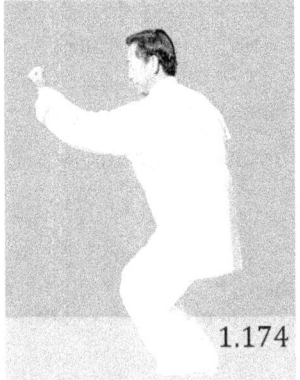
1.174

1.175

**Pointers**

o   Drill the left fist forward as the left foot advances a half-step.
o   Drill the right fist forward as the right foot lands forward.

**48.   Advance With a Tamping Hand**          jìnbù tāzhǎng        进步踏掌

ACTION 1: Withdraw the right foot a half-step and touch the ball of the foot down, shifting onto the left leg. Unclench the hands. Slide the left hand up along the outside of the right arm, palm out, to block up at eyebrow height with the forearm across the body. Bend the right elbow to bring the fist to the chest. Look forward. (image 1.176)

ACTION 2: Advance the right foot with the toes hooked in, following in the left foot and turning the torso ninety degrees leftward to land into a horse stance with the weight evenly distributed between the legs. Rotate the right palm out, thumb down, and push forcefully to chest height at the right. Brace up and pull leftward with the left hand, stopping above the head to the left. Look at the right hand. (images 1.177, 1.178)

1.176

1.177

1.178

## 70  THE XINGYI COMPOSITE FORM, *XINGYI ZONGHE QUAN*

**Pointers**

- The whole movement must be coordinated together – push the right hand, step the right foot, turn the body, brace and pull the left hand, and breathe out.
- Keep the right arm rounded to brace strongly.

**49.  Push the Shutter To Gaze At the Moon**

tuīchuāng wàngyuè                    推窗望月

ACTION 1: Lower both hands, swinging them leftward, upward, then rightward. Shift to the left leg and step the right foot across in front of the left foot with the foot turned out. Turn the body ninety degrees rightward. Look at the left hand. (image 1.179)

ACTION 2: Step the left foot forward without moving the right foot and keeping most weight on the right leg, to sit into a half-horse stance. Swing the hands downward, leftward, and upward. Turn the left palm out with the fingers down and the arm rounded, stopping at eyebrow height at the left of the body. Push forcefully to the left at chest height with the right hand, palm facing left, fingers up, and arm rounded. Press the head up and look past the right hand. (image 1.180)

1.179

1.180

**Pointers**

- Swing the arms as the right foot steps forward. Block up with the left arm and push with the right hand as the left foot steps forward. Settle the *qi* to the *dantian*.

**50.  Left Splitting Punch**      zuǒ pīquán              左劈拳

ACTION 1: Advance the right foot a half-step towards the left foot. Clench both hands and pull the right fist back to the belly, then drill it up and out to nose height. Pull the left fist back to the belly. Keep the head pressed up, and look at the right fist. (image 1.181)

ACTION 2: Advance the left foot a half-step wtihout moving the right foot, to sit into a *santi* stance. Drill the left fist along the top of the right forearm, then split forcefully forward to chest height. Pull the right hand down and back to the belly, palm down. Press the head up and look forward. (image 1.182)

### 51. Closing Move    shōu shì    收势

ACTION 1: Without moving the feet, clench the left hand and pull it back to the belly. Then shift forward and bring the right foot up beside the left foot, keeping the knees bent. (images 1.183, 1.184)

ACTION 2: Unclench the hands and lift them at the sides, then bend the elbows to bring the hands together at the front. Look at the right hand as it comes up, then look forward. (images 1.185, 1.186)

# 72 THE XINGYI COMPOSITE FORM, *XINGYI ZONGHE QUAN*

ACTION 3: Press the hands down in front of the belly and stand up to attention, letting the hands hang down to the sides. Look forward. The form is now completed. (image 1.187)

# THE MIXTURE OF MOVES

# 杂势捶

## Introduction To The Mixture Of Moves, ZASHICHUI

*Zashichui* is a classic form, also called Combined Shapes, and Integrated Form[2]. It is the longest traditional form of Xingyiquan. It is a relatively advanced level mixed form, meant to be learned after one has studied the five element techniques, the Five Elements Connected, the Eight Moves, and the twelve animals. It holds an important place among the traditional forms of Xingyiquan.

*Zashichui* does not contain all of the twelve animals, in fact, there are just a few. It contains some moves that are seldom seen: *cat washes its face, black dragon pours water, spread one wing, three basins land on the ground, push the shutter to gaze at the moon, lazy dragon lies in the road, dragon and tiger play together*. This form has a rich content, a good variety of moves, and smooth connections and power flow bewtween the moves. The move *cat washes its face*, however, occurs a great many times.

In some areas *Zashichui* is called the Floodgate Hits [闸势捶 zhá shì chuí] or the Pounding Hits [砸势捶 zá shì chuí]. This is due to dialect pronunciations of the first character.

## Names Of The Movements

1. Opening Move (left *santishi*)
2. Sparrow Hawk Folds its Wings
3. Sparrow Hawk Enters the Woods
4. Retreating Chopping Strike (Cat Washes its Face), twice
5. Black Dragon Pours Water
6. Stretch Out One Wing
7. Advance Left Crushing Punch (Hybernating Dragon Appears)
8. Right Aligned Stance Crushing Punch (Black Tiger Leaves its Den)
9. White Crane Flashes its Wings
10. Left Cannon, Pounding Punch

---

[2] Translator's note: The name doesn't translate well, and could also be translated as the Mixture of Hits. It is best to just call it *Zashichui*.

## THE MIXTURE OF MOVES, *ZASHI CHUI*

11. Spread Both Wings
12. Sparrow Hawk Enters the Woods
13. Retreating Chopping Strike (Cat Washes its Face), twice
14. Swallow Skims the Water
15. Swallow Spreads its Wings
16. Advancing Right Crushing Punch
17. Retreating Left Crushing Punch
18. Right Aligned Stance Crushing Punch
19. Spread Both Wings
20. Sparrow Hawk Enters the Woods
21. Retreating Chopping Strike (Cat Washes its Face), twice
22. Black Dragon Pours Water
23. Golden Rooster Pecks a Grain of Rice
24. Reverse Stance Eagle Grasp
25. Push the Shutter to Gaze at the Moon
26. Three Basins Land on the Ground
27. Lazy Dragon Lies in the Road
28. Black Dragon Roils the River (aligned stance left crossing punch)
29. Advancing Right Crushing Punch
30. Dragon and Tiger Fight Together
31. Right Aligned Stance Crushing Punch
32. White Crane Flashes its Wings
33. Left Cannon, Pounding Punch
34. Spread Both Wings
35. Sparrow Hawk Enters the Woods
36. Retreating Chopping Strike (Cat Washes its Face), twice
37. Black Dragon Pours Water
38. Stretch Out One Wing
39. Left Crushing Punch
40. Right Aligned Stance Crushing Punch
41. Wind Sways the Lotus Leaves (three times)
42. Advancing Left Crushing Punch
43. Sparrow Hawk Pierces the Sky
44. Sparrow Hawk Wheels Over
45. Sparrow Hawk Folds its Wings
46. Sparrow Hawk Folds Enters the Woods
47. Closing Move

# CHAPTER ONE: BAREHAND FORMS

**Description of the Movements**

1. **Opening Move (left *santishi*)**   qǐ shì   起势

Move to *santishi* the same as usual. Stand to attention, facing forty-five degrees to the direction of travel of the form. Gradually lift the hands at the sides to shoulder height, palms up, looking at the right hand. Bend the elbows to bring the hands in palms down, in front of the face, then press down to the belly, bending the legs to sit and turning the head to look forward. Clench both fists and roll the fist hearts up. Drill the right fist up and forward to nose height, twisting the little finger side up, looking at the right fist. Drill the left fist up and forward, sliding along above the right forearm. Advance the left foot, settling into a *santi* stance, unclenching the hands and rolling them palm down, splitting the left hand forward and down to chest height and pulling the right hand back to the belly. Press the head up and look past the left hand. (image 1.188)

See also Volume I, Chapter Two, for detailed description and images of *santishi*.

**Pointers**

- Relax the whole body during the opening move, and concentrate.
- Settle down into the legs as the hands press down.
- Land the left foot and the left hand simultaneously.

2. **Sparrow Hawk Folds its Wings**   yàozǐ shù shēn   鹞子束身

ACTION: Without moving the left foot, shift forward and take a long step forward with the right foot, lifting and dorsi-flexing the left foot by the right ankle without touching down. Bend the right leg slightly to stand firmly, and press the legs together. At the same time, clench both hands to fists, pull the left fist in to the belly with the fist heart in, and drill the right fist up past the sternum then forward to punch downward to solar plexus height with the fist eye forward. The right fist is outside the left fist, the elbows are tight to the ribs, the head presses up, and the eyes look forward. (image 1.189)

**Pointers**

- Step the right foot a long step forward and land firmly. Lift the left foot quickly, and pay attention to keeping the legs together.

- o The left fist must pull back and the right fist must punch forward and down at exactly the moment that the right foot steps forward. Pay attention to keeping the elbows in and the shoulders settled.

3. **Sparrow Hawk Enters the Woods**   yàozǐ rù lín   鹞子入林

ACTION: Take a long step forward with the left foot and follow in a half step with the right foot, keeping most weight on the right leg. At the same time, bend the right elbow to drill the right fist up to eyebrow height. Lift the left fist to the sternum then extend a punch to solar plexus height as the left foot steps forward. The left fist eye is on top, the elbow slightly bent, and the shoulder is extended forward. Rotate the right forearm to turn it out, keeping the elbow dropped, and bringing the fist to the right temple with the fist eye facing the temple. Release the shoulders and settle the elbows, press the head up. Look past the left fist. (image 1.190)

1.190

**Pointers**

- o The left punch must arrive at the same time as the left foot. Turn the waist and extend the shoulder into the punch, so that the body aligns sideways to the punch. Pay attention to keeping the right elbow down – do not allow it to rise. The right forearm should deflect with a rotation.
- o *Sparrow hawk folds its wings* and *sparrow hawk enters the woods* should be fully connected. There should be no hesitation between them, they are completed as one move.

4. **Retreating Chopping Strike (Cat Washes its Face)**

tuìbù pī quán (māo xī liǎn)   退步劈拳（猫洗脸）

ACTION 1 Retreat the left foot and shift back, withdrawing the right foot a half step. At the same time, open the hands. Cover inward with the left hand, pulling down and in to the left side, turning the body slightly left. Cover with the right hand, tucking in the elbow and pressing the forearm at the right of the head, palm in, and about a foot away from the face. The right fingers should be no higher than the nose, and the elbow at solar plexus height. Contain the chest and tuck in the belly. Look forward. (image 1.191)

1.191

# CHAPTER ONE: BAREHAND FORMS

ACTION 2: Retreat the right foot one step and withdraw the left foot a half step, shifting back and turning the body right. At the same time, cover with the right elbow and pull the hand in and down to the right side, palm in. Bend the left elbow and bring the hand first up and leftward, then across to cover to the right. The left hand is about a foot in front of the face, with the palm in, the elbow at solar plexus height. Contain the chest and tuck in the belly. Look forward. (image 1.192)

1.192

Repeat Actions 1 and 2.

**Pointers**

- This move is repeated twice. The repetitions should flow together smoothly, and the wrapping cover of the hands should allow no gaps. Retreat the left foot with the right elbow cover, and retreat the right foot with the left elbow cover, coordinating well together.

- The hands must continue to move throughout the *cat washes its face* actions, rotating the forearms externally while tucking in the elbows. The actions wrap downwards, using the waist to lead the shoulders, the shoulders to lead the elbows, and the retreating steps to turn the body sideways. In the form, the retreating steps should be quick and short. It is alright to just step back once, if your hands are quicker than your feet. Try to make the move quick, connected, and smooth.

5. **Black Dragon Pours Water**     wūlóng dàoshuǐ    乌龙倒水

ACTION 1: Without moving the feet, lower the right hand to circle it right, to the rear, then swing up over the head, palm forward. Tuck the left elbow in and lower the hand to in front of the belly. Look forward. (image 1.193)

ACTION 2: Press down with the right hand to in front of the belly, clenching the fist, fist heart in. Clench the left fist and drill it up past the sternum, then lift the elbow to do a framing block up with the forearm above the head, fist rotated so the fist heart faces out. Sit down slightly. Look forward. (image 1.194)

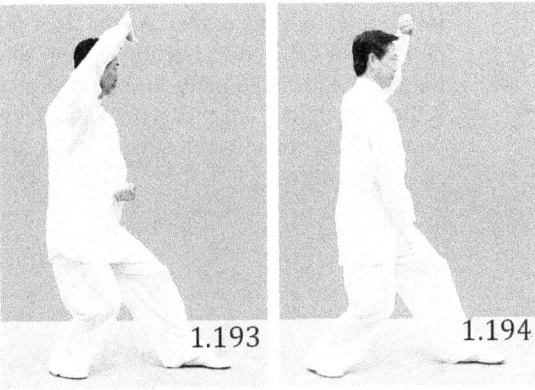
1.193   1.194

# 78   THE MIXTURE OF MOVES, *ZASHI CHUI*

**Pointers**

- Do not hesitate between actions one and two.
- The hands switch places up and down, so must be coordinated. Pay attention when drilling the left fist up to the framing block that the body has a forward intention. Brace up with the left elbow.

6. **Stretch Out One Wing**   dān zhǎn chì   单展翅

ACTION 1: Rotate the left fist to press down with the forearm across, pulling the fist in to the belly, fist heart in. Bring the right fist up past the sternum to drill up past the inside of the left arm to nose height. Then rotate the right fist inwards to turn the fist heart out, for a framing block above the head. Sit back slightly and lengthen the spine. Look forward. (image 1.195)

ACTION 2: Retreat the left foot then withdraw the right foot to in front of the left, sitting on the left leg. Rotate the right fist externally and tuck in the right elbow to turn the right fist heart up, bringing the forearm forward, then down to in front of the belly. The right fist lands into the left hand. Keep the right elbow tight to the ribs. Press the head up. Look forward. (image 1.196)

**Pointers**

- Drill the right fist up then cross for the framing block with a bracing power upwards. Be sure to shift the body back slightly and lengthen it.
- Swing the right fist into the left hand at exactly the same time that the left foot lands in its retreat. As the right fist pounds down, rotate the fist and tuck in the elbow, extend the right shoulder forward slightly, sit the buttocks, gather the belly, contain the chest, release the shoulders, and settle the elbows. All this gives a good power launch for the downward pound. The downward pound should also have a backward pulling, settling, power.

CHAPTER ONE: BAREHAND FORMS   79

7.   **Advance Left Crushing Punch (Hybernating Dragon Shows Itself)**

jìnbù zuǒ bēngquán, (zhélóng chūxiàn)   进步左崩拳（蛰龙出现）

ACTION: Advance the right foot and follow up the left foot a half step, keeping most weight on the left leg. At the same time, clench the left fist and punch directly forward with a crushing punch, fist eye up, elbow slightly bent. The right fist stays at the belly. Put the left shoulder forward into the punch. Look forward. (image 1.197)

1.197

**Pointers**

o   Land the left punch as the right foot lands.
    Foot and hand must arrive together. Put the shoulder forward to drive the punch, keeping the shoulders settled and the elbows down. Press the head up.

8.   **Right Aligned stance Crushing Punch (Black Tiger Leaves its Den)**

yòu shùnbù bēngquán, (hēihǔ chūdòng)   右顺步崩拳（黑虎出洞）

ACTION: Advance the right foot and follow up the left foot a half step, keeping the weight mostly on the left leg. At the same time, punch the right fist forward with a crushing punch to solar plexus height, fist eye up, elbow slightly bent, shoulder forward. Pull the left fist back to the belly. Press the head up. Look past the right fist. (image 1.198)

1.198

**Pointers**

o   The right foot lands, the right fist punches, and the left fist pulls back, all coordinated to arrive simultaneously. The upper and lower body work together so that the hands and feet arrive together. Turn the waist and extend the shoulder for the punch. The right and left fists must have equal power, one spitting and one swallowing. Punch with full power and gather in with full power.

# 80    THE MIXTURE OF MOVES, *ZASHI CHUI*

**9.     White Crane Flashes its Wings**    báihè liàngchì    白鹤亮翅

ACTION 1: Retreat the left foot a half step and turn in the right foot, setting down into a horse stance. Lower the right fist down to the belly so that the fists cross in front of the belly with the fist hearts inward. Then drill them up, right fist on the outside of the left, both fists drilling up to head height. Look at the right fist. (image 1.199)

ACTION 2: Without moving the feet, rotate the forearms to turn the fist hearts out then circle them outwards, each going to its own side. The arms brace outwards at shoulder height, slightly bent. Look at the right fist. (image 1.200)

ACTION 3: Sit back onto the left leg, withdrawing the right foot to beside the left foot, landing with a thump. Continue to circle the fists so that they come down, rotating them so the fist hearts face in, gathering them in front of the belly. Hit the belly with some force, sticking the elbows to the ribs, pressing up the head, and settling the *qi* to the *dantian*. Look forward. (image 1.201)

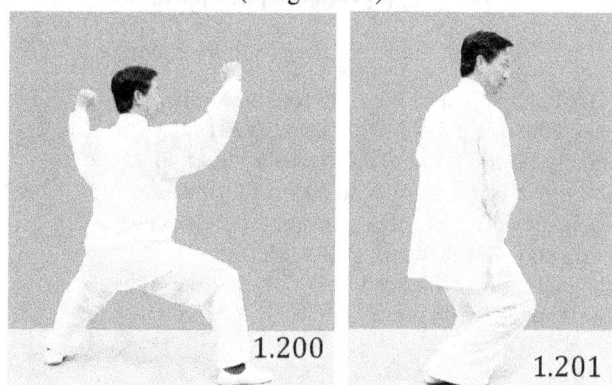

**Pointers**

o    The three actions must continue smoothly without pause, coordinating the whole body and having a full body power.

o    Pay attention when circling the fists that they have the powers of drilling, rolling over, bracing, wrapping, and hugging. When they go upwards they drill. When they rotate inwards they roll. When they open to the sides they brace. When they lower and rotate they wrap. When they pound into the belly they hug. Pay attention to the opening and closing of the chest and shoulders, to the release and tightening of the upper back, and to the settling of the elbows.

- o   The fists pound into the belly at the same time as the right foot thumps, fully coordinated. Settle the *qi* to the *dantian* to assist power output. When the right foot gathers in it must move along the ground, moving from the wrapping in of the waist and hips and the pulling in of the knee. Imagine you are pulling something in with your foot. The final trample of the foot should make a sound, but make sure you are not lifting to purposefully stamp the ground.
- o   Pay attention to the back and forth shifting of the body. Shift to the left leg when the fists drill up. Shift to the right leg when the fists brace outwards. Shift back to the left leg when the fists wrap and hug inwards.

**10.   Left Cannon, Pounding Punch**   zuǒ pàoquán   左炮拳

ACTION: Take a long step to the forward right with the right foot and follow in a half step with the left foot, keeping most weight on the left leg. At the same time, drill the right fist up past the chest to nose height and lift the left fist to the sternum. As the right foot steps, punch the left fist forward to solar plexus height, fist eye up, keeping the elbow slightly bent. Release through the shoulders and settle the elbows. Rotate the right fist and brace out with the elbow dropped, the fist eye by the right temple, fist heart forward. As the left shoulder pushes forward the right shoulder follows along. Tuck in the chin and press the head up. Look at the left fist. (image 1.202)

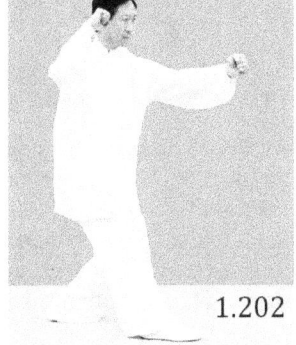

1.202

**Pointers**

- o   The left punch must arrive as the right foot lands – foot and hand working together. Pay attention to the power of the turn of the waist and shoulders. When you drill the right fist up, be sure to keep the elbow down – do not lift it.

**11.   Spread Both Wings**   shuāng zhǎn chì

ACTION 1: Retreat the left foot without moving the right foot. Bring both fists in front of the head, crossing them with the fist hearts in, right fist on the outside of the left. Look forward past the fists. (image 1.203)

ACTION 2: Shift to the left leg and withdraw the right foot to beside the left ankle, then stomp, putting the weight onto the right leg. Rotate the fists inwards and brace them out to their respective sides. Then rotate the fists outwards to turn the fist hearts

1.203

## 82    THE MIXTURE OF MOVES, *ZASHI CHUI*

up, and hug them down and in to the belly. Press the head up and settle the *qi* to the *dantian*. Look forward. (image 1.204)

1.204

**Pointers**

- The fists drill up as the left foot retreats, with a wrapping power. The fists pound into the belly as the right foot stomps.
- The drill, roll, brace, wrap, and hug of the fists use an internal rotation and external rotation that combines with the containing of the chest, the settling of the elbows, and the gathering of the belly to pound downwards. Settle the *qi* to the *dantian* when the fists hit the belly.

**12.    Sparrow Hawk Enters the Woods**    yàozǐ rùlín    鹞子入林

ACTION: Take a long step forwards with the left foot and follow up the right foot a half step. Drill the right fist up past the chest to nose height. Lift the left fist to under the right elbow then punch forward as the left foot steps forward. Punch to sternum height with the arm slightly bent, the fist eye on top. Rotate the right fist outwards to turn the fist heart out, and place the fist eye near the right temple, keeping the elbow dropped. Put the left shoulder forward into the punch. Look past the left fist. (image 1.205)

1.205

**Pointers**

- The pointers are the same as move 3.

**13.    Retreating Chopping Strike (Cat Washes its Face), twice**

    tuìbù pī quán (māo xī liǎn)    退步劈拳（猫洗脸）

- This is the same as movement 4. Repeat twice. (see images 1.191, 1.192)

**14.    Swallow Skims the Water**    yànzǐ chāo shuǐ    燕子抄水

ACTION 1: Complete the previous move with the left foot forward and the left hand up. Pull the right hand back, then lift it above the head, then press forward and down with the palm down. Lower the left hand and clench it, then drill it up past the sternum and forward to nose height, fist heart in. Press the right hand down at the side of the waist. Shift forward to the left leg. Look past the left fist. (image 1.206)

ACTION 2: Slice the right hand up in front of the outside of the left forearm and bend the left elbow to stab the left fist down. Continue to circle the right hand back. Open the left hand and slice it forward and up. Shift back. Look at the right hand. (images 1.207, 1.208)

ACTION 3: Advance the left foot a half step then push off to jump, lifting the right knee to step forward, landing with the foot turned out and the left knee raised in a right one legged stance. The body is turned slightly to the right. Slice the right hand forward and up above the

1.206

head, extending the arm. Bend the left arm and stab down, placing the back of the hand by the left ribs. Look forward to the left. (image 1.209)

ACTION 4: Squat fully on the right leg and dig the left foot forward, extending the leg with the foot tucked in, into a left drop stance. Thread the left hand down and forward along the left leg with the palm turned back, little finger up. Swing the right hand up behind with the arm rounded. Look past the left hand. (image 1.210)

1.207

1.208

1.209

1.210

# 84 THE MIXTURE OF MOVES, *ZASHI CHUI*

**Pointers**

- The hands work together in opposite directions, one up the other down, one forward the other back, one left the other right. This must be done in coordination with the body.
- Push off with the left leg, swinging the right leg forward and threading the right hand up at the same time. When the right leg sits into the drop stance, the the left hand slides along the left leg.
- The jump must go for both height and distance. Lift the *qi* to help this. The drop stance must be low. Settle the *qi* as you squat and thread out the hand.
- The move should be light and agile, with good coordination between the feet and hands. The actions should be connected and without pause, completed in one breath. Pay attention when threading the left hand along the leg that the head presses forward. As the left hand passes the left foot, shift forward. As the left elbow passes the left foot, bend the leg and move forward and up. You need to train waist strength and leg basics to be able to do this move well.

## 15. Swallow Spreads its Wings     yànzǐ zhǎnchì     燕子展翅

ACTION 1: Shift forward to the left leg, bending the knee to rise. Being the left shoulder forward, threading the left hand forward, extending it so it rises to shoulder height, palm to the right. Extend the right hand back. Press the head up. Look past the left hand. (image 1.211)

ACTION 2: Shift forward without stepping. Bend the left elbow to being the hand in to the chest, palm in. Lower the right hand behind, then slice it forward and up along under the left arm, then bend the elbow to bring the hand in front of the chest. The hands are now crossed in front of the chest, elbows down, palms in. Turn the body slightly to the right. Look forward. (image 1.212)

1.211     1.212

ACTION 3: Take a long step forward with the right foot, bending the right leg to stand steady. Follow in the left foot to the right ankle without touching down, keeping the knees together. Rotate both hands to turn the palm out and separate the arms forward and back, bending the elbows. The hands finish with upright sideways palms at shoulder height, the left in front and the right behind, palms facing right. Look at the left palm. (image 1.213)

**Pointers**

- The move must be done smoothly and well coordinated between upper and lower limbs, with equal attention given to right and left, completed in one breath.
- Take a long step forward and land firmly. Complete the opening of the arms as the foot lands.

1.213

**16. Advancing Right Crushing Punch**  jìnbù yòu bēng quán  进步右崩拳

ACTION: Step the left foot forward and follow up with the right foot to behind the left, weight on the right leg. Clench both hands and bring the right fist in to the waist, then punch it forward with a crushing punch to solar plexus height. Pull the left fist back to the left side. Press the head up. Look past the right fist. (image 1.214)

**Pointers**

- Bring the right foot in with a raking action, timing the punch with it.
- Whenever doing the crushing punch, one must try hard to accomplish its requirements that 'the hands never leave the heart, the elbows never leave the ribs, go in and out like in and out of a hole'.

1.214

**17. Retreating Left Crushing Punch**  tuìbù zuǒ bēng quán  退步左崩拳

ACTION: Retreat the right foot a half step and shift back. Retreat the left foot to the rear, landing with the whole foot. The right foot shifts a bit to allow this, turning out across the stance. Turn the body right, aligning the left shoulder forward. The stance is a scissors stance, with both legs slightly bent. Pull the right fist back to the right side and punch the left fist forward to solar plexus height with a crushing punch. Press the head up. Look past the left fist. (image 1.215)

1.215

## 86  THE MIXTURE OF MOVES, *ZASHI CHUI*

**Pointers**
- The left punch arrives as the left foot lands behind. The left foot should stomp when it lands.
- The waist and shoulders should work together to send the left fist out and the right fist back.

**18. Right Aligned stance Crushing Punch**

yòu shùnbù bēng quán            右顺步崩拳

ACTION: Advance the right foot and follow up a half step with the left foot, to take a right trinity stance. Pull the left fist back to the left side and punch the right fist forward with a crushing punch to solar plexus height. Press the head up. Look at the right fist. (see image 1.198)

**Pointers**
- The right punch arrives as the right foot lands. Turn the waist and send the shoulder into the punch. Settle the shoulders, drop the elbows, and breathe out to punch.

**19. Spread Both Wings**

This is the same as movement 11. (see images 1.203, 1.204)

**20. Sparrow Hawk Enters the Wood**

This is the same as movement 12. (see image 1.205)

**21. Retreating Chopping Strike (Cat Washes its Face), twice**

This is the same as movement 4. (see images 1.191, 1.192)

**22. Black Dragon Pours Water**

This is the same as movement 5. (see images 1.193, 1.194)

**23. Golden Rooster Pecks a Grain of Rice**    jīnjī shímǐ      金鸡食米

ACTION 1: Advance the left foot and shift forward without moving the right foot. Bring the left fist from the head to stab forward and down at the belly. Bring the right fist forward and up to scoop outside the left arm, then pull it back to the right to the right side. Open the left hand and extend it forward to solar plexus height, fingers up, palm to the left. Look past the left hand. (image 1.216)

1.216

## CHAPTER ONE: BAREHAND FORMS

ACTION 2: Bring the right foot in behind the left foot, landing with a thump, shifting to the right leg. Punch the right fist forward with a crushing punch to solar plexus height. Tuck the left hand onto the right wrist. Press the head up. Look at the right fist. (image 1.217)

1.217

**Pointers**

- The right punch comes as the right foot digs into the ground, completing the action as one
- Pull the right fist back as the left hand extends, using the shoulders to coordinate the action. Shift and use body technique to open and close – pre-load back to move forward, and pre-load left to move right.

**24.   Reverse Stance Eagle Grasp**   àobù yīng zhuō   拗步鹰捉

ACTION 1: Shift forward and step the right foot forward, bending the legs. Pull both hands back to the belly, clench the left hand, and drill them up and forward. Rotate the left fist so the little finger is turned up at nose height. Tuck in the chin and press the head up. Look at the left fist. (image 1.218)

ACTION 2: Take a long step to the forward left with the left foot then follow up a half step with the right foot, keeping most weight on the right leg. Drill the right fist up then forward and up along the left arm. As the fists cross, rotate them and open to eagle claws. Chop the right hand forward and down to waist height. Pull the left hand back to in front of the belly. Press the head up. Look down past the right hand. (image 1.219)

1.218

1.219

**Pointers**

- Drill the left fist out as the right foot steps forward. Chop the right hand down as the left foot steps forward.
- The eagle claw hand shape is: the fingertips are slightly tucked in, the palm is rounded, and the wrist is settled. Pay attention to releasing the shoulders and settling the elbows, and pressing the head up and tucking the buttocks under, when hitting out with the eagle grab. The legs have a

88   THE MIXTURE OF MOVES, *ZASHI CHUI*

scissoring power. Do not turn the head down to look down, but just look down with the eyes. This is a characteristic of the eagle claw.

**25.   Push the Shutter to Gaze at the Moon**   tuīchuāng wàngyuè   推窗望月

ACTION 1: Retreat the right foot a half step and withdraw the left foot to in front of the right foot. Circle the left hand from the belly forward and up, then back to by the left shoulder, palm up. Turn the right hand outward to bring the thumb side down, then circle down, forward, up, and back to by the right shoulder, palm down. Look at the left hand. Turn the body leftward. (image 1.220)

ACTION 2: Advance the left foot a long step and follow up a half step with the right foot, landing it turned out to sit into a half horse stance. At the same time, bring the left hand around down, forward, and up, finishing with the palm foward, thumb down, bracing with the arm in a framing high block at eye height. Push the right hand forward at solar plexus height with the fingers up. Tuck in the chin. The right hand is in front of the left ribs. Look past the right hand. (image 1.221)

**Pointers**

o   Circle the hands forward, up and back as the feet retreat and withdraw. Block and push as the left foot advances. The left brace and the right push must work together.

o   Pay attention to the bodywork for the move. When the hands move forward the body moves slightly back. When the hands move up the body sits slightly down. When the hands move back the body moves forward. When the hands push forward the body tucks to press up. The body sits down slightly and the head pushes up.

**26.      Three Basins on the Ground**   sānpán luòdì      三盘落地

ACTION 1: Withdraw the left foot to by the right ankle without touching down, not moving the right foot. Lower the right hand to the left ribs. Rotate the left hand out to turn the palm in, and settle the elbow to do an elbow cover to the right, lowering it to in front of the right shoulder. The arms are now crossed in front of the body. Look to the left. (image 1.222)

# CHAPTER ONE: BAREHAND FORMS 89

ACTION 2: Take a sideways bridging step with the left foot to the left and follow in slightly with the right foot, sitting into a horse stance. At the same time, brace the hands out to each direction, keeping the arms rounded. The hands brace out on opposite sides at hip height, palms down. Look at the left hand. (image 1.223)

1.222   1.223

**Pointers**

- Tuck the left hand in as the left foot withdraws, wrapping the elbow. Brace the hands out as the left foot advances.
- To do the rolling tuck of the left hand and elbow, close the shoulders, contain the chest, and tauten the upper back to store power. To brace out with the hands you need to open the chest, solidify the abdomen, release the waist, sit into the hip joints, settle the shoulders, brace the elbows, and set the wrists. Coordinate this power output with a breath out. The whole body has well balanced power and structure to front and back, left and right.

**27.  Lazy Dragon Lies in the Road**   lǎnlóng wòdào   懒龙卧道

ACTION 1: Shift forward to the left leg and clench the fists. Pull the left fist back to the right side, fist heart down. Rotate the right fist to fist heart up. and pull it back to the right ribs. Look to the forward left. (image 1.224)

ACTION 2: Lift the right knee, turning the foot out, then step forward with the foot turned out, sitting into a resting stance. At the same time, stab the right fist forward and down, out past the ribs and chest, to hip height. Look at the right fist. (image 1.225)

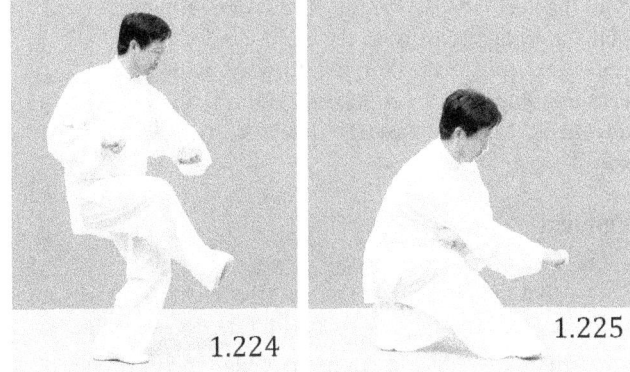

1.224   1.225

**Pointers**

- Coordinate the lifting of the right knee, step and sit into the resting stance with the stabbing down of the right fist.

## 90    THE MIXTURE OF MOVES, *ZASHI CHUI*

- o  When stabbing down, contain the chest, close the shoulders, tauten the upper back, and settle and release the shoulders. The left shoulder should angle to the front.

### 28. Black Dragon Overturns the Waves (Aligned stance Left Crossing Punch)

wūlóng fānjiāng (shùnbù zuǒ héngquán)    乌龙翻江（顺步左横拳）

ACTION: Take a long step straight forward with the left foot and follow in the right foot, keeping most weight on the right leg. At the same time, lift and roll over the right fist, pulling it back to the right waist, fist heart down. Rotate the left fist to turn the fist heart up, and do a crossing punch out from under the right arm, to shoulder height. Press the head up. Look forward past the left fist. (image 1.226)

1.226

### Pointers

- o  Complete the left crossing punch as the left foot lands. Twist the fists to complete both actions together with a complete power.

### 29.    Advancing Right Crushing Punch

This is the same as movement 16. (see image 1.214)

### 30.    Dragon and Tiger Play Together    lóng hǔ xiāngjiāo    龙虎相交

ACTION: Advance the left foot a half step and shift to the left leg, standing firmly with the leg slightly bent. Lift the right leg to do a strong heel kick forward, pulling the toes back to kick with the heel to waist height. At the same time, pull the right fist back to the right side of the waist and punch the left fist forward with a crushing punch to solar plexus height, fist eye up. Look forward past the left fist. (image 1.227)

1.227

### Pointers

- o  Coordinate upper and lower limbs so that the left fist punches, the right fist pulls back, and the right leg completes the heel kick with full, connected power.
- o  Turn the waist to put the shoulder into the punch. Tuck in the belly to kick, first lifting the knee, then extending into the heel. Pay attention to standing firmly on the left leg.

## 31. Right Aligned stance Crushing Punch

yòu shùnbù bēngquán　　　右顺步崩拳

ACTION: After the kick, land the right foot forward and down, and advance the left foot a half step to take a right trinity stance. Pull the left fist back and punch out the right fist with a crushing punch to solar plexus height, the arm slightly bent. Press the head up. Look at the right fist. (image 1.228)

1.228

### Pointers

- o  The pointers are the same as movement 8, just, because of the landing from the kick, the right foot has more trampling power.
- •  The following moves, 32 through 36, then 37 through 40, repeat combinations already done, those of moves 9 through 13, and 5 through 8.

| 32. | **White Crane Flashes its Wings** | see move 9 |
| 33. | **Left Cannon, Pounding Punch** | see move 10 |
| 34. | **Spread Both Wings** | see move 11 |
| 35. | **Sparrow Hawk Enters the Woods** | see move 12 |
| 36. | **Retreating Chopping Strike (Cat Washes its Face), twice** | see move 13 |
| 37. | **Black Dragon Pours Water** | see move 5 |
| 38. | **Stretch Out One Wing** | see move 6 |
| 39. | **Left Crushing Punch (Hybernating Dragon Shows Itself)** | see move 7 |
| 40. | **Right Aligned stance Crushing Punch (Black Tiger Leaves its Den)** | see move 8 |

## 41. Wind Sways the Lotus Leaves (three times)  fēng bǎi hēyè  风摆荷叶

ACTION 1: Turn around one-eighty degrees to the left to move back in the direction from which you came. Advance the left foot a half step to the forward left, without moving the right foot. Open both hands, and lower the right hand past the belly, so that both hands circle down to the left, then up, fingers up, palms facing each other. The left hand is in front of the right hand, both at shoulder height. Look at the right hand. (image 1.229 and from behind)

1.229 FROM BEHIND

ACTION 2: Step the right foot across to the front, turned out, so that the legs are crossed with the weight between them. Circle the hands from the left up, and back to the right, to lower. The hands now are upright at shoulder height, facing towards the rear right, with the arms slightly bent. Turn the body to the right. Look at the right hand. (image 1.230 and from behind)

1.230    1.230 FROM BEHIND

**Pointers**

- The hands swing to the front as the left foot advances, and swing to the rear as the right foot steps across.
- Both actions are repeated three times. The movement is soft and well coordinated the first and second times, then hit with power the third time. Pay attention to turning the waist well around to the rear right and swinging the arms with well settled shoulders and elbows. The right foot should cut across forcefully so that the whole move is stable with power – it must not become floating.

## 42. Advancing Left Crushing Punch

jìnbù zuǒ bēngquán     进步左崩拳

ACTION: Advance the left foot to the front and follow in the right foot slightly, keeping most weight on the right leg. Clench both hands and pull the right fist back to the right side of the waist. Bring the left fist down to in front of the chest, then, as the waist turns left, punch forward to solar plexus height. The arm is slightly bent and the fist eye is up. Press the head up. Look past the left fist. (image 1.231)

1.231

### Pointers

- Pay attention to first turn the body, and then step forward and punch.

## 43. Sparrow Hawk Pierces the Sky    yàozǐ zuāntiān    鹞子钻天

ACTION 1: Advance the left foot a half step and follow in the right foot to the left ankle without touching down. Rotate the left fist to turn the fist heart down, tucking the arm to press down across in front of the chest. Look at the left fist. (image 1.232)

ACTION 2: Step the right foot forward and follow in the left foot a half step, keeping most weight on the left leg. At the same time, drill the right fist up past the sternum and forward. Roll the little finger side of the fist up to punch to nose height. Tuck the left fist down, pulling back to the belly, fist heart in. Tuck the chin in and press the head up. Look forward past the right fist. (image 1.233)

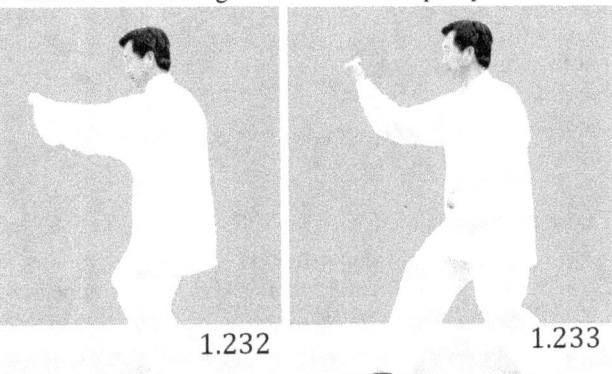

1.232        1.233

### Pointers

- Bend the left arm to tuck and press down as the left foot advances, arriving together. Drill the right fist out as the right foot steps forward, also arriving together
- Settle the body slightly down when the right fist drills up. Twist the waist and put the shoulder into the punch, keeping the shoulders settled and elbows dropped. Breathe out to exert power, and settle the *qi* to the *dantian*.

## 94  THE MIXTURE OF MOVES, *ZASHI CHUI*

### 44. Sparrow Hawk Wheels Over    yàozǐ fānshēn    鹞子翻身

ACTION 1: Pivot both feet on the spot, turning one-eighty degrees to face back in the direction from which you came. Lift the right elbow to bring the arm over the head as the body turns leftward, going forward, then covering down, fist heart down, to chest height. Drill the left fist up past the sternum and forward to nose height, twisting the little finger side up. Shift to the left leg. Look at the left fist. (image 1.234)

ACTION 2: Do a framing block up with the right arm, elbow across. Bend the left elbow and bring it back to the chest. Shift back to the right leg. Internally rotate the right fist and pull it back to the right side of the head. At the same time, internally rotate the left fist and lift the elbow, turning the fist eye in, then stab out along the left ribs towards the left hip. Look at the left fist. (image 1.235)

1.234

ACTION 3: Bend the right leg to squat down, and extend the left leg out to the left in a drop stance. Thread the left fist out along on top of the left leg and pull the right fist back to the right side of the waist, externally rotating it. Extend the left fist past the left foot. Look at the left fist. (image 1.236)

1.235      1.236

**Pointers**

- This move is done smoothly, all actions joining together without pause, completed in one breath. This move emphasizes bodywork. It takes expert body power, using the waist as the hub, and loosening the waist and shoulders, so that the entire body works together without slackening. The power is soft but not slack, hidden inside, not hard or stiff.
- Pay attention to shifting the weight back and forth, leading from the head and pressing from the waist.
- The fists and arms must work together as one. The left fist threads out inside the right arm, and the right arm blocks up along outside the left arm. When the right fist pulls back, use the elbow to draw it back, then use a wrapping, twisting power to lower the fist. Pay attention to the

shoulders, keep them slightly closed, roll them out, and release and settle them, coordinating with the arms and fists to twist and rotate.

**45.    Sparrow Hawk Folds its Wings**     yàozǐ shù shēn     鹞子束身

ACTION: Shift forward to the left leg and bend the left knee, moving forward and up, threading the left fist forward. Take a long step forward with the right foot and follow up the left foot to inside the right ankle without touching down, keeping the legs together. Tuck and press down with the left fist and pull it back to in front of the belly. Lift the right fist from the right side up to the sternum, then punch forwards and down to groin height. The right fist is rotated so the fist eye is forward. Press the head up. Look forward. (image 1.237)

1.237

**Pointers**

o   Pointers are the same as movement 2.

**46.    Sparrow Hawk Enters the Woods**    yàozǐ rùlín    鹞子入林

This is the same as movement 3. (image 1.238)

1.238

**47.    Closing Move**     shōu shì              收势

ACTION 1: Without moving the feet, lower the right fist to the belly and tuck and pull the left fist to the belly. both fist hearts face in. Press the left foot into the ground. Press the heaad up and tuck in the chin. Look forward. (image 1.239)

ACTION 2: Bring the right foot back beside the left foot, keeping the knees bent so that the height of the stance does not change. Unclench the hands and lift them at the sides to shoulder height, palms up, arms slightly bent. Then bend the elbows to bring the hands together at the front at shoulder height, fingers pointing to each other, palms down. Look at the right hand. (image 1.240)

## 96   THE MIXTURE OF MOVES, *ZASHI CHUI*

ACTION 3: Press the hands down in front of the belly and stand up to attention, letting the hands hang down to the sides. Look forward. (image 1.241)

1.239

1.240

1.241

**Pointers**

- Press into the left foot and press the head up as the left fist tucks and pulls in. Bring the right foot in as the hands move together.
- Stand up gradually as the hands push down, so that the actions of each are completed at the same time.
- The *closing move* is completed without a pause. Pay attention that the spirit remains full, the manner remains dignified, and that the entire movement is completed without slackening.

CHAPTER TWO

# THE EIGHT SKILLS

# 八字功

## INTRODUCTION TO THE EIGHT SKILLS, *BAZIGONG*

The Eight Skills are an important component of the Xingyiquan system. They are the functional techniques of traditional Xingyiquan, that is, training them improves your ability to apply your power – they are combat effective. The classics say, "the Xingyiquan system is composed of the five elemental techniques and the twelve animal models for training the body, and the other techniques for practicality. The functional techniques are learned in order to be used. The path of learning must develop both the body and train combative applications. Mastery of both is mastery of the system."

The Eight Skills are spread, intercept, wrap, bridge, scoop, butt, pass, and guide. Each skill is practised as a short sequence of actions that have a specific method, power application, and combative application. Each skill can be trained on its own or within the eight skills form. Training the Eight Skills enhances the movement vocabulary of the five elemental techniques and the twelve animals – bringing additional power applications through each segment of the body, and the ability to issue power to many directions and angles.

The Eight Skills were not taught lightly to outsiders of the Xingyiquan system, so they are not widespread. The set of Eight Skills presented here was developed in 1919 by the Baoding Military School, and written up in 'The records of the Wushu Research Society,' but the book only roughly describes the movements with simple diagrams. I studied this old book for many years and asked many elder masters about the skills, and gradually worked out the actions and their requirements. I describe them here thoroughly, and have added many images and created poems as memory aids. I present these so that readers can learn and understand the Eight Skills.

# ONE: THE SKILL OF SPREADING

# 展字功

## INTRODUCTION TO SPREAD, *ZHAN*

The classics say, "Spread means to stretch or open out, that is, to open out the hands and feet." Spread means to open up, expand, stretch out, or unfold. Among the Eight Skills, the Skill Of Spreading gives the imagery of an expansive, opened posture, spreading the feet and hands, turning the body sideways to enter and strike.[3]

The short sequence for training the Skill Of Spreading is: *opening move, right step forward tiger carries, right spread, step forward left splitting fist, left spread,* and *step forward right splitting fist.*

**1a  Opening Move (left *santishi*)    qǐ shì    起势**

**Description:**

ACTION 1: Stand to attention, facing forty-five degrees to the line on which you will travel. You may also start facing directly in the way you will travel, with the right foot turned out to almost forty-five degrees. (image 2.1)

ACTION 2: Without moving the feet, gradually lift the hands at the sides to shoulder height, palms up and arms naturally bent. Look at the right hand. (image 2.2)

---

[3] Author's note: Some classics write 'break' [折 zhé] instead of 'spread' [展 zhǎn]. This sounds similar, but means something quite different. Break means to snap something by hacking or by knocking with the forearm. It is something similar to a splitting fist, so the movement structure, actions, and application would not be the same as spreading.

ACTION 3: Bend the elbows so that the hands point to each other in front of the face, palms down. Then press the hands down to the belly, bending the legs to sit with the knees together. Press the head up and look forward to the left. (image 2.3)

ACTION 4: Clench the fists at the belly and turn the fist hearts up. Keep the left fist at the belly and drill the right fist up by the sternum then forward to nose height. Twist the ulnar edge of the right forearm up. Look at the right fist. (image 2.4)

ACTION 5: Advance the left foot without moving the right foot. The stance length should be the length of your own shin. The left leg is slightly bent and the right leg more bent, with more weight on the right leg.[4] Bring the left fist up by the sternum and out to the right elbow, drilling forward by sliding along the right forearm, fist heart up. When the left fist arrives at the right fist, unclench both hands and turn the palms down. Split the left hand forward and down with the arm slightly bent and the wrist cocked, fingers at shoulder height. Pull the right hand back to the belly, palm down. Press the head up and look past the left hand. (image 2.5)

**Pointers**

- Press the hands down as you sit – complete all actions together.
- Time the left hand split to finish as the left foot lands.
- The spirit of the opening move must be full and shown in the eyes.

**1b**   **Right Step Forward, Tiger Carries**   yòu shàngbù hǔtuō   右上步虎托

ACTION 1: Advance the left foot a half-step and follow in the right foot beside the left ankle without touching down. Keep the knees together to take a one-legged stance with the left leg bent. Thread the right hand forward, palm down, under the left forearm. Once the wrists cross, circle the hands out to the sides, palms angled

---

[4] Author's note: The proper weight distribution of a *santi* stance is between seventy-thirty and sixty-forty. The 'sweet spot' is 0.618 weighted on the rear leg.

forward. Complete the circles by bringing the hands back to the waist, palms forward and fingers down. Press the head up and look forward. (images 2.6, 2.7)

ACTION 2: Take a long step forward with the right foot and follow in a half-step with the left foot to take a *santi* stance with the right foot forward. Do a carrying technique with the palms, to push forward and down with the palms forward and the fingers down. The hands should be a fist width apart at belly height. Look past the hands. (image 2.8)

**Pointers**

- Circle the hands while advancing the left foot.
- You must apply an integrated power by completing the carrying action of the hands as the right foot lands.

**1c    Spread, Right Side**    yòu zhǎnshì    右展势

ACTION 1: Retreat the left foot a half-step and withdraw the right foot to just in front of the left, shifting the weight mostly onto the left leg. Clench the hands with the fist hearts up. Drill the left fist up to nose height outside the right forearm. Bend the right elbow to do a hooking cover leftward in front of the body, also with the fist at nose height. Finish with both fist hearts face in and a gathering, embracing power in the elbows. Look past the fists, facing in the direction of the technique. (image 2.9)

ACTION 2: Advance the right foot a long step and hook-in the foot as it lands. Follow in the left foot a half-step, turning the foot out as it lands. Turn the body ninety degrees and sit down with more weight on the left leg to take a half horse stance, with the right leg leading. Pull the left fist up and back to the left temple, rotating the fist and bending the elbow so that the fist eye is down and the arm braces out. Rotate the right fist and lift the elbow so that the fist eye is down with the elbow at shoulder height. Turn the body as you step forward and punch forward to sternum height with the right fist, completing the punch with the arm slightly bent and the fist eye down. Look at the right fist. (image 2.10 and images from the other side and from the front)

2.10

2.10 OTHER SIDE    2.10 FRONT

**Pointers**

- Complete three actions together: retreat the left foot, drill the left fist up, and cover leftward with the right fist.

- Complete the planting punch as the right foot lands. Sit well down into a half horse stance.

**1d    Step Forward, Left Split**         shàngbù zuǒ pīquán    上步左劈拳

ACTION 1: Withdraw the right foot a half-step and shift back, turning the torso slightly right. Pull the left fist down the left side to the waist, fist heart up and elbow hugging the ribs. Rotate the right fist out toward the thumb side and pull it back to the belly, fist heart up. Press the head up and look forward. (image 2.11)

ACTION 2: Advance the right foot a half-step and follow in the left foot beside the right without touching down. Drill the right fist up to the sternum and forward to nose height with the ulnar edge

2.11

## 102　THE SKILL OF SPREADING, *ZHAN ZIGONG*

turned up. Do not move the left fist yet. Press the head up and look past the right fist. (image 2.12)

ACTION 3: Take a long step forward with the left foot and follow in a half-step with the right foot, keeping most weight on the right leg. Bring the left fist by the sternum then out along the right forearm, then unclench it and split forward. Unclench the right hand, turn it over, and pull it back to the belly, palm down. The split is done to sternum height. Press the head up and look forward. (image 2.13)

2.12　2.13

**Pointers**

- These three actions are done as one movement – it is a stepping forward split.
- The actions should be done without pause and the hands and feet must be tightly coordinated: Pull the right fist back as the right foot withdraws; Drill the right fist up as the right foot advances; Split with the left hand as the left foot steps forward.

**1e　Spread, Left Side　　zuǒ zhǎnshì　　左展势**

ACTION 1: Retreat the right foot a half-step and continue by withdrawing the left foot a half-step, keeping most weight on the right leg. Clench both fists. Rotate the left fist so the fist centre is up and bend the elbow to cover rightward to the body's midline. Turn the right fist heart up and slide it forward outside the left forearm to drill up to nose height. Then bend the left elbow and bring it in, turning both fist hearts in and closing in with the elbows. Look forward. (image 2.14)

2.14　2.15

ACTION 2: Advance the left foot a long step and land with it hooked in. Follow up the right foot with a half-step advance, turning it out. Turn the body ninety degrees rightward and sit down into a half horse stance. Rotate the right fist and pull it up and back to the right side of the head, fist eye down, bending the elbow to brace outward. Roll the left fist down so the fist eye is down, and lift the elbow to shoulder height. As the left foot steps forward and the body turns, plant the left fist forward to sternum height. Complete the punch with the left arm slightly bent and the fist eye down. Look at the left fist. (image 2.15)

**1f    Step Forward, Right Split**    shàngbù yǒu pīquán    上步右劈拳

ACTION 1: Turn the torso slightly to the left and withdraw the left foot a half-step. Rotate the right fist and pull it down the side to the waist with the fist heart up and the elbow snug to the ribs. Rotate the left fist and pull it back to the belly, fist heart up. Look forward. (image 2.16)

ACTION 2: Advance the left foot a half-step and follow in the right foot beside the left without touching down, keeping the knees together. Drill the left fist forward and up to nose height, twisting the ulnar edge up. Press the head up and look forward. (image 2.17)

ACTION 3: Take a long step forward with the right foot and follow in a half-step with the left foot. Bring the right fist by the sternum, along the left forearm, and then unclench it and split forward to sternum height. Unclench the left hand and pull it back to the belly. Press the head up and look past the right hand. (image 2.18)

- Continue on, alternating the left and right *skill of spreading* without the opening moves.

**1g    Turn Around for the Skill of Spreading**

zhǎnzìgōng zhuànshēn        展字功转身

You may perform a *split turn around* or a *tiger carry turn around*, but more usually the *tiger carries*. For more detail on *split turn around*, see Volume I.

## 104 THE SKILL OF SPREADING, *ZHAN ZIGONG*

- If the <u>left</u> foot is forward, to turn with *tiger carries*:

ACTION 1: Hook-in step the left foot in front of the right toes and shift onto the left leg, turning the body around rightward two-seventy degrees to face back in the way you came. Lift the right foot at the left ankle without touching down. Turn the unclenched hands palm out, crossing them in front of the body, then circle them up, out to either side, then in to the side of the torso with the palms forward and fingers down. Press the head up and look forward. (image 2.19)

ACTION 2: Step the right foot diagonally to the forward right and follow in the left foot a half-step. Push the hands forward and down to belly height. Finish with the hands fist-width apart, palms forward, fingers down, elbows bent and close together. Sit the torso down, press the head up, and look forward. (image 2.20)

- If the <u>right</u> foot is forward, to turn with *tiger carries:*

ACTION 1: Hook-in the right foot toward the left toes to turn the body around one-eighty to the left, facing back in the way you came. Shift onto the right leg and lift the left foot by the right foot without touching down. Bend the knees and keep them together to stand firmly on the right leg. Cross the forearms in front of the chest with the palms out, left hand inside the right hand. Circle the hands up and out to the left and right then bring them back to the sides, palm forward, fingers down. Press the head up and look forward. (images 2.21, 2.22)

CHAPTER TWO: THE EIGHT SKILLS    105

ACTION 2: Take a long step diagonally to the forward left with the left foot and follow in the right foot a half-step, keeping most weight on the right leg. Do a low carrying action to belly height with the hands. Finish about fist width apart, palms facing forward, fingers down. Look forward. (image 2.23)

2.23

**Pointers**

- Circle the hands as you step around. Be sure to take a good hook-in step so that the turn around is quick.
- Complete the tiger carries as the foot lands forward, so that the hands and feet work together.

**1h    Closing Move for the Skill of Spreading**

zhǎnzìgōng shōushì          展字功收势

Continue on until you are at your starting point facing in the same direction that you did the *opening move*.

- To start the closing from *tiger carries* in <u>left</u> stance:

ACTION 1: Withdraw the left foot to inside the right foot. Clench the right hand and pull it back to the belly. Turn the left hand over and cover, pressing down with the palm down at shoulder height with the elbow bent. Drill the right fist up by the sternum and forward to nose height, ulnar edge turned up. At the same time, press down and pull the left hand back to the belly, clenching it. Press the head up and look forward. (image 2.24)

ACTION 2: Step the left foot forward without moving the right foot to sit into a *santi* stance. Drill the left fist out from the sternum to the right elbow and forward until the fists cross. Then unclench the hands and split forward with the left hand while pulling the right hand back to the belly, palms facing down. Press the head up and look forward. (image 2.25)

2.24

2.25

# 106 THE SKILL OF SPREADING, *ZHAN ZIGONG*

- From a *tiger carries* with the right foot forward:

ACTION 1: Withdraw the right foot to inside the left foot. Land the right foot firmly and shift onto the right leg, lifting the left foot a bit and keeping the knees together. Turn the left hand over and cover, pressing down with the palm down at shoulder height with the elbow bent. Pull the right hand back to the belly, clenching it, then drill the right fist up by the sternum and forward to nose height, ulnar edge turned up. At the same time, press down and pull the left hand back to the belly, clenching it. Press the head up and look forward. (images 2.26, 2.27)

2.26

2.27

ACTION 2: Step the left foot forward without moving the right foot, to sit into a *santi* stance. Perform a splitting action, splitting forward with the left hand while pulling the right hand back to the belly. Press the head up and look forward. (image 2.28)

2.28

- When you arrive in *santishi* then close as you would normally.

**Pointers**

- Drill the right fist up and cover with the left forearm as the lead foot withdraws. Be sure to move all together and to sit back to the right leg.

- Split forward with the left hand as the left foot advances into the *santi* stance. Step an appropriate distance so that the right foot does not need to move, so that you can keep your spirit full and settled.

## POWER GENERATION FOR THE SKILL OF SPREADING

The short sequence for the Skill Of Spreading is comprised of a spread technique combined with a split done to both sides. Looking at the structure of the spread technique, it is a planting punch with the body turned sideways. Its power launch is long range with considerable strength. Its long range comes from adding a shoulder width to the length of the arm. Its strength comes from combining a forward step, a body turn and an arm extension to deliver the planting punch.

The final spread position aligns the feet and the body in one plane. Prior to spreading, the lead arm covers in and the rear fist drills up so that the elbows close together in front of the chest. The elbows should use a bracing out power, closing the chest and stretching the upper back to gather energy.

When the feet retreat and withdraw and the fists drill up, the body should rise slightly and shift back to gather energy. Just prior to the planting punch, the shoulder of the punching side should draw back to gather power for the punch.

Launch power forward and down for the planting punch. It should finish between belly and chest height. The lead foot should land with a trampling power. At the instant of launching the punch, the body should have a crossways shoving power in the same direction as the punch. The fist and arm use a drilling power that rolls, tucks, twists, and rotates. Turn the waist and extend the shoulder into the punch to turn the body sideways to complete the punch.

Use the rear hand to give more power to the lead hand by pulling the rear fist back by the head, twisting as it goes, and bracing back with the elbow. The entire strike is fully connected, as the body core leads the shoulders, the shoulders urge the elbows, and the elbows urge the fists forward. The power flows smoothly between each segment. Exhale to complete the whole body connection in the power launch.

The key to getting power when connecting the spread to the split is, as you withdraw the foot, bring the fist back by turning and pulling it from the shoulder and elbow. Bring the shoulder back and stretch it out, then settle it down. Close the elbow in and then settle it down. In this way the shoulders draw the elbows and the elbows draw the fists into the rotation, pulling it back to the belly as the foot withdraws. Then you can roll the fist over and step forward into the split.

- When first learning do not try too hard to get whole body power. First get a feel for the line of action. Concentrate on getting the main actions, hand placement, body shape and footwork smooth. Once the movement is correct then you can get comfortable with it. You can work on whole body power once you have a comfortable foundation. Correct and perfect your technique continually in your practice.

## PRACTICAL APPLICATIONS FOR THE SKILL OF SPREADING

The kernel of the Skill Of Spreading's short sequence is the right and left spread techniques. Analysing this spread position, it is a turned planting punch. The whole sequence contains both attack and defense. The retreat and withdrawal of the feet together with the rolling and closing of the elbows closes off any attack, tightly protecting the chest and head area. A quick advance and turn to plant the punch goes for the opponent's chest, belly, or floating ribs. The key lies in entering the lead foot through into the opponent's groin area.

# THE SKILL OF SPREADING, ZHAN ZIGONG

- The spread technique can be either a counter attack that flows from a defensive move or a direct attack, using the theory of 'you do what you want and I'll do what I want'. In Xingyiquan, we often go for a direct hit without bothering to block. If your opponent attacks to your head, you turn sideways and attack his head. Because you have added the length of the shoulder to your extended arm, if you both punch at the same time your punch will land while your opponent's will fall short.
- When counter attacking, retreat the rear foot. When directly attacking, step the rear foot forward.

Duck the head back, protect the chest with the elbows, and protect the head with the fists. The rear fist can drill up in a scooping upper block, or can hook and pull back. The lead fist takes its opportunity to strike forward.

- Of course, in combat you cannot count on one technique finishing the job. The classics say, "once you start, do ten techniques." Attack continuously until you win. As you continue on from the spread to the split, the lead hand does a backfist punch or a drilling punch, and then you step further forward into the split. This is just a simple analysis of the technique; in a combative situation you need to adjust to whatever comes.

## THE POEM ABOUT THE SKILL OF SPREADING

展字功歌诀

展势侧身劲力雄，

一展一劈练其功。

掩肘上钻胸前抱，

拧腰栽打贯腹胸。

The spread position with the body turned has great strength,

Train this skill with a spread and a split.

Cover with the elbows and drill up to hug in front of the chest,

Twist the waist and plant a punch through the belly or chest.

# TWO: THE SKILL OF INTERCEPTING

## 截字功

### INTRODUCTION TO INTERCEPT, *JIE*

The classics say, "intercept means to cut out, to cut off the opponent's attack." The action of intercepting is to obstruct and break with a cutting action, and so combines breaking, checking, cutting off, and trapping. The Skill Of Intercepting is thus a trapping cut of the opponent's arm. It can be performed as a single arm or a double arm technique. Intercept's power application is a short, quick hit. It is done just before the opponent's attack is completed, trapping with a hard force vertically across his attack, trapping and checking to attack quickly. Intercept can be seen as simply a defensive move, but since it is able to break the opponent's arm it can finish a fight.

Within the sequence you can either perform intercept alone or you can combine it with a trundle. Trundle means to push or shove straight forward with both hands. You should first learn the standard way, and then work on the alternate ways. Then when you need to use it you will be able to react spontaneously. Beginners should train hard and carefully seek to understand through practice.

The short sequence for the Skill Of Intercepting is *opening move, right step forward tiger carries, intercept,* and *advance and trundle*.

**2a**  **Opening Move (left *santishi*)**   qǐ shì    起势

Start with *santishi* as described movement 1a above.

**2b**  **Right Step Forward, Tiger Carries**   yòu shàngbù hǔtuō   右上步虎托

This is the same as described above in 1b.

**2c**  **Intercept, Left Side**   zuǒ jiéshì   左截势

ACTION 1: Retreat the left foot a half-step and shift back towards the left leg. Withdraw the right foot a half-step. Clench the left fist and drill it up towards the forward right. Unclench it and rotate it into a hooking position, then pull in an arc to the left, bending the arm in front of the left chest. Clench the right fist and draw it back by the right waist, then without stopping, bend the elbow and lift it, taking it forward and rolling it to cut across to the left, just to the left of the midline. Then rotate the right arm ulnar edge up. The right fist is at nose height with the elbow bent about one hundred degrees. Turn leftward, twisting the waist, sitting the torso, and settling the shoulders and elbows. Press the head up and look past the right fist. (image 2.29)

**Pointers**

- Hook with the right hand as the left foot retreats.
- Cut across with the right forearm and elbow as the right foot withdraws.
- Compress the torso slightly as you intercept with the elbow.
- Turn the waist and close the shoulders to put power into the elbow as it cuts across to intercept.

2.29

**2d   Advance and Trundle**   jìnbù gǔnshǒu   进步滚手

ACTION: Advance the right foot a long step and follow in a half-step with the left foot to take a *santi* stance with the right foot forward and left back. Unclench the right hand and rotate the thumb outward, settling the elbow down and extending the arm to push forward at sternum height, finishing with the arm slightly bent. Place the left hand at the right forearm, palm forward. Put equal power into both hands and close in the elbows. Contain the chest, lengthen the spine, release the shoulders, settle the elbows, and press the head up. Look forward. (image 2.30)

2.30

**Pointers**

- Take a long step with the right foot and follow in quickly with the left. Make sure the weight shift is quick and stable.
- Complete the double push as the right foot lands, with an integrated power.

**2e   Intercept, Right Side**   yòu jiéshì   右截势

ACTION: Advance the left foot a half-step and shift slightly forward. Lift the left heel slightly and place the weight between the legs. Clench the right fist and pull it down, then drill it forward and up in front of the left side of the body. Unclench it and rotate the thumb inward to hook with the hand, pulling across in front and to the right in an arc towards the right chest with the arm bent and the palm facing down. Clench the left fist and lift the elbow, then cut the elbow across towards the right to just right of the midline. Rotate the left fist into the ulnar edge. The fist is at nose height and the elbow is at sternum height. The left elbow is bent about one hundred degrees. Turn the body a bit to the right. Twist the waist, sit into the torso,

CHAPTER TWO: THE EIGHT SKILLS    111

settle the shoulders and elbows, and lift the head up. Look past the left fist. (images 2.31 and 2.31 front)

2.31

2.31 FRONT

**Pointers**

- This is the same intercept technique, but to the right. Be sure to use the power from the body core.
- When intercepting, gather the power in the body core and contain the chest. Tighten the fists when cutting across with the forearms.
- Complete the trundle and intercept as one action, keeping the movement connected and quick.

**2f    Step Forward and Trundle**    shàngbù gǔnshǒu    上步滚手

ACTION: Take a long step forward with the left foot and follow in a half-step with the right foot. Keep most weight on the right leg. Unclench the left hand and turn it forward, settling the elbow and extending the arm to push forward, finishing with the arm slightly bent and the hand at the sternum. Push forward with the right hand at the same time, just behind the left wrist, palm also facing forward. Apply force equally into the hands, both elbows held in. Contain the chest, lengthen the spine, release the shoulders, steel the elbows, and press the head up. Look forward. Breathe out to assist the power launch. (image 2.32)

2.32

- Carry on alternating left and right as long as the practice area and your fitness allow.

**Pointers**

- Advance the right foot a good distance and use the combined force of the step and both hands to push. Unite the power of the whole body to arrive all at the same time.
- Perform the intercept to the right as the right foot advances a half-step.
- Do not stop between intercept and trundle, but complete them as one move. Think of them as one move.

## 2g  Turn Around for the Skill of Intercepting

jiézìgòng zhuànshēn    截字功转身

Turn around with a *tiger carries*, as described in movement 1g, then continue on repeating the combination sequence.

## 2h  Closing Move for the Skill of Intercepting

jiézìgòng shōushì    截字功收势

Continue until you are back at your starting place facing in the same direction as you started, then perform a left split as described above in movement 1h. Then close as you would normally from *santishi*.

## POWER GENERATION FOR THE SKILL OF INTERCEPTING

The main application in the sequence of the Skill Of Intercepting is the hand hook and elbow cover to break, and then the entry to trundle and push away. If you retreat you must be agile, and if you advance or step forward you must be quick.

Turn the body slightly to get power into the elbow interception, so that one hand hooks and pulls while the other hand cuts across. Use the ulnar side of the forearm for the crossing elbow-cover. Twist your waist, reach the shoulder into the move, settle the elbows down and turn the wrists, twisting to get the cutting power. You need to get the full use out of both elbows, with a settled power, quick and short. Launch an instantaneous power that is hard and fierce but settled.

When you step forward for the trundle and push, take a long step in to charge the body forward. To trundle up the opponent, the lead hand rolls, hooks, and grabs, applying a rolling pressure down, and the rear hand closes in and releases. To do the action of the lead hand, first contain the chest, settle the elbows, flex the waist, and use the body's power to roll and press – close the elbows. Then push forward with both hands simultaneously. When releasing power, lengthen the spine, extend the arms, release the shoulders forward, and charge in with the footwork, driving the body forward to shove. Compress the torso as the hands rise, lengthen the torso as they land. Step forward quickly, get the hands in quickly. Breathe out to launch power. Press the head up. Focus on sending the opponent away a good distance.

- The above has described the single-handed intercept. There is also a double-handed intercept. The double-handed intercept is similar to *tiger intercepts*. The skill of intercept has many variations, such as upper intercept, lower intercept, left intercept, and right intercept. They are just variations on the same power, changing directions, placements, and angles to train the skill in a variety of ways.

## PRACTICAL APPLICATIONS FOR THE SKILL OF INTERCEPTING

Intercept is mainly a retreating defense to block the opponent's hands. The trundle then shoves him away.

- The classics say "straight, use intercept; crossways, use jam." This simply means that when the opponent comes at me with a straight technique, then intercept is effective. If the opponent comes at me with a crossing or swinging punch then a jam is effective. That is, jam him at the root of the arm to prevent him from throwing the punch.

When using intercept you must master the timing and wait for the right moment. It works when the opponent has thrown the punch but it has not yet landed – neither earlier nor later will work. If you block too early then he can easily pull his punch away and you will miss him altogether. If you block too late then his punch will land. You must time it just right, and hit the right spot, after his punch has entered your space.

- Another important concept is "far, intercept the middle segment; near, intercept the tip." This means that if you are at a bit of a distance when you intercept, then you should go for the opponent's elbow. If you are close, then intercept his hand, wrist, or forearm.

Intercept is a defensive move, but your goal is to attack. After the intercept you must immediately step in to get your body close, and trundle. The lead hand changes immediately to push, using both hands to shove at the same time. Use an explosive power if you want to injure the opponent. Use a longer power to just throw him down or away.

- When actually using the technique you must adapt to the situation. Techniques come from the heart out to the hands. To really use any technique you must practise hard and get combative experience.

## THE POEM ABOUT THE SKILL OF INTERCEPTING

截字功歌诀

截法意在敌肘手，

单双进退随意走。

远找中节近截梢，

打人全凭后手有。

Focus on the opponent's elbow or hands to intercept,

Use whatever works – advance or retreat, one hand or two.

When at a distance attack the middle segment, when close block the tip.

Hitting the opponent depends entirely on the rear hand making contact.

# THREE: THE SKILL OF WRAPPING

# 裹字功

## INTRODUCTION TO WRAP, *GUO*

The classics say, "Wrap means to enclose. You wrap up your opponent so that he loses effectiveness. The body rotates with soft strength. It uses the secret of softness to beat hardness." Wrap means to coil around, to encircle. The character contains both wrapping and coiling meaning.[5]

The short sequence for the Skill Of Wrapping is *opening, right step forward tiger carries, double wrap* (to left and right), and *step forward double shove*.

**3a**  **Opening Move (left *santishi*)**     qǐ shì      起势

Start with *santishi* as described above in movement 1a.

**3b**  **Right Step Forward Tiger Carries**   yòu shàngbù hǔ tuō    右上步虎托

See the description and images in movement 1b.

**3c**  **Double Wrap to Left and Right**

  zuǒ yòu shuāng guǒshǒu      左右双裹手

ACTION 1: Move the body forward slightly, retreat the left foot, and shift onto the left leg. Withdraw the right foot to beside the left without touching down. Bend the knees, keeping them together, and stand firmly on the left leg. Extend the left hand to the left, forward, and up, palm facing right, fingers up. Once it reaches forward, circle it horizontally rightward across to in front of the right shoulder. Keep the right hand at the right side. Move the torso slightly leftward. Look forward. (image 2.33)

2.33

---

[5] Author's note: Some writings and teachers refer to this technique as 果, which sounds the same, but simply means fruit. Combined with other characters it has a variety of meanings, but none of them apply to martial arts techniques. 裹 is the correct character.

ACTION 2: Step the right foot diagonally forward and follow in the left foot to beside the right without touching down. Shift onto the right leg, bending the knees to stand firmly on the right leg with the knees together. Extend the right hand to the right, forward and up with the palm facing left and fingers up. After it reaches forward, circle it flat across to in front of the left shoulder. At this time the arms are crossed as if holding something, the left inside the right, both palms turned in, about twenty centimetres in front of the chest. Settle the shoulders, drop the elbows, contain the chest, and stretch the upper back. Look forward. (image 2.34)

2.34

**Pointers**

- Roll the left hand rightward as the left foot retreats, so that both move together.

- Roll the right hand leftward as the right foot steps forward, both moving simultaneously.

- Wrapping to the right and left is a soft, continuous movement. Be sure to turn the body sideways as the arms pass across.

**3d   Step Forward, Double Shove**

shàngbù shuāng zhuàng zhǎng          上步双撞掌

ACTION 1: Take a long step forward with the left foot and follow in the right foot a half-step, keeping most weight back on the right leg. Roll the hands over in front of the chest to face the palms out, thumbs down, then as the left foot steps forward, push forward. Push with the arms curved, the fingers pointing to each other, and the palms out at shoulder height. Release the shoulders forward, press the head up, and look forward. (images 2.35 and 2.35 front)

2.35          2.35 FRONT

**Pointers**

- Complete the pushing shove as the left foot lands.

- As the hands do the pushing shove, rotate the arms inward so that they maintain a bracing curve.

# 116 THE SKILL OF WRAPPING, *GUO ZIGONG*

o The *double wrap* and *double shove* should be done as one action, with no break between them.

**3e      Double Wrap              shuāng guǒshǒu            双裹手**

ACTION 1: Retreat the right foot a half-step and shift to the right leg, withdrawing the left foot to beside the right without touching down. Keep the knees bent and together, and stand firmly on the right leg. Lower the right hand then bring it forward and left, circling it horizontally across to in front of the left shoulder. Circle with the palm facing left and the fingers up, and then turn the palm in. Lower the left hand to the left side. Move the torso to the right and turn the body sideways to the right a bit. Look forward. (image 2.36)

ACTION 2: Take a long step diagonally forward with the left foot and follow in the right foot to inside the left without touching down. Bend the knees and keep them together to stand firmly on one leg. Extend the left hand forward and up, and then circle it across to the right to in front of the right shoulder, palm right and fingers up. Shift to the left leg and turn the torso slightly sideways leftward. Cross the forearms in front of the chest, hands about twenty centimetres from the chest, right hand inside the left hand, palms facing in. Contain the chest and make the upper back taut. Look forward. (images 2.37, 2.38)

**3f      Step Forward, Double Shove**

shàngbù shuāng zhuàng zhǎng            上步双撞掌

ACTION 1: Take a long step forward with the right foot and follow in the left foot a half-step, keeping most weight on the left leg. Rotate the forearms in front of the chest to turn the palms out and thumbs down. As the left foot steps forward, extend the arms to push forcefully forward. Complete the push with the arms curved to brace, the fingers facing each other, and the palms forward at shoulder height. Release the shoulder forward, press the head up, and look past the hands. (image 2.39)

- Continue on, alternating right and left techniques, as many times as you wish.

**3g  Turn Around for the Skill of Wrapping**

guǒ zìgōng huíshēnshì          裹字功回身势

Turn around from the *double shove* with a *tiger carries*, as described above in movement 1g.

- *Turn around* is the same on either side, just transpose right and left.

**3h  Closing Move for the Skill of Wrapping**

guǒ zìgōng shōushì          裹字功收势

You may do the closing once you get back to where you started, facing the same direction. Close as described above in movement 1h.

## POWER GENERATION FOR THE SKILL OF WRAPPING

The double wrapping action is actually an inward circle, wrap, and draw with both hands. The hands must first go forward, then go out to the opposite side, and finally circle back. Wrap combines an inward checking power with a drawing back power. It also hides a transverse checking power applied inwards.

Keep the bodywork soft, going along with the forward and backward stepping. When advancing to the left and right, the torso moves left and right. Lead from the head, that is, when wrapping rightward with the left hand, move the head slightly to the left, and when wrapping leftward with the right hand, move the head slightly to the right. The actions of the hands and arms must be a coordinated twisting rotation – left and right, forward and back, up and down. This action must be coordinated with the torso – as the hands move forward the torso moves slightly back. When the hands go left the torso goes right. When the hands draw back the torso moves forward. In this way, the hands and body are coordinated according to the rules of biomechanics, which bring out the internal power of the movement.

# THE SKILL OF WRAPPING, *GUO ZIGONG*

When wrapping inward, transfer power from the waist and shoulders to the elbows, and from the elbows to the hands. Empty the chest and stretch the upper back. When crossing the arms in front of the chest, cover in with the elbows with a hidden inflating energy. Sit the torso down slightly and set backward slightly to store energy to prepare for a forward launch of power.

- The whole movement should be soft and well coordinated. Seek the action's power and coordination according to the rule of 'pre-load right to go left, pre-load back to go forward.' When your movements can express this principle and use it well, then you can find the proper power.

- The step forward double-handed shove is the power launch portion of the sequence, and continues smoothly from the wrapping move. Just before launching power, gather the torso, bend the knees, settle the buttocks down, empty the chest and gather the lower back. Press the knees down and forward to prepare for a good push off. When you cross the arms in front of the chest, relax the shoulders, and brace the elbows forward slightly in an embracing posture.

When launching power, charge the whole body forward by pushing off the rear foot to drive the lead foot forward. Turn the palms and forcefully extend the arms to push or shove forward. Close the elbows in by using the shoulder girdle, and urge the hands forward from the elbows. Exhale to gain power when launching. Push forward by pressing the head up, lengthening the spine, releasing the shoulders, and extending the arms. Pretend you are using your whole body to push a heavy object away from you.

- When practising the Skill Of Wrapping, focus on soft power for the wrapping portion, and on hard power for the pushing portion.

## PRACTICAL APPLICATIONS FOR THE SKILL OF WRAPPING

From its action, you can see that wrap is a defensive move. It covers inward, controlling the outside of the opponent's elbows. Together with the footwork that retreats and dodges, it avoids an opponent's attack, going along with his line of attack to guide him to one side. Grab if you can, if not, then slap aside.

If the opponent punches towards your head with his right fist, you quickly extend your left hand forward and cover his arm, continuing it along his rightward direction. Dodge your head to the left and step either back or to the side. If the opponent punches with the left fist, then quickly use your right hand to cover and follow his leftward force, dodging your head to the right and stepping right. After the wrapping technique, then quickly step forward and attack.

Defense is just the means to an end, which is to attack.

The two-handed shove attacks the opponent's chest. When using it, charge in with your footwork, drive hard from your body, and launch your power into your hands. To be most effective use an explosive force focusing on a point a foot behind the opponent's back. The ideal time to apply the shove is when you have covered your opponent's elbows, tying him up with crossed arms. Then you can step in and shove him away. This ideal situation is not so easy to achieve, though. In a real combat situation you are not always going to be dealing with a simple situation, so you need to be flexible to deal with whatever happens. You need to train hard in your daily exercises, and practise applications often to gain experience. Once your skill is natural to you then you can use techniques freely and control your opponent. The key to this is the deep skills that you gain from training.

## **THE POEM ABOUT THE SKILL OF WRAPPING**

裹字功歌诀

裹手掩肘技法严，

顺势进退头微闪。

以柔克刚身法妙，

上步撞掌意推山。

Wrapping with the hands and covering with the elbows is deadly,

Enter or retreat along the line of the oncoming action, ducking the head slightly.

With skillful body technique, softness conquers hardness,

Step forward and shove as if you are pushing a mountain.

# FOUR: THE SKILL OF BRIDGING

跨字功

## INTRODUCTION TO BRIDGE, *KUA*

The classics say, "Bridge is like bestriding a horse. It takes the position of lifting the hip."[6] The character 'kua' also means to ford a stream, or to jump over. 'Kua' contains the meaning of taking a big stride to span a distance, and also implies lifting a foot to take a big stride. It implies a horse stance, as the movement is like bestriding a horse. It also has the idea of pushing off the rear foot to jump forward.[7]

The short sequence for the Skill Of Bridging is: *opening move, right step forward tiger carries, retreat close the shoulders, step forward and bridge, stamp and drill,* and *aligned stance driving punch.*

**4a**  **Opening Move**            qǐ shì              起势

As described in movement 1a.

**4b**  **Right Step Forward, Tiger Carries**   yòu shàngbù hǔ tuō  右上步虎托

As described in movement 1b.

---

[6] Translator's note: 'Bestriding' is possibly a better translation than bridging, but is an awkward word in English. Bridging has close to the same meaning, and contains the meaning of fording. I have used stride and hurdle previously, but do not like either of those translations. The final position resembles a bridge, and I like the combination of movement and structure: taking a bridging step to finish with a strong bridge-like structure.

[7] Author's note: Some classics write 'kua' with the muscle or hand radical instead of the foot radical. These characters are pronounced the same but differ in meaning – each refer to different parts of the body and describe different basic actions. 'Kua' with the hand radical means to hook with the upper arm to carry something against the body, or to carry over the shoulder. 'Kua' with the muscle radical means the hip. The technique strikes the waist or hip, so this name reminds you to attack with the hip or towards the hip. Most martial arts skills have been passed on through verbal transmissions, and with the diverse accents in China and various different understandings of techniques and characters, it is no wonder that there is some diversity in the names. I have examined many old classics and photographs and decided that the best way to write this technique is with the foot radical, as it describes the technique the best.

CHAPTER TWO: THE EIGHT SKILLS   121

**4c   Left Retreat Close the Shoulders (T Stance Stab Down)**

zuǒ tuìbù héjiān (dīngbù xiàchāzhǎng)   左退步合肩（丁步下插掌）

ACTION 1: Retreat the left foot without moving the right foot, shifting the weight to between the feet. Rotate the left hand thumb inwards to turn the palm forward and lift it up, then circle it forward with the arm bent. Then pull it down and back to beside the left hip, palm down. Internally rotate the right hand (thumb turns in towards the palm) to lift the arm with the elbow bent, palm up to the right of the head. Rise slightly and look at the left hand. (image 2.40)

ACTION 2: Shift back to the left foot and withdraw the right foot to inside the left foot, touching the ball of the foot down. Stand on the left leg with the knees bent and together. Sit the torso down slightly. Bring the left hand up and cover with the elbow to the right shoulder, placing the hand in front of the right shoulder with the fingers up. Rotate the right hand fingers down and palm to the rear, bend the elbow and stab down past the left hip. Turn the torso leftward to bring the right shoulder forward. Look forward. (image 2.41)

2.40

2.41

**Pointers**

o   Coordinate the actions of the feet and hands. Retreat the rear foot, withdraw the lead foot, and position the hands. Be sure to close the lead shoulder in, that is, tuck the right shoulder across towards the left. Stab the lead hand down as the torso closes down and you squat on the rear leg.

o   Retreat and withdraw the feet quickly and sit back quickly. The final squat position must be stable. The movement must be completed without a pause.

**4d   Step Forward Left Bridge**   shàngbù zuǒ kuàshì   上步左跨势

ACTION 1: Step the right foot straight forward, landing with the foot turned outward. Turn the right hand so the thumb web is down and the palm forward and slice forward and up in a curving manner to shoulder height. Lower the left hand and bring it back to beside the left waist, palm forward, fingers down, elbow tight to the ribs. Look at the right hand. (image 2.42)

## 122 THE SKILL OF BRIDGING, *KUA ZIGONG*

ACTION 2: Take a long step to the front with the left foot, landing with the foot turned slightly inward. Follow-in the right foot a bit, landing it turned crossways, sitting down into a half-horse stance with the torso turned ninety degrees. Slice the right hand up, clenching it in front of the head, the pulling it back to the right above the head with the fist eye down. Extend the left arm to push forward from the left side to hip height, elbow slightly bent, palm forward, fingers down. Look past the left hand. (images 2.43 and 2.43 front)

**Pointers**

o   The bridging step is done in two steps. Advance the lead foot a half step as the hand slices up. Take a long step forward with the lead foot and follow-in the rear foot quickly as you push one hand forward and pull the other hand back.

o   Be sure to turn the torso as you push forward. The push should be on line with the plane of the torso. Sit down into a half-horse stance.

**4e      Stamp, Right Drill**      zhènjiǎo yòu zuānquán      震脚右钻拳

ACTION 1: Advance the left foot a half-step and shift forward onto the left leg. Turn the left palm and hook it to press down, palm down at shoulder height. Lower the right fist and pull it back to beside the waist, fist heart up. Look at the left hand. (image 2.44)

ACTION 2: Follow in the right foot to land with a thump beside the left foot, immediately lifting the left foot by the right ankle. Drill the right fist forward and up to nose height with the ulnar edge turned up. Cover and press down with the left hand, pulling it back to the belly and clenching it, fist heart down. Press the head up and look past the right fist. (image 2.45)

**Pointers**

- Drill the right fist up as the right foot stamps. Three actions occur together: the right stamp, the right fist drill, and the left hand pull back.
- Be sure to do a shoveling thump. Do not lift the foot to stamp down.

**4f   Left Aligned Stance Driving Punch**   zuǒ shùnbù bēngquán 左顺步崩拳

ACTION: Advance the left foot a long step and follow in the right foot a half-step, keeping most weight on the right leg. Turn the right fist to tuck and press down, then pull it back to the belly, fist heart in. Punch the left fist forward to sternum height with the elbow slightly bent. Reach the left shoulder slightly forward. Press the head up and look forward. (image 2.46)

**Pointers**

- The entire move must be well integrated, using whole body power.
- Three actions are completed at once: advance the left foot, punch the left fist, and pull the right fist to the belly.

**4g   Right Retreat, Close the Shoulders**   yòu tuìbù héjiān 右退步合肩

ACTION 1: Retreat the right foot without moving the left foot, and shift the weight to balance between the feet. Unclench the hands and circle the right hand up, forward and then down to pull back to beside the right hip, palm down. Bend the left arm and lift it up at the left of the head, palm obliquely up, fingers back. Raise the torso slightly. Look at the right hand as it moves, then as it pulls back to the hip, look forward. (image 2.47)

ACTION 2: Shift back onto the right leg and withdraw the left foot to beside the right foot, touching the ball of the foot down. Bend the knees to squat to lower the torso, keeping the knees

together. Thread the right hand up and do an elbow cover by the left shoulder, palm and fingers up just in front of the left shoulder. Bend the left elbow and turn the hand fingers down, stabbing down past the right ribs with the palm back at the right hip. Turn right to bring the left shoulder forward. Look forward. (image 2.48)

**Pointers**

- This is the same as movement 4c, just transposing right and left.

**4h    Step Forward Right Bridge**    shàngbù yòu kuàshì    上步右跨势

ACTION 1: Advance the left foot a half-step, landing with the foot turned out. Turn the left hand so that the thumb web is down and the palm is forward, and then circle it forward and up to slice forward to shoulder height. Lower the right hand to beside the right hip, palm forward, fingers down, elbow tight to the ribs. Look at the left hand. (image 2.49)

ACTION 2: Take a long step forward with the right foot, landing with the foot turned slightly in, and following in a half-step with the left foot, turned crossways. Sit down with the body turned leftward ninety degrees, into a half-horse stance. Continue the slice with the left hand, circling up to in front of the head, and clenching. Then pull it back to above the left side of the head, fist eye down. As the right foot steps forward, push the right hand forward to hip height. Keep the elbow slightly bent;

the palm faces forward and the fingers are down. Look past the right hand. (image 2.50)

**Pointers**

- This is the same as movement 4d, just transposing right and left.

CHAPTER TWO: THE EIGHT SKILLS   125

**4i    Stamp, Left Drill**    zhènjiǎo zuǒ zuānquán    震脚左钻拳

ACTION 1: Advance the left foot a short half-step and shift forward without moving the right foot. Turn the right palm down and tuck and press down. Lower the left fist and pull it back beside the left waist, fist heart up. Look at the right hand. (image 2.51)

ACTION 2: Follow in the left foot to land by the right foot with a thump, lifting the right foot by the left ankle. Drill the left fist forward and up to nose height, twisting the ulnar edge up. Cover and press the right hand down, pulling it back to the belly and clenching it, fist heart down. Press the head up and look past the left fist. (image 2.52)

**Pointers**

o   This is the same as movement 4e, just transposing right and left.

**4j    Right Aligned Stance Driving Punch**   yòu shùnbù bēngquán 右顺步崩拳

ACTION: Advance the right foot a long step and follow in the left foot a half-step, keeping most weight on the left leg. Rotate the left fist to tuck and press down, then pull it back to the belly, fist heart in. Punch the right fist forward to solar plexus height, elbow slightly bent, right shoulder slightly forward. Press the head up and look past the right fist. (image 2.53)

**Pointers**

o   This is the same as movement 4f, just transposing right and left.

•   Continue on alternating right and left sides, depending on the space available.

## 126  THE SKILL OF BRIDGING, *KUA ZIGONG*

### 4k  Turn Around for the Skill of Bridging

kuà zìgōng huíshēn shì       跨字功回身势

Once you get to the end of your area and need to turn around, use *tiger carries*. The turn is done from the *aligned stance driving punch*, so begins slightly differently than usual.

- Starting from the <u>right</u> side punch:

ACTION 1: Hook-in the right foot in front of the left toes and shift onto the right leg, lifting the left foot by the right ankle and turning the body around one-eighty to face in the way you just came. Lower the right fist to the belly and unclench both hands, crossing them and lifting them, and then circling out to the sides, palms forward. Continue to circle the hands until they are back down to the sides, palms forward, fingers down. Press the head up and look forward. (images 2.54, 2.55)

2.54

2.55

ACTION 2: Take a long diagonal step with the left foot to the left front and follow in the right foot a half-step. Do a carrying action with both hands to the front to belly height, palms forward, with a fist width between them. Press the head up and look past the hands. (image 2.56)

2.56

- Right and left are the same, just transposing directions.

**Pointers**

- Take a good sized hook-in step, turn the body quickly, and keep stable.
- Complete the *tiger carries* with the hands at exactly the same time as the lead foot lands.

CHAPTER TWO: THE EIGHT SKILLS   127

**4l      Closing Move of the Skill of Bridging**

kuàzìgōng shōushì              跨字功受势

- Continue back and forth until you get back to your starting point in an *aligned stance driving punch*, facing in the same direction that you did the *opening move*.

- From a <u>left</u> *aligned stance driving punch*:

ACTION 1: Withdraw the left foot to beside the right foot. Bend the left elbow to pull the left back to the belly, turning it to tuck in. Drill the right fist up and forward to nose height, turning the ulnar edge up. Look at the right fist. (image 2.57)

ACTION 2: Advance the left foot without moving the right foot, to take a *santi* stance. Perform a left split, splitting with the left hand and pulling the right hand back to the belly. (image 2.58)

- From a <u>right</u> *aligned stance driving punch*:

ACTION 1: Withdraw the right foot to beside the left foot, landing it and shifting onto the right leg. Unclench the right hand and pull it back to the belly, then clench it again and drill it up and forward to nose height, turning the ulnar edge up. Look at the right fist. (image 2.59)

ACTION 2: Advance the left foot without moving the right foot, to take a *santi* stance. Perform a left split. (see image 2.58 above)

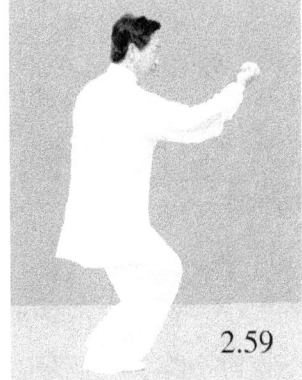

- Then close the form the same as usual from left split, or *santishi*.

## Power Generation For The Skill Of Bridging

The skill of bridging sequence consists of a *withdrawing shoulder close*, a *step forward to bridge*, a *stamp and drill*, and an *aligned stance driving punch*.

*Withdrawing shoulder close*

The footwork is Xingyiquan's characteristic footwork, 'first retreat and then withdraw'. As the classics say, "To retreat, first retreat the rear foot, once you retreat, then you must withdraw [the lead foot]. To advance, first advance the lead foot, once you advance then you must follow in [the rear foot]". Since in Xingyiquan, most weight is on the rear leg, when the rear foot retreats the weight first shifts slightly forward, so that you use the lead foot to push back and the rear leg to extend back. The buttocks must settle down and the weight must shift back quickly. Be sure to pull in at the hips and close the knees.

The power of the hands is: stab the lead hand down towards the rear while threading the rear hand forward with an inner covering action, so that there is a twisting power between the hands. The lead shoulder first opens then closes. The shoulder closes when the lead hand stabs down, to empty the chest and tauten the upper back, pull in the abdomen and tuck in the torso.

This stance is low, sitting down to gather power in order to release it, like pressing down on a spring. Turn the body and pull the shoulder in as the hand stabs down, but be sure to press the head up.

Exhale when you release power, and relax as soon as you have done so. Whenever you release power, always immediately relax.

*Step forward to bridge*

The bridging step is to cover distance, and the follow-in step must be fast. The lead foot should land with a trampling power that acts as a brake.

When doing the slice up with the hand, the lead shoulder must extend forward so that the shoulder leads the elbow and the elbow leads the hand. The hand should be held in a hooked shape to be able to strike with a slicing up action.

When doing the pushing carry, put power to the root of the palm and tuck the elbow into the ribs, sitting down into the lumbar back, settling the shoulders, turning the waist so that the body is sideways, and extending the arm.

To release power into the bridge action: Step forward, landing with a trampling power; turn the waist and put the shoulder into the action with a twisting power; sit into the lumbar area, sit into the hips, settle the shoulders and drop the elbows with a settling power; slice the lead hand up and hook and pull back with a bracing power.

Coordinate the actions with an exhalation of breath. In this way the complete technique will be coordinated and have whole body power. It will be balanced and full. The emphasis is on the turn of the waist, the reach of the shoulder, and the sit into the hips.

*Stamp and drill*

The weight shifts slightly forward then back. This shifting is in order to coordinate the power, to make it fuller, integrated, and able to release more effectively.

The torso, shoulders, and elbows lead the movement of the hands. When the lead hand turns to tuck and press down, do this by rotating the shoulder to lead the elbow and hand. When the rear hand lowers, do this by taking the elbow back and down, rotating the forearm as it lowers.

The stomp is a raking action, not a lift and stamp. Roll the hips in and close the knee to bring the foot into the stomp.

*Aligned stance driving punch*

Keep the elbow tight to the ribs, turning the torso and reaching the shoulder forward, releasing the shoulder and settling the elbow to send the punch out.

Launch power equally into both the lead and the rear hands, to send one forward and one back. "Go out like a steel rasp, return like a grappling hook."

## PRACTICAL APPLICATIONS FOR THE SKILL OF BRIDGING

Looking at the action of *retreat close the shoulders*, it is a defensive move. Retreat and duck out of the way, protecting the chest with the elbows, and the ribs with the arms. Tuck the waist and empty the chest to gather power for the strike. This defensive move places the body in a preparatory position for the counter-attack while awaiting an opportunity.

- If you advance when you close the shoulders, then you can do a shoulder strike. One hand protects the head while the other protects the groin. The hands and arms need to twist and roll in to protect you. When practising, do the actions large and open. When using it, keep the actions small and compact.

*Bridging* is a close range attack, so you must get the body in tight. During the lead hand slice, if you can get a grasp then pull, otherwise use the slice to knock away. The step in must charge into the opponent's groin area, the rear hand can then strike his belly, ribs, or hip area. If you get close enough then you can strike with your hip or shoulder.

- The key to bridging is the advancing footwork to get the body in. When you advance, advance everything. When you retreat, retreat everything. To use this properly, watch what the opponent is doing and take whatever opportunity presents. Using the technique courageously will guarantee success.

## THE SKILL OF BRIDGING, *KUA ZIGONG*

*Stamp and drill* together with *aligned stance driving punch* can be seen as a high fake combined with a low strike. They must be used together without hesitation. Use them to alternate from insubstantial to substantial – the drill is insubstantial and the driving punch is substantial. You can either advance or retreat, according to what is necessary. The drill can also be used as a defensive move or a full attack, combining with the following driving punch.

- When using techniques, don't try to think what technique is a counter to what technique, and exactly how it would work. You must be able to take whatever chance presents, make opportunities for yourself, fully use your own potential, and persevere until you win. If you want to reach a high level in combat, then during regular practice you must train hard and try out techniques with partners, gaining experience and examining the techniques.

### THE POEM ABOUT THE SKILL OF BRIDGING

跨字功歌诀

退步合肩要含胸，

上下撩托跨步冲。

拧要沉肩坐胯力，

震脚钻拳紧连崩。

Empty your chest, retreat and close the shoulders,

Charge in with a bridging step, slicing up and carrying down.

The strength comes from turning the waist, settling the shoulders, and sitting into the hips,

Stomp the foot and drill the fist, followed tightly by a punch.

# FIVE: THE SKILL OF SCOOPING

# 挑字功

## INTRODUCTION TO SCOOP, *TIAO*

The classics say, "The strength of the scoop comes from the shoulders and legs, when the right hand scoops, the right foot opens fiercely, and the left leg braces strongly, so the shoulder is able to exert all the force. It is like the snake technique, but with the hand a bit higher." The Xinhua dictionary definition of scoop is, "to use a long and pointed weapon to stab and lift,"[8] and "to knock away or cause something to move." Scooping is both the application and the way of applying of power. The definition within the martial arts is "a palm or fist technique that exerts force upward and forward from below while the arm maintains a certain flexion." It is both a defensive and offensive technique. Scooping is the opposite of splitting, as split exerts force down and forward while scoop exerts force up and forward. So, while you press the head up to split, you sit the buttocks down to scoop.

The short sequence for the Skill Of Scooping is: *opening move, right step forward tiger carries, withdraw and close the shoulders, advance and scoop, withdraw and chop, advance and scoop, step forward eagle grasps.*

**5a**     **Opening Move (left *santishi*)**     qǐ shì     起势

As described in movement 1a.

**5b**     **Right Step Forward, Tiger Carries**

yòu shàngbù hǔ tuō     右上步虎托

As described in movement 1b.

**5c**     **Withdraw, Close the Shoulders**[9]     chèbù héjiān     撤步合肩

As described in movement 4c.

---

[8] Translator's note: The best action to think of is stabbing a pitchfork into a bale of hay and lifting it onto a platform in one smooth motion.

[9] Translator's note: Called *retreat, close the shoulders* in movement 4c. The rear foot retreats and the lead foot withdraws, so the name can go either way.

# THE SKILL OF SCOOPING, *TIAO ZIGONG*

## 5d    Advance, Scoop    jìnbù tiǎozhǎng    进步挑掌

ACTION: Take a long step forward with the right foot and follow in a half-step with the left foot, keeping most weight on the rear leg, to take a *santi* stance. Turn the right hand and bring it from the left hip to in front of the belly, fingers up and palm forward, and keeping the elbow hugging the ribs. Then do a scooping strike upwards to nose height with the elbow bent and the power going through to the heel of the palm. Turn the left hand palm down and pull down and back to the belly. Sit down into the buttocks. Look past the right hand. (image 2.60)

### Pointers

- Three actions must be completed simultaneously with integrated power: land the right foot, scoop the right arm, and pull back the left hand.
- When the right hand scoops up the elbow must first hug the ribs. Release and settle the shoulder, drop the elbow, and apply force to the heart of the palm.

## 5e    Withdraw, Chop    chèbù pīquán    撤步劈拳

ACTION: Withdraw the right foot a half-step to touch the ball down in front of the left foot. Shift back without moving the left foot. Slide the left hand along the top of the right arm to chop forward and down. Pull the right hand back and down to the belly. Complete the chop at chest height with the left shoulder reaching forward. Lean the torso slightly forward, press the head up and look at the left hand. (image 2.61)

### Pointers

- Three actions must be completed simultaneously with integrated power: withdraw the right foot, pull back the right hand, and chop forward with the left hand.
- As the left hand chops, it should first slide along the right arm, so that it is a sliding grab. Tuck in the abdomen and empty the chest, turn the waist and reach the shoulder into the technique.

## CHAPTER TWO: THE EIGHT SKILLS    133

**5f    Advance, Scoop**        jìnbù tiǎozhǎng        进步挑掌

ACTION: Take a long step forward with the right foot and follow in a half-step with the left foot. Scoop the right hand forcefully up from the right hip to nose height. Keep the elbow bent, the fingers up and palm forward. Pull the left hand palm back to the belly. Sit down into the buttocks, press the head up, and look past the right hand. (images 2.62 and 2.62 front)

2.62

2.62 FRONT

**Pointers**

- Perform movements 5d, 5e, and 5f with no hesitation between them, increasing in strength.

- Turn the waist and shoulders to the right and left to put force into the palms to the right and left.

**5g    Step Forward, Eagle Grasps**    shàngbù yīngzhuō    上步鹰捉

ACTION 1: First withdraw the right foot slightly and then advance it a half-step, following in with the left foot beside the right ankle without touching down. Clench the right hand and pull it back to the belly, and then drill it up by the sternum and forward to head height with the ulnar edge twisted up. Place the left fist tightly at the right elbow, fist heart up. Keep the left elbow tucked into the solar plexus so that the elbows are both tucked in. Look past the right fist. (image 2.63)

ACTION 2: Take a long step forward with the left foot and follow in a half-step with the right foot to take a sixty-forty *santi* stance. Slide the left fist along the right arm to drill up until the fists cross. Then unclench the hands, chop the left hand down, palm forward, and pull the right hand back to the belly. Chop the left hand down to waist height with the arm slightly bent and palm down. Straighten the

2.63    2.64

# THE SKILL OF SCOOPING, *TIAO ZIGONG*

neck and press the head up. Look past the left hand. Flex the fingers slightly to form eagle claws. (image 2.64)

**Pointers**

- Drill the right fist up as the right foot advances. Remember to withdraw the right foot before advancing it.
- Chop the hands down as the left foot lands. Pay attention to pressing the head up, and to the height of the palm strikes. Do not hesitate during the actions.

**5h    Retreat, Close the Shoulders**     tuìbù héjiān     退步合肩

ACTION: Retreat the right foot and shift onto the right leg. Withdraw the left foot to beside the right foot, touching the ball down. Flex the knees to squat down with the knees together, weight on the right leg. Turn the left hand palm up and bend the arm to circle it up and across in front of the face to do an elbow cover towards the right shoulder. Then turn the fingers down to stab past the right ribs to the right hip, palm in. Bring the right hand up and do an elbow cover to the left shoulder, palm turned up. Turn right and tuck the left shoulder towards the right shoulder, so that the left shoulder is forward. Tuck in the abdomen, empty the chest, press the head up, and look past the right hand. (image 2.65)

- Repeat movements 5d, 5e, 5f and 5g, that is, *advance scoop, withdraw chop, advance scoop, step forward eagle grasps*, performing them on the other side. Repeat both sides as long as your space and fitness allows.

**5i    Turn Around for the Skill of Scooping**

tiǎo zìgōng huíshēnshì            挑字功回身势

- The *turn around* is *tiger carries* as described in movement 1g. After turning, continue on with the *advance, scoop* and the rest of the sequence.

**5l    Closing Move for the Skill of Scooping**

tiǎo zìgōng shōushì            挑字功收势

- Once you get back to where you started, sit into *santishi* and then close the form, as described in movement 1h.

## POWER GENERATION FOR THE SKILL OF SCOOPING

The power of the first three movements of the sequence is described in the section on the Skill Of Bridging.

*Advance, scoop*

Advance a long step forward and follow in quickly.

Before applying the scoop, fix the right upper arm tightly to the ribs, placing the elbow between the waist and belly and keeping the elbow bent a hundred degrees. Then flex the waist and settle the shoulder using the waist and abdomen to lift up, keeping the shoulder and elbow dropped. Release the shoulder to send it forward, and extend the arm to do a scooping hit forward.

Both the upward scoop and the downward pull are done on the same plane. Strike the belly with the hand that pulls back to aid the *qi* to settle to the *dantian*, and exhale to launch power.

Lengthen the spine to urge the shoulder forward. Settle the shoulders to send the elbow forward. Drop the elbow to urge the hand forward, finishing with an upward exertion of power into the scoop. Drop into the buttocks at the instant that you launch power.

*Withdraw, chop*

This exerts power forward and down. The lead hand should clench and pull down and back forcefully. Put equal force into the lead and rear hands. The rear hand should slide along the lead forearm, rubbing before pushing out.

Press the head forward, tuck in the abdomen and empty the chest. Settle the shoulder and drop the elbow, turn the waist and reach the shoulder, turning the shoulders into the action to do the chopping palm. Keep the elbow rolled in when chopping. Lean the torso slightly forward to create a downward pressure.

*Step forward eagle grasps*

During the half-step advance, drill both fists up simultaneously, one behind the other. Expand the body core, lengthen the spine, hug the elbows together in front of the chest, empty the chest, close the shoulders, and stretch the upper back.

During the step forward splitting action, tuck in the abdomen, flex the body core, and draw the elbows down forcefully. The torso should have a forward butting, pressing down power as the foot lands. In the final position, the head should have an upward butting power, the legs should have a scissoring power. The entire body must be integrated and show the clear spirit of the eagle.

## PRACTICAL APPLICATIONS FOR THE SKILL OF SCOOPING

The use of the *eagle grasps* is the same as described in the eagle model, see Volume I, Chapter Ten.

# 136 THE SKILL OF SCOOPING, *TIAO ZIGONG*

The heart of the Skill Of Scooping is the scoop itself, which strikes upward and forward through the palm. It is intended to inflict heavy damage on your opponent, knocking him far away. Because the scoop exerts power up and forward, it you strike the opponent's chest you can easily break his root and send him away.

- Both of the main actions of the scoop – the scoop of the rear hand and the withdrawal of the lead hand – are circular actions along the same plane as the body. From the point of view of biomechanics, when the centre of gravity of every segment is in motion, the closer their line of action to the body's centre of gravity the more effective the action will be. From the point of view of combat effectiveness, this 'protects the centre and hits the centre'. To protect your own centre and strike your opponent's centre, use your footwork to trample into him, taking over his centre. The scoop strikes directly to your opponent's core, between the chest and abdomen, and your goal is to knock him away, knock him down, or heavily injure him.

The short sequence for the Skill Of Scooping consists of three palm techniques: advance scoop, withdraw chop, and advance scoop. You can use them as continuous attacks, each one faster and stronger than the previous one. The classics say, "Launch the first punch but hit with the second punch; success depends on the following punch coming quickly." You can use the strikes as a fake and following attack. You can also use one hand to block up, trap, hook, or draw in the opponent, to allow the next hand to get in. There are no set rules on to how to use the techniques – you need to assess the situation.

- When using the scoop you must turn the torso sideways to get in. This presents a smaller surface area to your opponent and gives you more reach as you turn the torso, extend the shoulder, and reach the arm, thus giving you a greater force.

- The classics say, "never send a hand out without purpose, never bring it back without purpose." When you bring the hand back after the strike, hook onto something, grab something, press something down – anything to prevent the opponent from launching a counter attack.

To apply the Skill Of Scooping you need to take advantage of the timing and placement, you need to be flexible, don't do it like it is set in stone.

## The Poem About The Skill Of Scooping

挑字功歌诀

挑掌去意敌胸膛，

坐臀长腰臂伸长。

上挑下劈连环进，

护中打中是主张。

Scooping palm is meant for the opponent's chest or groin.

Sit the buttocks down, fill up the kidney area, extend the arm to lengthen your reach.

Scoop up and chop down in one continuous advancing attack.

The main goal is to protect your centre and hit your opponent's centre.

# SIX: THE SKILL OF BUTTING

# 顶字功

## INTRODUCTION TO BUTT, *DING*

The classics say, "The strength of butting is in the head, so the most important thing is to straighten the neck and drop the shoulders. Combine this with a cover and punch." *Ding* means to support something on the head, to brace up, or to carry. It also means to go against the flow of something, butting up against something. As a technique in Xingyiquan it means to strike with the head, "the head strikes as the feet go in, it starts and ends in the centre. When the feet take over the central gate and take over the space, even a skilled player cannot defend against the attack."

The short sequence for training the Skill Of Butting is: *opening move, step forward tiger carries, advance double elbow covers, step forward head butt, pull and knee butt, step forward elbow butt, stroke and driving punch, step forward split.*[10]

**6a**   **Opening Move (left *santishi*)**   qǐ shì   起势

As described in movement 1a.

**6b**   **Right Step Forward, Tiger Carries**   yòu shàngbù hǔtuō   右上步虎托

As described in movement 1b.

**6c**   **Advance, Double Elbow Covers**   jìnbù shuāng yǎnzhǒu   进步双掩肘

ACTION: Advance the right foot a half-step and lift the left foot by the right ankle without touching down. Keep the legs together and stand firmly on the right leg. Clench the right hand and bend the right elbow to drill the right hand up to head height, then do an elbow cover leftwards, lowering the fist to the left ribs, fist heart in.

Clench the left hand and bend the left elbow, drill the fist to head height, then do an elbow cover rightwards, lowering the fist to the right ribs, fist heart in. When

---

[10] Author's note: My reference text described a head butt, a straight push and a cover to punch in the short sequence. Since in martial arts, elbow and knee strikes are also called butt [*ding*], the Skill Of Butting should include elbow and knee strikes as well as head strikes, so I have added them.

the forearms cross in front of the chest the right arm is inside the left. Empty the chest, stretch the upper back and press the head up slightly. Look ahead. (images 2.66, 2.67, 2,68)

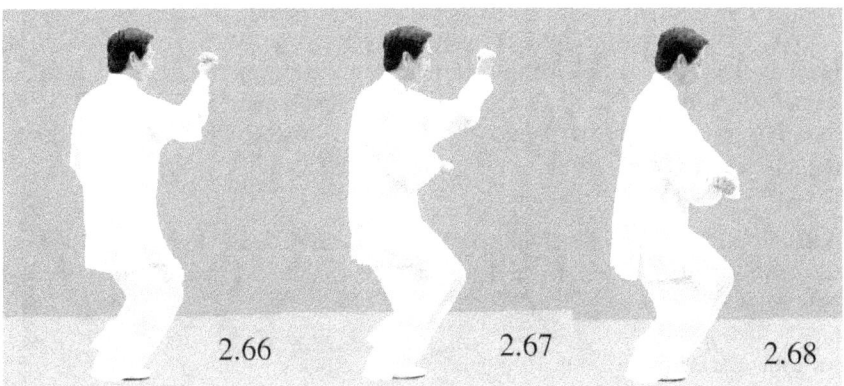

**Pointers**

- Coordinate the right foot advance with the outward circles and inward covers of the arms. The elbow covers must be done quickly.

- When doing the elbow covers to left and right, transfer power from the waist to the shoulders, the shoulders to the elbows, and the elbows to the arms. Complete the actions without pausing.

**6d    Step Forward, Head Butt**        shàngbù tóudǐng    上步头顶

ACTION: Take a long step forward with the left foot and follow in a half-step with the right, putting most weight on the left leg. Keep the fists clenched and the forearms crossed and push / press them forward and down to belly height. Shift forward and lean the torso forward, tucking in the chin, pulling in the abdomen and emptying the chest in order to butt forward with the forehead. Settle the shoulders down, close the teeth, straighten the nape of the neck and look forward. (images 2.69 and 2.69 front)

**Pointers**

- Butt with the head as the left foot lands, hitting at exactly the same time.

# 140  THE SKILL OF BUTTING, *DING ZIGONG*

- Advance double elbow covers and step forward head butt should be done as one move with no break between them.

## 6e  Pull and Knee Butt    lǔshǒu xīzhuàng    捋手膝撞

ACTION 1: Advance the left foot forward diagonally to the left and shift forward, bending the right leg and lifting the right heel. Unclench the hands and extend them to the forward left, fingers forward, left palm forward, right hand in front of the left elbow. Turn the left palm to face right and turn the right hand thumb down, palm also facing right. Both hands are chest height as if grabbing to pull. Look past the left hand. (image 2.70)

ACTION 2: Shift onto the left leg to stand on it with the knee slightly bent, leaning the torso slightly forward. Bend the right knee and shove forward with it to chest height. Clench the hands and pull back towards the right – pull the left fist back to in front of the chest, fist heart up, and pull the right fist back on the ride side, fist heart down. Look at the left fist and stand firmly on the left leg. (image 2.71)

### Pointers

- Extend the hands forward as the lead foot advances. Grab and pull the hands back as the knee butts forward. Be sure to flex the supporting leg slightly and to grab the ground with the toes to stand firmly.

- Dodge the torso to the left so that the entire move is coordinated and the use of power is balanced throughout the body.

## 6f  Step Forward, Right Elbow Butt    shàngbù yòu dǐngzhǒu    上步右顶肘

ACTION: Take a long step straight forward with the right foot and follow in the left foot a half-step. Bring the right elbow into the right ribs, and then as the right foot lands, butt forward and up with the elbow bent. Bring the right fist to above the right shoulder with the fist heart in, so that the elbow butts up above shoulder height. Place the left hand behind the right elbow to support it, tucking the left elbow into the solar plexus. Shift partially onto the right leg. Look straight forward. (image 2.72)

CHAPTER TWO: THE EIGHT SKILLS   141

**Pointers**

- o  The elbow strike must come as the lead foot lands, so that the whole body is coordinated. Be sure to shift slightly forward.

- o  Land the foot well forward and bring the rear foot in quickly. The stance should be long enough that the body is fairly low.

**6g    Stroke and Driving Punch**         lǔshǒu bēngquán         捋手崩拳

ACTION 1: Shift back and withdraw the right foot a half-step to touch the ball of the foot down in front of the left foot. Do not move the left foot yet. Extend the right hand forward then cover and press down, clench to grab, and pull back to the right side. Slide the left hand along the right arm to chop out to chest height, fingers up, palm forward. Put the left shoulder forward into the action, lean the torso slightly forward and lift the buttocks slightly. Look past the left hand. (image 2.73)

ACTION 2: Advance the right foot a long step and follow in the left foot a half-step, keeping the weight mostly on the left leg. Punch the right fist forward to solar plexus height, fist eye up and fist surface angled forward slightly. Clench and pull the left hand back to the belly, fist heart in. Press the head up and look past the right fist. (image 2.74)

**Pointers**

- o  Push the left hand forward as the right hand covers and pulls back, so that the whole action works as a unit.

- o  The *Advance driving punch* must be fast. Drive the footwork forward for distance and punch quickly.

- o  Chop the left hand down when the right foot withdraws for the pull back. Then advance the foot and punch at exactly the same time.

## 142  THE SKILL OF BUTTING, *DING ZIGONG*

### 6h   Step Forward, Left Split    shàngbù zuǒ pīquán    上步左劈拳

ACTION 1: First withdraw the right foot slightly and pull the right fist back to the belly. Then advance the right foot a half-step and follow in the left foot, lifting it beside the right without touching down. Drill the right fist up by the sternum and forward to nose height. twisting the ulnar edge up. Press the head up and look forward. (image 2.75)

ACTION 2: Take a long step forward with the left foot and follow in the right foot a half-step. Drill the left fist up by the sternum and out along to the right elbow. When the fists meet, unclench the hands and turn the palms down, splitting the left hand forward and down to chest height while pulling the right hand back to the belly. Press the head up and look forward. (image 2.76)

- Carry on, repeating the same moves on the other side: *left advance double elbow covers, step forward head butt, pull and knee butt, step forward left elbow butt, stroke and driving punch*. The actions are the same, just switching right and left.

### 6i   Turn Around for the Skill of Butting

     dǐng zìgōng huíshēn shì      顶字功回身势

- The turn around is the same as *split turn around*. Whichever hand is forward, pull the lead hand back and hook-in the lead foot to turn around. Then advance with a drilling fist and step forward into a split. (See Volume I for details on *split turn around*.)

### 6l   Closing Move for the Skill of Butting

     dǐng zìgōng shōushì      顶字功收势

- Once you get back to where you started, and are sitting in left split, you may close the form. Close as is usual from *santishi*.

# CHAPTER TWO: THE EIGHT SKILLS

## POWER GENERATION FOR THE SKILL OF BUTTING

*Double elbow covers*

The hands wrap around to bring the elbows in to cover, so the forearms have a sticky wrapping power. The forearms need to rotate, drawn by the waist and shoulders. The whole action is circular. When the right hand extends forward and the left elbow covers, the right shoulder should reach forward slightly. When the left hand reaches forward and the right elbow covers, the left shoulder should reach forward slightly. Empty the chest, tuck the elbows in tightly, and keep the action smooth. Relax the waist to be able to do the bodywork.

*Head butt*

Settle the shoulders as the arms cross and stab down. The arms have a bracing power forward and down.

As the head butts forwards, empty the chest and spread the upper back, bow from the waist and tuck in the abdomen, releasing power from the body core to transfer to the spine, linking through each segment of the body.

Tuck in the chin, straighten and tighten the nape of the neck, clench the teeth, and hit with the forehead. Coordinate the strike with an exhalation. Be sure to shift forward.

*Knee butt*

The knees strike either up or across. Both work well. When striking with the knee the body should lean about fifty degrees. Tuck in the abdomen, empty the chest, and use both hands to pull back to create an equal and opposite force for the knee strike. The body core is the fulcrum, so that the lower and upper limbs work together to release the integrated power of the whole body.

*Elbow butt*

Drive the footwork forward and shove with the body. Reach the shoulder forward and put power from the lower back upward, sitting the buttocks down. Shift forward and lean slightly into the action.

Keep the elbow tight to the ribs at first, then drive forward and up.

When releasing power, connect through the whole body.

*Pull back and punch*

This consists of a withdrawing step and covering chop followed by a step forward into a driving punch. The footwork is to first withdraw and then advance; withdraw only a little, then advance a good distance, remembering that the rear foot must then follow in. The hand technique has a hooking pull back, first with the right hand and then with the left.

The whole movement must link together without hesitation. When releasing power be sure to turn the waist and reach the shoulder. When withdrawing, press the head up and lift the torso slightly. When punching, drop the torso slightly to focus forward.

- The power in Xingyiquan movements can only be found by practice, and in practicing with a mind to fulfilling all the requirements of Xingyiquan in each body segment. On this foundation, when you release power you should focus on feeling and understanding the laws of physics. Transitional moves between each position must follow the structure of the body and follow the principles of movement. This focus helps you to find both the internal and the external aspects of each movement. Of course, it is vital to follow the principles of combat. If you leave the principles of combat then you are no longer doing martial arts. The martial arts are intrinsically combative.

## Practical Applications For The Skill Of Butting

The main techniques in the sequence of the skill of butting are the head butt, the knee butt, and the elbow butt. These are all close range techniques. The classics say, "use the hands and feet for long range, use the knees and elbows for short range." Xingyiquan emphasizes the 'seven fists' and the fourteen targets. The head is one of the 'seven fists' so the skill of butting emphasizes its training and application.

*Head butt*

To hit with the head the hands must open up the opponent's defense. "Stomp into his main door to steal his position," get the body in close. As lead foot lands the rear foot must drive to push into the head to hit the opponent's face or chest.

This technique only works when you are wholly committed to victory. Be sure to use both hands to control the opponent's hands to protect your head from possible attack. A head butt is like a kiss – you cannot do it if you are not close.

*Knee butt*

A knee strike can be used as a dodging counter attack to an opponent's straight attack. You grab his arm with both hands, pulling him along his line of attack and striking his chest or belly strongly with the knee. If you can get a grip, then grab, otherwise knock his arms aside.

Be sure to dodge the body to the side to make space, then you can step forward to hit with the knee.

You must hit hard and fast and get in tight to your opponent in order to be effective.

*Elbow butt*

*Step forward elbow butt* is actually an upward scooping elbow strike. You have to get close for this to work. You have to react to your opportunities in order to get in for an elbow strike, and this depends on your footwork and courage. You

## CHAPTER TWO: THE EIGHT SKILLS

have to dare to step into your opponent's groin, taking his 'central gate,' getting close enough to shove with your whole body.

- Because this is a short range technique it puts you at risk. You must protect your head, and "use long and short together, use long to reinforce the short and use short to control the long."

*Stroke and punch*

This can be done together with the elbow butt to 'use long to reinforce the short' or it can be used on its own. It is a fast attack that protects the centre while attacking the centre, 'eating a fist and returning a fist.'

*Withdraw and cover to split*

This is essentially a defensive move, but it could also be done as a high fake before a low strike. Additionally it serves to gather power for the punch.

Punch directly into the opponent's heart, focussing a foot behind him.

- The butting techniques are all close range. This means that you have to get your whole body in close, so courage is vital to their effectiveness. You have to have a no holds barred spirit that oppresses your opponent, otherwise you are just 'discussing tactics on paper'. To use a technique you must master its principles, practise its power, and thoroughly examine what attacks it is effective against. You need to fully use your own abilities, be flexible and natural to be able to change with the situation, to "get the feeling when you see the view."

## THE POEM ABOUT THE SKILL OF BUTTING

顶字功歌诀

顶技三法头膝肘，

全凭步法往里走。

节短势险护己身，

贴身打法强中手。

The three methods of butting are the head, knee, and elbow.

They all depend on the footwork getting you inside.

It is dangerous to use short segments, so you must protect yourself.

To use short range techniques you must take over and control the centre.

# SEVEN: THE SKILL OF PASSING

# 云字功

## Introduction To Pass, *Yun*

Clouds [*yun*] pass by in the sky, turning and flowing, so the word passing [*yun*] is often used for smooth turning techniques. The technique pulls to the side with both hands, flowing like clouds. 'Cloud hands' in Taijiquan is a passing technique, as are flat brandishing techniques of weapons. The Skill Of Passing in Xingyiquan describes the spinning of the hands in front of the head, and also includes an upward block, a knocking draw, and a grabbing pull, all used as compact defense. If well used, pass is very effective. It can be combined with a reverse stance drill, combining defense with offense. It develops quick and agile hand and body techniques, quick footwork, and should show the continuity of passing clouds or flowing water.

Pass can be done with either large or small actions. The hands perform large, expansive movements for the large pass, one hand circling above the head while the other hand circles in front of the body. The hands perform a small circle in front of the face for the small pass, with a compact movement. Pass can be practised alone with advancing and retreating footwork. When combined with the drill, it must be done with advancing footwork.

The short sequence for training the Skill Of Passing contains *opening move, right step forward tiger carries, left pass, right pass,* and two *reverse stance drills.*

**7a**     **Opening Move (left *santishi*)**     qǐ shì     起势

As described in movement 1a.

**7b**     **Right Step Forward, Tiger Carries**    yòu shàngbù hǔtuō    右上步虎托

As described in movement 1b.

## 7c    Step Forward, Left Pass    shàngbù zuǒ yúnshì    上步左云势

ACTION 1: Advance the right foot a small step forward and then take a step forward with the left foot, bending the legs and shifting the weight to between the feet. Turn the left hand palm up and bend the elbow, lifting the elbow up so that the forearm blocks across above the head. Turn the right palm up and bring it by the sternum then extend out to the left front at nose height, keeping the elbow tucked in. Empty the chest and stretch the upper back. Look at the right hand. (image 2.77)

ACTION 2: Without moving the left foot, take a step forward with the right foot, turning it out as you land. Shift more weight onto the left leg. Circle the left hand above the head, back at the left to the left side of the body, then carry forward and up to shoulder height on the midline of the body with the elbow slightly bent and the palm up. At the same time, circle the right hand across to the right. When it arrives in front at the right, bend the elbow and turn the palm up, circling past in front of the face. When it circles to the left side, turn the palm out and thumb down with the thumb web open, finishing with the right hand at the right side of the head. Look past the left hand. (images 2.78 and 2.78 front)

**Pointers**

- Take small quick steps for the left and right stepping during *left pass*. The right foot must land turned out, across the line. Keep the centre of gravity low to move with stability.

- The hands should circle at the same time. When one hand is above the head the other is in front of the body. The hands draw opposite circles. When they arrive in front of the body then the left hand carries and the right hand pulls back. This action should happen as the right foot steps forward.

- The hands and feet must be coordinated, and the movement must be completed smoothly as one action.

## 7d  Reverse Stance Right Drill     àobù yòu zuānquán  拗步右钻拳

ACTION: Take a long step forward with the left foot and follow in a half-step with the right foot, keeping most weight on the left leg. Turn the left hand palm down and tuck it in, pulling down, left, and back while bending the arm and clenching the fist, and then circle it up to the left side of the head, fist heart out, fist eye down, elbow a bit higher than the shoulder. At the same time, clench and draw the right fist back slightly and lower it by the right waist, turning the fist heart up, and then drilling forward and up to nose height. Press the head up and look past the right fist. (image 2.79)

### Pointers

- The right drill must be completed as the right foot lands. The punch must have a focal point. Keep the body well balanced and use whole body power.

## 7e  Step Forward, Right Pass     shàngbù yòu yúnshì     上步右云势

ACTION 1: Advance the left foot a short step and then step the right foot forward, bending the knees and shifting between the legs with a bit more weight on the rear leg. Unclench the right hand and rotate it thumb inward, lifting the elbow to block up above the head with the forearm across, hand at the left side of the head, palm up. Unclench the left hand and rotate it thumb outward, bringing it by the sternum and extending it to the right front to nose height palm up, elbow tucked into the solar plexus. Empty the chest and stretch the upper back. Look at the left hand. (image 2.80)

ACTION 2: Step the left foot forward without moving the right foot, land with the foot turned out, bend the knees and keep most weight on the right leg. Circle the right hand back and right above the head. Then lower it down the right side to sternum height with the elbow slightly bent, palm up. Complete the action with a carry on the midline of the body, palm up at shoulder height. Circle the left hand, palm up, to the forward left, using the elbow as the pivot point. When it arrives at the forward left, bend the elbow and turn the palm out, thumb down, and

stretch the thumb web open. Then pull the left hand down, left, and back, pulling it to the left side of the head, palm out, fingers forward. Look at the right hand. (image 2.81)

**Pointers**

- Do not pause between actions 1 and 2. The hands should circle like carrying plates, using body action. Keep the waist relaxed, compress the torso slightly, keep the movement smooth and continuous, and coordinate the feet with the hands.

- Focus on the hand techniques while circling. One closes off, blocks up, hoists and pulls while the other settles, brushes aside, and hooks.

**7f    Reverse Stance Left Drill**          àobù zuǒ zuānquán        拗步左钻拳

ACTION: Take a long step forward with the right foot and follow in a half-step with the left foot, keeping most weight on the left leg. Rotate the right hand thumb inward to tuck it in, palm down, and circle down, right, and back to brush aside and draw. Bend the elbow and clench the fist to pull back to above the right shoulder, fist heart out, fist eye down. Draw the left fist back a bit then lower it to the left waist, fist heart up. Once it arrives at the waist, drill forward and up to nose height, twisting the ulnar edge up. Press the head up and look past the left fist. (image 2.82)

- Continue on, alternating left and right, the number of repetitions determined by the space and your fitness.

**Pointers**

- Be sure to rotate the fist and arm before doing the drill.

- Three actions must be completed at the same time: the right foot lands, the right hand draws back, and the left fist drills.

- This move should be explosive.

**7g    Turn Around for the Skill of Passing**

yún zìgōng huíshēnshì         云字功回身势

Turn around when you are in a *reverse stance drill*, turning into a *tiger carries*. See movement 1g for the description of the *tiger carries* turn.

- To turn from a *reverse stance left drill*, hook-in the right foot and turn around, advancing the left foot into *tiger carries*.

# 150 THE SKILL OF PASSING, *YUN ZIGONG*

- To turn from a *reverse stance right drill*, hook-in the left foot and turn around, advancing the right foot for *tiger carries*.

The exact hand actions will differ slightly, you will need to bring the rear hand forward and drop the lead hand slightly to cross the hands. Note that you are turning from a reverse stance instead of an aligned stance, so the feeling will be a bit different.

- After you turn around, then continue on to repeat the passing sequence.

**7h  Closing Move for the Skill of Passing**

yún zìgōng shōushì            云字功收势

When you are back to the starting point, in a *reverse stance drill* facing in the same direction that you started from, you may close the form.

- From *reverse stance left drill*:

Withdraw the right foot and place it beside the left foot, feet parallel. Tuck the left fist to cover / press with the forearm across the body and lower the right fist to the waist. Drill the right fist up to nose height and pull the left fist back to the belly. Look at the right fist. (image 2.83)

- From *reverse stance right drill*:

Withdraw the left foot to beside the right foot. Circle the right fist right, down, and then drill forward and up. Unclench the left hand and circle it left and up, then right and down to cover and press down, pulling back to the belly. Look at the right fist (image 2.84)

- Advance the left foot without moving the right foot, to settle into a *santi* stance. Split the left hand forward and pull the right hand back to the belly to take a *santishi*. Then close as usual from *santishi*. See the description in movement 1h.

# CHAPTER TWO: THE EIGHT SKILLS

## POWER GENERATION FOR THE SKILL OF PASSING

*Pass*

Analyzing the action of passing, the hands each draw a circle in front of the face in a nonstandard elipse. Using the left pass as example, the left hand rotates and lifts the forearm up, opening out the left shoulder. The right hand extends forward, closing in the right shoulder. You need to empty the chest and gather in the lower back, keeping the waist relaxed and lively to draw the arms into action, so that the hands guide, the waist urges, and the shoulders follow.

When the right hand circles in front, the right shoulder reaches forward. When the left hand circles in front, the left shoulder reaches forward. When the left hand has the carrying power, then the right hand has a drawing back power. The power comes from the body core. With the coordination of the footwork, the actions alternate left and right.

*Reverse stance drill*

The torso must first draw back before the drill. This gathers power by 'pre-loading back to launch forward.' If you will punch the right fist then the right shoulder should roll and draw to the right, compressing down, and the right upper arm should be tight to the ribs. In this way the lower back will urge the shoulder forward, the shoulder will urge the elbow, and the fist will twist and drill to the midline of the body. This makes the drilling punch solid and heavy, completed with whole body power.

- The completed drilling punch should be neither too short nor too long – "too bent lacks reach, too straight lacks strength" – an elbow angle of one hundred and twenty degrees is ideal.

In addition, when the left hand tucks in and presses down, then brushes aside to draw back, keep the arm relaxed and settled. Do not use brute force. Transfer power from the waist to the shoulder and from the shoulder to the elbow, which in turn draws the hand. The power should be heavy, sudden, shaking. The right hand drills forward and the left hand draws back, completely connected through the waist, using the power of the body core.

- During the short sequence of the *skill of passing*, during the pass the chest should be empty and the upper back stretched, the abdomen should be pulled in and the lower back compressed, and the torso should be lowered. During the drill, the lower back should first gather and then straighten and hump. The buttocks should first drop down slightly. Breathe out to release power, settling the breath to the *dantian* to increase the whole body power of the drill.

## PRACTICAL APPLICATIONS FOR THE SKILL OF PASSING

Passing is essentially a defensive move, lifting the elbow and hand to protect the head. The rear hand comes through to protect your chest and ribs. You need to close in your chest and close in the rear shoulder to better protect your upper body's upper portion and midline.

The rear hand knocks aside as it circles, catching the opponent's arm and pulling it to the side and back as the lead hand comes through. It works whether you advance or retreat, but it works best with a retreating step. You need to coordinate the hand action with the footwork. To use it advancing, both hands need to continuously and quickly circle in front of the body to protect you. This serves also to confuse the opponent and create an opportunity to get in with another technique.

*Reverse stance drill* covers the opponent's arm and presses it down, using the power from your back to shake him and take him sideways so that the rear hand can come through with an uppercut to his chest or jaw. The key is to drive the footwork into the opponent to get a tight punch. Drill is a close range technique, so if you can't get in close then you won't be able to use its full potential as a strong hit.

- Talking about fighting is not fighting. Similarly, knowing techniques without having deep skills is useless. You need to get a feel for applications with a lot of thoughtful practice. As you gain practical experience and learn from others you will gradually improve. Remember that in actual combat the techniques are not set in cement. You have to react according to the situation and use techniques fluidly, according to your own natural abilities.

## THE POEM ABOUT THE SKILL OF PASSING

云字功歌诀

云势两手绕身前，

架拨挦带神意联。

搂手钻打腰肩劲，

快步进身拳上钻。

The hands circle in front of the body to pass.
Block up, knock away, pull and guide, connecting your spirit and mind.
Brush aside and drill using the power of your back and shoulders.
Quick footwork gets the body in close so that you can drill up.

# EIGHT: THE SKILL OF GUIDING

# 领字功

## INTRODUCTION TO GUIDE, *LING*

Guide means to catch or to accept an oncoming force and guide it along the same direction – to draw something along, accepting and taking it somewhere else – so the Skill Of Guiding is that of redirecting an attack off to the side. If the opponent strikes down the midline you defend with both hands, quickly grabbing and drawing him along, guiding him to the outside line. Take the force of the opponent and add a little along the same direction, so that he misses his target, 'guiding his attack to land in emptiness.' Once he is turned away from you, you are in a smooth position to counter attack at will. Guide can also be used as a direct grabbing attack, pulling your opponent forcefully to the side to put him off balance and throw him off stride.[11] Guide can be practised alone, as advance guide, retreat guide, aligned stance guide, reverse stance guide, and so on.

The short sequence for the Skill Of Guiding is: *opening move, right step forward tiger carries, left guide, left aligned stance cannon punch, turn around tiger carries, pivot triple palm strikes, advance left driving punch, right guide*, and so on.

**8a     Opening Move (left *santishi*)**     qǐ shì     起势

As described in movement 1a.

**8b     Right Step Forward, Tiger Carries**     yòu shàngbù hǔtuō     右上步虎托

As described in movement 1b.

**8c     Step Forward, Left Guide**     shàngbù zuǒ lǐngshì     上步左领势

ACTION 1: Advance the right foot a half-step and bring in the left foot by the right ankle without touching down. Stand firmly on the right leg with the knees bent and together. Cross the wrists with the left on the outside, left palm facing in

---

[11] Author's note: Some classics write, "guide is the snake model," but looking at the technique and line of action of snake model, guide is quite different. Snake model is mainly a slice up, a scoop, or a low drag. Guide, on the other hand, follows the line of attack smoothly. Perhaps in some branches of Xingyiquan the Skill Of Guiding is similar to the snake model's technique, but as far as we are concerned they are not at all alike.

## 154 THE SKILL OF GUIDING, *LING ZIGONG*

and right palm facing out. Push and block up in front of the head, hands to nose height. Empty the chest, stretch the upper back, and drop the elbows. Look past the hands. (image 2.85)

ACTION 2: Step the left foot a long step forward and follow in a half-step with the right foot, shifting back a bit into a sixty-forty stance. Entwine the wrists around each other, rotating the right hand thumb outward and the left hand thumb inward, so that the hands draw a small circle at the right in front of the body. When the palms both face forward then clench the hands and pull down and back to the left with a guiding action. The left hand completes the move behind the body with the palm down, and the right hand pulls back below the left armpit, fist heart up. Press the head up and look forward. (images 2.86 and 2.86 front)

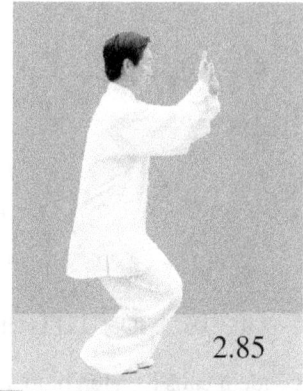

2.85

2.86

2.86 FRONT

**Pointers**

- Complete the upward crossed block as the right foot lands. Sit the torso down.

- Complete the guiding back action as the left foot lands. Be sure to rotate and grab, and to draw a small circle.

**8d     Left Aligned Stance Cannon Punch** zuǒ shùnbù pàoquán 左顺步炮拳

ACTION: Advance the left foot and follow in the right foot a half-step, keeping most weight on the right leg. Turn the right fist heart in and drill up toward the left temple. Bend the left elbow and bring the fist in to in front of the chest. As the left foot advances, punch the left fist forward to sternum height and draw the right fist across to the right temple, rotating the thumb in. Reach the left shoulder forward and settle the right elbow down. Press the head up and look past the left fist. (image 2.87)

2.87

CHAPTER TWO: THE EIGHT SKILLS    155

**Pointers**

- Complete the left punch as the left foot lands.
- Turn the waist and extend the shoulder into the punch. Keep the right elbow down and rotate the thumb side of the fist in towards the palm [called internal rotation]. In this high position, this action will turn the fist heart out.

**8e    Turn Around, Tiger Carries**    huíshēn hǔtuō    回身虎托

ACTION 1: Hook-in step the left foot at the right toes and turn the body around one-eighty degrees to the right, sitting onto the left leg. When you have turned around, withdraw the right foot to just in front of the left. Bring the left fist to in front of the chest, and stab the right fist from under the right armpit behind the body out to sternum height, fist eye down. Keep the right arm slightly bent. Look at the right fist. (image 2.88)

ACTION 2: Advance the right foot a half-step and bring the left foot up by the right foot without touching down. Thread the left fist forward along under the right arm. When the fists cross, unclench the hands and lift them, crossed, then open out to the sides. Continue to circle them down to the sides, palms forward, fingers down. Press the head up and look forward. (images 2.89, 2.90)

ACTION 3: Step the left foot forward and follow the right foot in a half-step, keeping most weight on the right leg. Push the hands forward and down, palms forward at belly height, a fist width apart. Keep the arms slightly bent, empty the chest, stretch the upper back, sit into the buttocks, and settle the shoulders. Look past the hands. (image 2.91)

## 156   THE SKILL OF GUIDING, *LING ZIGONG*

**Pointers**

- Hook-in the lead foot as the fist stabs out towards the rear.
- Turn the body and step forward as the hands circle and come into the waist.
- Push the hands forward and down as the foot lands.

**8f      Pivot, Triple Palm Strikes**   zhuànshēn sānzhǎng   转身三掌

ACTION 1: Hook-in the left foot towards the right toes and turn around one-eighty to the right to face back in the way which you came. Shift onto the left leg and, after you have pivoted, advance the right foot a half-step without moving the left foot. Rotate the right hand so the thumb is down and the little finger is up and bring it past the left side of the body, up, forward, and then down in a circular chop, hitting with the ulnar edge at sternum height with the arm slightly bent. Look at the right hand. (image 2.92)

ACTION 2: Step the left foot forward without moving the right foot. Bend the left arm and lift the hand, then circle it from the back up, forward and down with a circular chop, finishing at sternum height with the arm slightly bent. Pull the right hand back to the right side. Look at the left hand. (image 2.93)

ACTION 3: Shift back and withdraw the left foot a half-step to touch the ball down in front of the right foot. Do not move the right foot. Circle the right hand up and forward in a circling chop and cover with the palm down at sternum height. Pull the left hand back to the left side and clench it. Reach the right shoulder forward and lift the torso slightly. Look at the right hand. (image 2.94)

**Pointers**

- The hook-in to pivot should be a large range movement, hooking to take a T stance.

## CHAPTER TWO: THE EIGHT SKILLS

- o Complete the inverted hand circular chop as the body turns. Complete the left circular chop as the left foot steps forward. Complete the right covering chop as the left foot withdraws.

- o These three palms – one inverted chop, one straight chop, and one covering chop – should be fully connected without a pause between them, completed as one action.

**8g   Aligned Stance Left Driving Punch** shùnbù zuǒ bēngquán 顺步左崩拳

ACTION: Advance the left foot and follow in a half-step with the right foot. Clench the right hand and pull it back to the belly, fist heart in. Do a left driving punch forward to sternum height, arm slightly bent. Press the head up and look past the left fist. (image 2.95)

**Pointers**

- o Complete the left punch at exactly the same time that the left foot lands.

- o Do not pause between *pivot three palms* and *left driving punch*. They are connected and completed as one action.

**8h   Right Guide**   yòu lǐngshì   右领势

ACTION 1: Advance the left foot a half-step and follow in the right foot to beside the left without touching down, bending the left leg to stand firmly. Thread the right fist out under the left arm until the fists meet, then unclench them with the wrists crossed, left hand above the right, palms angled up. Drill and block up in front of the head with the hands at nose height. Empty the chest and stretch the upper back. Look past the hands. (image 2.96)

# 158   THE SKILL OF GUIDING, *LING ZIGONG*

ACTION 2: Take a long step forward with the right foot and follow in the left foot a half-step. Keep the wrists crossed and rotate the left thumb outwards and the right thumb inwards. When both palms face forward, clench the hands. Pull, guiding down to the rear right until the right fist is behind the body, fist heart down, and the left fist is under the right armpit, fist heart up. Press the head up and look forward. (image 2.97)

**Pointers:**

The same as *left guide*, see pointers for movement 8c.

**8i   Right Aligned Stance Cannon Punch**   yòu shùnbù pàoquán   右顺步炮拳

ACTION: Tuck the left elbow in and drill up, fist heart in, to the right temple. Bend the right elbow and bring the fist to the chest. Advance the right foot and follow in the left foot a half-step. Punch with a *right cannon punch* as the right foot lands. The right fist punches to sternum height, fist eye up. The left fist rotates the thumb inward and moves to beside the left temple. Keep the left elbow down. Press the head up and look past the right fist. (image 2.98)

**Pointers:**

- o   The same as *left aligned stance cannon punch*, see pointers for movement 8d.

**8j   Turn Around, Tiger Carries**   huíshēn hǔtuō   回身虎托

The same as movement 8e described above, just transposing left and right.

**8k   Pivot, Triple Palm Strikes**   zhuànshēn sānzhǎng   转身三掌

The same as movement 8f described above, just transposing left and right.

**8l   Aligned Stance Right Driving Punch**

   shùnbù yòu bēngquán      顺步右崩拳

The same as movement 8g described above, just transposing left and right.

- Since the sequence for the *skill of guiding* contains turning moves within it, it is practiced without a 'turn around' move.

CHAPTER TWO: THE EIGHT SKILLS    159

**8m    Closing Move for the Skill of Guiding**

lǐng zìgōng shōushì            领字功收势

On getting back to the starting place, you will close from a *driving punch*.

- From a <u>left</u> *aligned stance driving punch*:

ACTION 1: Without moving the feet, tuck in and pull the left fist back to the belly. (image 2.99)

ACTION 2: Bring the right foot back to the left, feet parallel. Unclench the hands and lift them to the sides, palms up, until they reach shoulder height. Look at the right hand. (images 2.100, 2.101)

ACTION 3: Without moving the legs, bend the elbows to bring the hands together in front of the face at shoulder height, pointing to each other with the palms down. (image 2.102)

ACTION 4: Press the hands down and stand up. Bring the hands to hang at the sides, to stand at attention. (image 2.103)

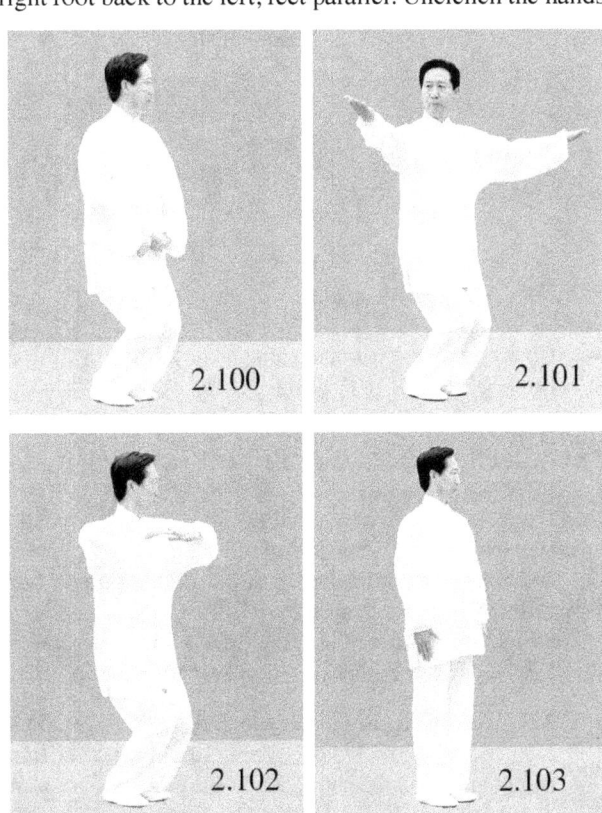

# 160 THE SKILL OF GUIDING, *LING ZIGONG*

- If you are in a <u>right</u> *aligned stance driving punch*:

ACTION 1: Retreat the right foot and then retreat the left foot behind the right, landing with the whole foot. Shift back with the weight between the legs and turn the right foot out slightly to take a crossed stance. Rotate the right fist heart up and pull it back to the belly. Punch the left fist forward to sternum height. Press the head up and look at the left fist. This is a *retreating driving punch*. (images 2.104, 2.105)

ACTION 2: Step the left foot forward without moving the right foot, to take a *santi* stance. Tuck in the left fist and pull it back to the belly. Press the head up and look forward. (image 2.106)

- Continue on to close the same as described in Actions 2, 3, and 4 above (see images 2.100, 2.101, 2.102, 2.103)

## POWER GENERATION FOR THE SKILL OF GUIDING

When the hands cross and push/block up in front, you should empty the chest and stretch the upper back, putting an inflating energy, or bracing power, into the arms. As the hands grab and rotate, just before they guide back, they should pre-load forward and rightward, as they will be pulling back and to the left. In order to guide back, the hands should first draw a small circle forward. This helps to get a feel for the whole body power, and help to gather power.

- The waist needs to be relaxed and supple so that its natural elasticity leads the actions of the hands. When guiding, power transfers from the waist to shoulders, from the shoulders to the elbows, and from the elbows to the hands.

When guiding to the left, the right shoulder is forward. When guiding to the right, the left shoulder is forward. In this way the shoulders have a hidden shove. Turn the waist to align the shoulders into the action, and lean the torso slightly.

- The lead foot should have a raking power as it lands and the head should butt forward, so that your entire intention is to charge forward. The hand that guides back should have a pulling power back and a settling power down.

*Aligned stance cannon punch*

Keep the elbow tightly hugging the ribs and punch to the midline. Turn the waist and extend into the shoulder to launch power. Tuck in the elbow to drill the fist up. Exhale to assist the power release by combing internal with external movement.

*Pivot, triple palm strikes*

Relax the shoulders during the hook-in step, turn around, and inverted circling chop. Transfer power from the shoulders to the elbows, and from the elbows to the hands. As the circling chop lowers it should have heavy power. As the arm circles, keep the elbow bent at a certain angle, then bend it and move forward, and then extend it as it reaches forward. This increases the force and speed of the circle. This is how to use both angular and linear velocity effectively. The angular velocity achieves a quick turn around, and the linear velocity gains a greater strength for the hit.

The inverted chop, straight chop, and covering chop are all achieved by transferring power from the waist to the shoulders, from the shoulders to the elbows to turn, and then to the hands as the elbows extend, so that the power reaches to the hands at the point of contact. Be sure to chop to the midline of the body.

*Turn around tiger carries*

Lift the elbow, close the shoulders and rotate the arms to do the stab to the rear, so that the whole body is connected without a weak point.

- If you want to use whole body power in every position and technique, you must first clearly understand the correct trajectory of the feet and hands, and absolutely understand the fixed positions, the coordination between the hands and feet, and the height of the stances. In addition, you must understand the power release – what is the order of the release? Where is the origin of the power? Where is the hitting surface? How do the hands and feet work together? How do you use the torso? You also need to understand the breathing coordination with the power launch. Once you are clear on the movements and how to do them, then you need to undergo a period of intense training. The classics say, "from familiarity grows skill, and from skill grows the true essence." During intense training you need to study and examine whether or not your movements are in accordance with the principles of physics. Do they fit the laws of physics? Do they fit the structure of the body? Of course, the most important thing is to fit the principles of combat. While you are concentrating on all this, you also must remember that the body should feel comfortable, smooth and unimpeded, clear minded, and carefree.

## PRACTICAL APPLICATIONS FOR THE SKILL OF GUIDING

The Skill Of Guiding uses a crossed upper pushing block that can be a defense against a straight line punch. The block also prepares for the two handed grab and pull. When you step forward and turn the body then you can guide the attack back by pulling forcefully on the opponent's arm. Grab clothes or 'meat' depending on what's there.

- The optimal situation would be: I grab the opponent's right arm with both hands and guide it towards the rear on my right side. Or, if I grab his left arm then I guide it back on my left. This way I prevent him from counter attacking with his other arm as I pull. But in reality, where is an ideal situation awaiting us? You have to create your opportunity and take advantage of whatever opportunity might present itself, and use the technique as best you can. When using guiding as an independent technique you can retreat as you pull. Otherwise, try to step in with a cannon punch afterwards.

The *pivot triple palm strikes* are meant to deal with an attack from the rear. They must be done quickly, and immediately connected to a driving punch. If someone comes at you from the rear, you can turn around and defend with an inverted chop. Attack then with the second palm, striking to his face, and add the third chop to his face, immediately following up with a driving punch to his solar plexus. This combination prevents him from responding to your attack and he will lose the exchange.

- You can never expect to use any technique in a combat situation without altering it. You will need to change the exact movement from what you normally practise. But if you utilize the power that you have trained then you can change the techniques and make combinations as needed to control your opponent and win. The principle of combat is, "control your opponent and do not let him control you."

General Qi Jiguan said in his classic manual on the martial arts, "To win you must understand your enemy. Winning and losing is not determined by magic but by the will to win. Whoever has the strongest desire to win, will win. If the enemy has low skill but is talented at tactics then he should be considered skilled. The ancients say, 'The skilled man is brave. He believes in himself, so will win.'" I suggest that the reader should consider this carefully.

## THE POEM ABOUT THE SKILL OF GUIDING

领字功歌诀

双手抓捋侧身领,
暗藏肩撞炮拳攻。
转身顾后连三掌,
得机得势进步崩。

Grab with both hands and turn sideways to guide.
This hides a shoulder strike and a cannon punch attack.
Turn around to deal with the back with three continuous palms.
Take the opportunities offered to advance and punch.

# THE EIGHT SKILLS CONNECTED FORM

# 八字功连还拳

## Introduction To The Eight Skills Connected Form, Bazigong Lianhuan Quan

The Eight Skills Form is a form that connects the individual eight skills, and which is widespread and popular amongst traditional Xingyiquan practitioners. It includes all of the most important and representative techniques of each of the eight skills of spread, intercept, wrap, bridge, scoop, butt, pass, and guide. There are some additional techniques in the form, necessary to smooth out the transitions and maintain a good power flow, so the Eight Skills Form is quite rich in content.

The Eight Skills Form teaches you techniques outside the standard five elements and twelve animals. You use different body parts, directions, angles, power, techniques, and applications. This will give you a richer and better movement vocabulary in Xingyiquan and improve your combative ability.

You should learn the Eight Skills Form only after you have mastered the individual eight skills, then you can master the form fairly quickly. Of course, if you have a good foundation and are good at Xingyiquan forms, you could learn the form directly, but you will need to work very hard at it to get it properly

### Names of the Movements
1. Opening Move (left *santishi*)
2. Advance, Right Driving Punch, or Crushing Punch
3. Step Forward, Tiger Carries
4. Step Forward, Spread, Right Side
5. Step Forward Swinging Chop with Crossing Cut
6. Advance, Double Intercept on Left Side
7. Step forward, Double Intercept on Right Side
8. Push a Boat Downstream
9. Dodging Double Wrap
10. Step Forward, Double Shove
11. Withdraw, Close the Shoulders
12. Step Forward Left Bridge
13. Step Forward, Left Split
14. Step Forward, Right Eagle Grasps

## CHAPTER TWO: THE EIGHT SKILLS

15. Turn Around, Snake Coils its Body
16. Step Forward, Right Scoop
17. Withdraw, Left Chop
18. Advance, Scoop
19. Retreat, Elbow Cover
20. Advance, Head Butt
21. Pull and Knee Butt
22. Step Forward, Elbow Butt
23. Stroke and Driving Punch, or Crushing Punch
24. Pass, Pull and Drag
25. Reverse Stance Left Drill and Hit
26. Left Guide
27. Step Forward, Left Cannon Punch, or Pounding Punch
28. Turn Around, Tiger Carries
29. Push the Shutter to Gaze at the Moon
30. Closing Move

**Description of the Movements**

1. **Opening Move (left *santishi*)**   qǐ shì       起势

ACTION 1: Stand to attention, facing forty-five degrees, ninety degrees, or directly facing the line on which you will travel. (image 2.107)

ACTION 2: Without moving the feet, gradually lift the hands at the sides to shoulder height, palms up and arms naturally bent. Look at the right hand. (image 2.108)

ACTION 3: Bend the elbows so that the hands point to each other in front of the face, palms down. Then press the hands down to the belly, bending the legs to sit with the knees together. Press the head up and tuck the chin in. Turn the head to look forward to the left, along the line which you will travel. (image 2.109)

# 166 THE EIGHT SKILLS CONNECTED, *BAZIGONG LIANHUAN*

ACTION 4: Clench the fists at the belly and turn the fist hearts up, keeping the elbows tight to the ribs. Drill the right fist up by the sternum then forward to nose height, twist the ulnar edge of the forearm up. Turn leftward to look in the direction that the form will take. Press the head up, and look at the right fist. (image 2.110)

ACTION 5: Advance the left foot without moving the right foot, settling into a *santi* stance, with more weight on the right leg. Bring the left fist up by the sternum and out to the right elbow, drilling forward by sliding along the right forearm, fist heart up. When the left fist arrives at the right fist, unclench both hands and turn the palms down. Split the left hand forward and down with the arm slightly bent and the wrist cocked, fingers at shoulder height. Pull the right hand back to the belly, palm down. Press the head up, tuck in the chin, and look past the left hand. (image 2.111)

2.110

2.111

**Pointers**

o   See pointers for details on *santishi* in Volume I, Chapter Two.

2.   **Advance, Right Driving Punch, or Crushing Punch**

jìnbù yòu bēngquán       进步右崩拳

ACTION: Advance the left foot a long step and follow in the right foot a half-step, keeping most weight on the right leg. Turn the left fist to tuck and press down, then pull it back to the belly, fist heart in. Lift the right fist to sternum height then punch straight forward with the elbow slightly bent and the fist eye up. Reach the right shoulder slightly forward. Press the head up, tuck in the chin, and look past the right fist. (image 2.112)

2.112

**Pointers**

o   The entire move must be well integrated, the right fist landing as the right foot comes in. The right foot should shovel in with a thump. Coordinate the power impulse with an expulsion of breath.

## CHAPTER TWO: THE EIGHT SKILLS 167

3. **Step Forward, Tiger Carries**   shàngbù hǔtuō   上步虎托

ACTION 1: Advance the left foot a half-step and follow in the right foot beside the left ankle without touching down. Rotate both palms in and thread the left hand forward, under the right forearm. Once the wrists cross, circle the hands out to the sides, palms angled forward. Complete the circles by bringing the hands back to the waist, keeping the elbows snug to the ribs, palms forward, and fingers down. Press the head up and look forward. (images 2.113, 2.114)

2.113

2.114

ACTION 2: Take a long step to the forward right with the right foot and follow in a half-step with the left foot into a stance with most weight on the left leg. Do a carrying technique with the palms to belly height, pushing forward and down. The hands should be about ten centimetres apart, with the palms forward and the fingers down. Press the head up, settle the shoulders, tuck in the elbows, and look past the hands. (image 2.115)

2.115

**Pointers**
- Circle the hands while advancing the left foot.
- You must apply an integrated power by completing the carrying action of the hands as the right foot lands.

4. **Step Forward, Spread, Right Side**   shàngbù yòu zhǎnshì   上步右展势

ACTION 1: Advance the right foot a half-step. Tuck the left hand down, first circling left, up, and forward, to to do a crossing cover in front of the body at chest height. Clench the right fist and bring it back to the belly. Look at the left hand. (image 2.116)

ACTION 2: Step the left foot forward a half-step, turning the foot out as it lands. Bring the right fist up past the sternum then drill forward and up along inside the left forearm to nose height. Press the left hand down towards the waist. Look forward. (image 2.117)

168    THE EIGHT SKILLS CONNECTED, *BAZIGONG LIANHUAN*

ACTION 3: Take a long step forward with the right foot, landing with the foot turned in. Bring the left foot a half-step in, turned parallel to the right foot, and sit down with more weight on the left leg, in a half horse stance. Bring the left forearm across to block above the head. Bend the right elbow and bring it back to the armpit, rolling the fist over so that the fist eye is down and the fist heart faces back. Punch forward to sternum height with the right fist, completing the punch with the arm slightly bent and the fist eye down. Pull the left fist up and back to the left of the head, rotating the fist and bending the elbow with the fist eye down and the arm bracing out. Turn leftward, turning the waist and reaching forward with the shoulder. Press the head up, look past the right fist. (image 2.118)

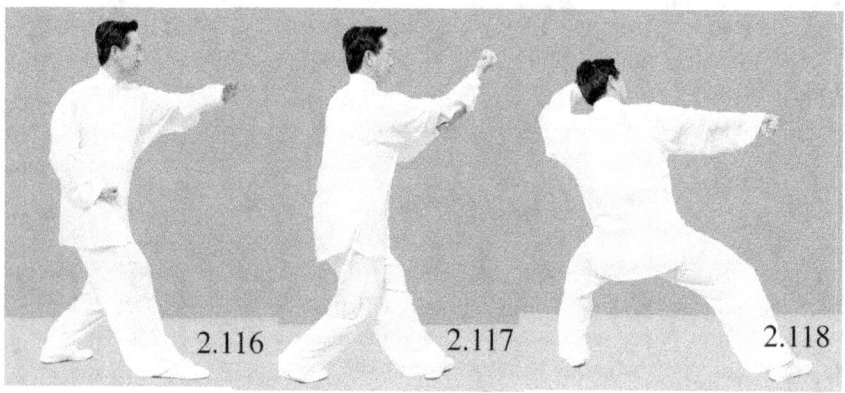

**Pointers**

- Complete the whole movement without pausing, with full connected power.
- Complete the right planting punch as the right foot lands. Put power into the right fist by turning the lower back and extending the right shoulder, turning the body sideways to hit. Brace back with the left elbow as the left fist pulls back. Lean slightly into the left side and grab the ground with the right foot. Be sure to connect the lower back, shoulders and elbows, and coordinate the hit with an expulsion of breath.

5.   **Step Forward, Swinging Chop with Crossing Cut**

shàngbù lūnpī héng zhé    上步抡劈横折

ACTION 1: Rise slightly and withdraw the right foot a half-step, then advance it a half-step. Lower the left hand by the left waist. Lower the right fist in front of the body, then circle it back, up, and finally forward in a swinging chop downwards. Finish with the right open palm vertical at chest height. Look at the right hand. (image 2.119)

ACTION 2: Step the left foot forward to touch down beside the right foot, turning the body a one-eighty degrees rightward by pivoting on the right foot. Rotate the left hand so the palm faces in, and bend the elbow to bring the forearm to block across in front of the body as it turns. Finish with the left hand at nose height in front of the right shoulder, palm down. Place the right palm under the left armpit. Look to the forward left. (image 2.120)

ACTION 3: Take a long step forward with the left foot and follow in a half-step with the right foot. Cut across tranversely with the full left arm, keeping the arm slightly bent. Brace back with the right hand with the arm slighly bent. The left hand is at neck height and the right hand is at shoulder height, both palms down. Look at the left hand. (image 2.121)

**Pointers**

- The right swinging chop is connected to the right foot, so the waist must remain relaxed to transfer power to the arm through the shoulder. The power must remain settled.
- The crossing cut of the left arm must get its power from the waist by containing the chest and closing the shoulders.
- Three actions are done as one: the left arm cuts across, the left foot steps forward, and the right arm braces back. The arms must remain rounded. Open the chest, solidify the abdomen, and breathe out to launch power.
- The two actions must be done as one, with no pause between them.

6. **Advance, Double Intercept on Left Side**

jìnbù zuǒ shuāng jié          进步左双截

ACTION 1: Withdraw the left foot a half-step and shift back onto the right leg without moving the right foot. Clench the left fist, bring it down, then drill it up in front of the right shoulder, fist heart in, elbow protecting the solar plexus. Clench the right fist, bend the elbow, and draw the fist to in front of the right shoulder at head height, fist eye facing back. Look forward. (image 2.122)

ACTION 2: Advance the left foot a long step to the forward left, following the right foot in a half-step. Turn the waist to pull the fists to the left, bending the elbows to intercept with the forearms across the body. Rotate the right fist heart to face in at mouth height and the left fist heart to face out at shoulder height. The

## 170   THE EIGHT SKILLS CONNECTED, *BAZIGONG LIANHUAN*

right elbow is covering in front of the body. Press the head up, tuck in the jaw, and look forward. (image 2.123)

**Pointers**

- Withdraw the left foot as the left fist drills upward. Be sure to turn the waist right and sit down into the torso to gather power.
- Cut across with the fists and forearms as the left foot lands forward. Turn the waist and reach with the shoulders, rotate the arms and settle the elbows. The power comes from the lower back and is expressed in the elbows, forearms and fists. Be sure to keep the waist relaxed and lively.

**7.   Step Forward, Double Intercept on Right Side**

shàngbù yòu shuāngjié                         上步右双截

ACTION 1: Advance the left foot a half-step and bring in the right foot without touching down. Slightly extend the arms and lower the fists in front. Bend the right elbow and drill the fist up past the sterum to in front of the left shoulder, fist heart in. Circle the left fist back and up, then bend the elbow and twist the fist heart out beside the left shoulder at ear height. Turn the body a bit to the left. Look to the forward right. (image 2.124)

ACTION 2: Advance the right foot a long step to the forward left, following the left foot in a half-step, keeping most weight on the left leg. Pull the fists to the right, bending the elbows to intercept with the forearms across the body by turning the waist rightward. Rotate the left fist heart to face in at mouth height and the right fist heart to face out at shoulder height. The left elbow is covering in front of the body. Press the head up, tuck in the jaw, and look past the left fist. (image 2.125)

**Pointers**

- Complete the intercept as one action, keeping the movement connected.
- Be sure to lead the movement of the shoulders from the body core, and to lead the movement of the elbows from the shoulders. The left and right action of the torso follows the principle of 'to go forward first pre-load back, to go left first pre-load right.'

8.    **Push a Boat Downstream**     shùn shuǐ tuī zhōu     顺水推舟

ACTION 1: Retreat the left foot a half-step then withdraw the right foot a half-step, keeping most weight on the left leg. Unclench the hands, extend the right hand forward, and turn both palms down. Do a pulling drag with both hands from the forward right – pulling left, down and back – with the right hand forward of the left. Complete the pull with the left hand by the left waist and the right hand in front of the belly. Solidify the abdomen and contain the chest, turning the torso slightly left. Press the head up and look forward. (image 2.126)

ACTION 2: Take a long step forward with the right foot and follow in a half-step with the left foot, keeping most weight on the left leg. Push forcefully forward with both hands, extending the arms with the palms facing forward. The right hand is in front at chest height and the left hand is just in front of the right elbow. Press the head up, tuck in the chin, and look straight ahead. (image 2.127)

2.126     2.127

**Pointers**

- When the left foot retreats and the right foot withdraws, the feet must move quickly. Then when the right foot advances it must go for a good distance, and the left foot must follow in quickly.
- The cover, press, pull and drag should follow a full circle and move together with the backward weight shift. When the hands push forward they must move with the forward advance of the right foot. When issuing power the elbows must stay tucked in, and shoulders and elbows must setttle. Lengthen the waist, extend the arms, and exhale to issue power.

172    THE EIGHT SKILLS CONNECTED, *BAZIGONG LIANHUAN*

9.    **Dodging Double Wrap**    yáoshēn shuāng guǒ    摇身双裹

ACTION 1: Shift the right foot a half-step to the forward right and bring in the left foot to beside the right. Extend the right hand forward, palm facing left, fingers up. Extend it at the right, then once it reaches forward, circle it horizontally leftward across to in front of the left shoulder. Lead to the right with the head. Bring the left hand back to the belly. Look at the right hand. (image 2.128)

ACTION 2: Step the left foot to the forward left and follow in the right foot to beside the right without touching down. Extend the left hand to the left, forward and up with the palm facing right and fingers up. After it reaches forward, circle it flat across to in front of the right shoulder, palm in. Lead to the left with the head and the body action. Look at the left hand. (image 2.129)

**Pointers**

- The circling action of the hands works together with the dodging action of the feet. Lead the action of the hands from the shoulders, and the action of the shoulders from the waist.
- Wrapping is a soft, continuous movement. Be sure to dodge the body sideways as the arms pass across. Dodge with the body and turn the head to the right as the hands wrap to the left, and vice versa.

10.    **Step Forward, Double Shove**

   shàngbù shuāng zhuàng zhǎng    上步双撞掌

ACTION: Take a long step forward with the right foot and follow in the left foot a half-step, keeping most weight back on the left leg. Roll the hands over in front of the chest to face the palms out, fingers pointing to each other, thumbs down, then shove forward forcefully. Shove straight forward with the arms slightly rounded and the palms out at chest height. Expand the upper back, contain the chest, and breathe out forcefully, settling the breath to the *dantian*. Press the head up, and look forward. (image 2.130)

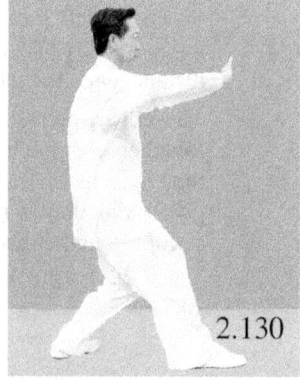

**Pointers**

- Complete the pushing shove as the right foot lands.
- Contain the chest and open the upper back to put strength forward. Use the expulsion of breath to put power into the shove. Keep the arms rounded to brace forward.

11. **Withdraw, Close the Shoulders**  chèbù héjiān shì   撤步合肩势

ACTION: Retreat the left foot a half-step and withdraw the right foot inside the left foot, touching the ball of the foot down and shifting the weight to the left foot. Bend the knees and sit the torso down slightly. Turn the body leftward to bring the right shoulder in front. Circle the right hand past the chest, down, and stab down by the left hip, rotating the thumb outwards to turn the palm in. Pull the left hand back and lower it to by the left waist. Then bring the left hand up and forward, and wrap it towards the right shoulder, palm in. Both elbows are in front of the chest. Tuck in the abdomen and close the chest. Compress the body in and squat. Look past the right shoulder. (image 2.131)

**Pointers**

- Coordinate the actions of the body, feet, and hands; retreat the rear foot, withdraw the lead foot, tuck the body, stab the right hand down, and wrap the left hand forward.
- Try to shrink the torso as you squat down. Contain the chest and expand the upper back. This move stores power for the following strike.

12. **Step Forward, Left Bridge**  shàngbù zuǒ kuàshì   上步左跨势

ACTION 1: Step the right foot straight forward, landing with the foot turned outward. Don't move the left foot, and settle the weight between the feet. Turn the right hand so the thumb web is down and the palm forward and slice forward from the hip, up in a curving manner, clenching the fist as it arrives at head height. Lower the left hand and bring it back to beside the left waist, palm forward, fingers down. Look at the right hand. (image 2.132)

ACTION 2: Take a long step to the front with the left foot, landing with the foot turned slightly inward. Follow-in the right foot a bit, landing it turned crossways, sitting down into a half horse stance. Extend the left arm to push forward at hip height, elbow slightly bent, palm forward, fingers

down. Pull the right fist back to the right above the head with the fist eye down. Turn the torso leftward. Look past the left hand. (image 2.133)

**Pointers**
- Advance the right foot a half-step as the right hand slices up.
- Step the left foot forward as the left hand pushes out at the hip. Use the waist and shoulders, turning and settling. Be sure to coordinate upper and lower hands so that they act together.

**13. Step Forward, Left Split**      shàngbù zuǒ pīquán      上步左劈拳

ACTION 1: Advance the left foot slightly and shift between the two feet. Turn the left hand and cut with the forearm to cover and press down at chest height, palm down. Lower the right hand by the right waist. Look past the left hand. (image 2.134)

ACTION 2: Step the right foot forward with the foot turned out. Clench the left fist and pull it back to the belly. Drill the right fist up to the sternum and forward to nose height with the ulnar edge turned up. Look past the right fist. (image 2.135)

ACTION 3: Take a step forward with the left foot and follow in a half-step with the right foot, settling into a *santi* stance. Bring the left fist by the sternum then out along the right forearm, then unclench it and split forward. Pull the right hand back to the belly, palm down. The split is done to shoulder height. Press the head up, tuck in the chin, and look past the left hand. (image 2.136)

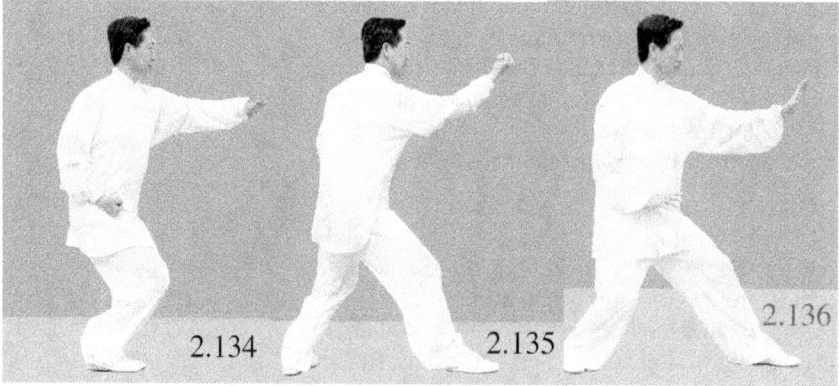

## Pointers

- These three actions are done as one movement – a stepping forward split. The actions should be done without pause and the hands and feet must be tightly coordinated.
- Split with the left hand as the left foot steps forward.

**14.** **Step Forward, Right Eagle Grasps**

shàngbù yòu yīngzhuō　　　　上步右鹰捉

ACTION 1: First withdraw the left foot slightly and then advance it a half-step, following in with the right foot beside the left ankle. Clench the left hand and pull it back to the belly, and then drill it up by the sternum and forward to nose height with the ulnar edge twisted up. Place the right fist at the left elbow, fist heart up. Press the head up. Look past the left fist. (image 2.137)

ACTION 2: Take a long step forward with the right foot and follow in a half-step with the left foot, keeping the weight slightly back. Slide the right fist along the left arm to drill up to head height. Once the fists cross unclench the hands, chop the hands down, right hand finishing palm forward at waist height, and left hand pulling back to the belly, both palms down. Straighten the back and press the head up. Look past the right hand. (image 2.138)

## Pointers

- You may hook the fingers slightly into eagle claws, or you may use a normal palm shape.
- Chop the right hand down as the right foot lands. Pay attention to pressing the head up, settling the elbows, sitting into the buttocks, and keeping a scissoring pressure between the legs.

**15.** **Turn Around, Snake Coils its Body**

huíshēn shé chánshēn　　　回身蛇缠身

ACTION 1: Stand up and pivot around a full one-eighty degrees on the feet to face around in the opposite direction. Turn the left hand thumb inward and lift the elbow to swing the left hand up, back and down to the left hip, arm slightly bent. Lift the right hand to the right of the head, keeping the arm slightly bent, thumb web forward, and palm up. Follow the movement of the left hand with the eyes. (image 2.139)

# 176    THE EIGHT SKILLS CONNECTED, *BAZIGONG LIANHUAN*

ACTION 2: Twist the body and sit down into a resting stance with the left foot forward. Stab the right hand down outside the left hip, palm out. Wrap the left hand in, threading up to the right shoulder, palm in. In the resting stance, the right heel is raised and the left foot is turned out, the thighs crosssed and squeezing together. Look past the left hand. (image 2.140)

**Pointers**

- Rise up as the arms circle around.
- Stab the right hand down as you turn and sit into the resting stance. The whole movement must be done in one action with no pausing.

### 16.    Step Forward, Right Scoop    shàngbù yòu tiǎozhǎng    上步右挑掌

ACTION: Advance the left foot a half-step then take a long step forward with the right foot and follow in a half-step with the left foot. Turn the left hand palm down and pull down and back to the belly. Turn the right hand and bring it from front of the belly, fingers up and palm forward, to do a scooping strike upwards to chest height with the elbow bent. Settle the shoulders and elbows and press the head up. Look past the right hand. (image 2.141)

**Pointers**

- Complete the right arm scoop as the right foot lands. Before the right hand scoops up the elbow must first hug the ribs. Sit into the hips, lengthen the lower back, release and settle the shoulders, and drop the elbows.

CHAPTER TWO: THE EIGHT SKILLS    177

17.    **Withdraw, Left Chop**    chèbù zuǒ pīquán    撤步左劈拳

ACTION: Withdraw the right foot a half-step to touch the ball down in front of the left foot. Shift back without moving the left foot. Slide the left hand along the top of the right arm to chop forward and down. Pull the right hand back and down to the belly. Complete the chop at chest height with the left shoulder reaching forward. Press the head up and look past the left hand. (image 2.142)

2.142

**Pointers**

o   The hands must work together simultaneously with integrated power: pull back the right hand and chop forward with the left hand as you withdraw the right foot.

o   Tuck in the abdomen and empty the chest, turn the waist, lean slightly into the movement, and reach the shoulder into the technique.

18.    **Advance, Right Scoop**    jìnbù yòu tiǎozhǎng    进步右挑掌

ACTION: Advance the right foot a long step forward and follow in a half-step with the left foot, keeping the weight back on the left leg. Scoop up the right hand from in front of the belly, fingers up and palm forward at shoulder height with the elbow bent. Pull the left palm back to the belly. Press the head up, tuck the jaw in, and look past the right hand. (image 2.143)

2.143

**Pointers**

o   This is the same as movement 16 described above.

o   Movements 16, 17, and 18 are done continuously without pausing between them. Be sure to apply force forward and upward to each of the scoops.

19.    **Retreat, Elbow Cover**    tuìbù yǎnzhǒu    退步掩肘

ACTION 1: Retreat the left foot a half-step and shift the weight back, then withdraw the right foot a half-step. Clench the right hand and rotate the right elbow to do an elbow/forearm cover leftwards with the fist at nose height and the elbow below shoulder height. Keep the left fist at the belly. Look past the right fist. (image 2.144)

## 178  THE EIGHT SKILLS CONNECTED, *BAZIGONG LIANHUAN*

ACTION 2: Retreat the right foot a step, shift the weight back, and withdraw the left foot a half-step to in front of the right foot. Lower the right fist with a covering action down the left to the left ribs, fist heart in. Bring the left fist up and rightward, bending the left elbow to do an elbow cover rightwards. Turn rightward. Lower the left fist to the right waist, fist heart in. When the forearms cross in front of the chest the left arm is inside the right. Empty the chest and stretch the upper back. Look ahead. (image 2.145)

2.144

2.145

**Pointers**

- Coordinate the left foot retreat with the right elbow cover and the right foot retreat with the left elbow cover.
- Complete the two actions without pausing. Turn the body as the feet move. You need to turn sideways to do the elbow covers, so keep the waist lively and the shoulders settled.

**20.   Advance, Head Butt**   jìnbù tóudǐng   进步头顶

ACTION: Advance the left foot and follow in a half-step with the right, shifting the weight to a forward weighted sixty-forty stance. Brace the arms forward, the wrists crossed and the fists clenched at belly height, fist hearts down. Butt forward with the forehead, leaning the torso forward, tucking in the chin and putting the head slightly forward of the body. Stiffen the nape of the neck, clench the teeth, and look forward. (image 2.146)

2.146

**Pointers**

- Butt with the head and brace with the arms as the left foot lands, hitting with hands, feet and head at exactly the same time.
- Be sure to shift the weight forward to be able to hit with the head. Tuck in the abdomen and close the chest. When head butting, remember "to hit with the head you must use the feet, controlling the centre from

beginning to ending; no one can defend against a foot charging through the front door."

### 21.  Pull and Knee Butt  lǔshǒu xīzhuàng  捋手膝撞

ACTION: Advance the left foot a half-step forward diagonally to the left and shift forward. Shift onto the left leg and stand with the knee slightly bent, leaning the torso slightly forward. Unclench the hands and extend them to the forward left at shoulder height, left hand in front, right hand at the left elbow. Stretch open the thumb webs. Bend the right knee and shove forward and up with it to waist height. As the right knee strikes, clench the hands and pull back towards the right. Pull the left fist back to in front of the chest, fist heart up, left elbow at the solar plexus, and pull the right fist back on the ride side, fist heart down. Press the head forward and look past the left fist. (image 2.147)

### Pointers

- Grab and pull the hands back as the knee butts forward, exerting force both forward and back. Tuck in the belly, lift the knee, and rotate the waist to pull back. Dodge the torso to lean a bit to the left.

### 22.  Step Forward, Elbow Butt  shàngbù dǐngzhǒu  上步顶肘

ACTION: Take a long step straight forward with the right foot and follow in the left foot a half-step, shifting the weight forward to a forward weighted sixty-forty stance. Bring the right elbow into the right ribs, and then as the right foot lands, butt forward and up with the elbow bent. Bring the right fist to above the right shoulder with the fist heart in, so that the elbow butts up at shoulder height. Place the left hand behind the right elbow to support it. Reach the right shoulder forward. Press the head up and look straight forward. (image 2.148)

### Pointers

- Land the foot well forward, land firmly, and bring the rear foot in quickly. Be sure to shift slightly forward to be able to strike with the elbow.

# 180   THE EIGHT SKILLS CONNECTED, *BAZIGONG LIANHUAN*

### 23.   Stroke and Driving Punch, or Crushing Punch

lǔshǒu bēngquán                             捋手崩拳

ACTION 1: Shift back and withdraw the right foot a half-step without moving the left foot. Unclench the right hand and extend it forward then cover and press down, clenching to grab and pull back to the right side. Slide the left hand along the right arm to chop out to chest height. Put the left shoulder forward into the action, tuck in the belly and empty the chest. Look past the left hand. (image 2.149)

ACTION 2: Advance the right foot a long step and follow in the left foot a half-step, keeping the weight mostly on the left leg. Punch the right fist forward to chest height. Clench and pull the left hand back to the belly. Press the head up, tuck in the chin, and look past the right fist. (image 2.150)

### Pointers

- Chop the left hand down as the right hand pulls back, both when the right foot withdraws.
- Advance the right foot and punch the right fist at exactly the same time.

### 24.   Pass, Pull and Drag     yún shì lǔ daì     云势捋带

ACTION 1: Advance the right foot a half-step and follow in the left foot to beside the right foot without touching down. Unclench both hands and bend the right arm to lift the elbow above the head, close by the ear. Circle the right hand up and back at the right, and then forward, finishing at the forward right, palm up. Turn the left palm up and circle it past the chest, forward, and then left. When the left hand arrives at the left side, bend the elbow and bring it in front of the face then around to the forward right. At this time, the right hand is at the forward right with the palm up and the left hand is at the right elbow, palm forward, thumb down, and thumb web stretched open. Look past the right hand. (image 2.151)

ACTION 2: Take a long step forward with the left foot, foot turned out. Bend the legs and shift the weight between the feet. Drag the hands down, forward and up in a carrying position, the right palm angled up at nose height, arm slightly bent. The left hand finishes to the left of and above the head, palm out. Turn the waist, reach the right shoulder forward, and look past the right hand. (image 2.152)

2.152

**Pointers**
- The right hand passes and circles above the head while the left hand circles in front of the body. The hands are performing an opposing passing action, so they must coordinate together.
- The left foot steps forward as the hands carry up and then drag back to the left. Get power from the waist so that the movement is coordinated.

**25. Reverse Stance, Left Drilling Punch** àobù zuǒ zuāndǎ 拗步左钻打

ACTION: Take a long step forward with the right foot and follow in a half-step with the left foot. Turn the right hand palm down and tuck it in, bending the wrist, then bend the elbow and clench the fist, circling it up to the right side of the head. Clench and lower the left fist back to the left waist, then, keeping it tight to the ribs and rotating the ulnar edge in, drill forward and up to nose height. Press the head up, tuck in the chin, and look forward. (image 2.153)

2.153

**Pointers**
- Punch with the left fist as the right foot lands.
- Use the waist and shoulder to get power to the right wrist to hook and drag back. Use a shaking power from the waist, keeping the shoulders and elbows settled. Keep the waist, shoulders, and elbows relaxed before using power. Be sure to keep the elbow snug to the ribs during the drilling punch, to get power into it from the lower back.

## 26. Left Guide    zuǒ lǐngshì    左领势

ACTION 1: Advance the right foot a half-step and follow in the left foot without touching down. Bring the right fist in to cross the wrists with the right inside the left, unclenching the hands with the left palm facing up and right palm facing forward. Draw a circle forward, up, and then rightward. When the hands arrrive at the forward right, externally rotate the right hand and internally rotate the left hand so that the palms are angled to the left. Reach the right hand forward to the right to nose height and the left to the right elbow. Look past the right hand. (image 2.154)

ACTION 2: Step the left foot a long step forward and follow in a half-step with the right foot. Clench both hands and pull down and back to the left with a guiding action. The left hand completes the move behind the body with the fist heart down, and the right hand pulls back to the left ribs, fist heart up. Press the head up and look at the left hand. (image 2.155)

### Pointers

- Complete the guiding back action as the left foot lands. Press the head up as the hands pull down. Press the right shoulder forward as the hands pull back. In this way the body works as a unit, applying force in equal and opposite directions.
- The hands do a grappling action as they circle, and then pull back. The intent is grabbing an opponent's arm and pulling it down to the left.

## 27. Step Forward, Left Cannon Punch, or Pounding Punch

shàngbù zuǒ pàoquán      上步左炮拳

ACTION: Take a big step forward with the right foot and follow in the left foot a half-step. Drill the right fist forward and up. Bring the left hand in to the waist then hit out with a cannon punch – punch the left fist forward to sternum height, reaching the left shoulder forward. The right fist finishes at the right temple with the fist eye in and elbow down. Press the head up and look past the left fist. (image 2.156)

CHAPTER TWO: THE EIGHT SKILLS    183

**Pointers**

- Complete the left punch as the left foot lands. You must turn the waist and extend the shoulder into the punch.

**28.   Turn Around, Tiger Carries**   huíshēn hǔtuō   回身虎托

ACTION 1: Hook-in step the right foot at the left toes and turn the body around to the left, lifting the left foot at the right ankle without touching down. Cross the hands in front of the body and unclench them, palms out. Then lift them, open out to the sides, and continue to circle them down to either side, palms forward, fingers down. Tuck the elbows in snug to the ribs. Press the head up and look forward. (images 2.157, 2.158)

ACTION 2: Step the left foot forward and follow the right foot in a half-step, keeping most weight on the right leg. Push the hands forcefully forward and down, palms forward at belly height about a fist's width apart. Press the head up and sit into the buttocks. Look past the hands. (image 2.159)

**Pointers**

- Hook-in the foot well to get around, and turn around quickly in one coordinated action
- Push the hands forward and down as the left foot lands. To get power, sit into the hips, reach the shoulders, settle the elbows, squeeze the ribs, and breathe out.

184    THE EIGHT SKILLS CONNECTED, *BAZIGONG LIANHUAN*

### 29.    Push the Shutter to Gaze at the Moon

tuī chuāng wàng yuè              推窗望月

ACTION 1: Withdraw the left foot to touch down in front of the right foot, most weight on the right leg. Turn the left palm up and rotate the right ulnar edge up, palm rightward. Circle the hands in front of the belly forward, up, and then back. Bring the right hand down to beside the right waist, fingers up. Bring the left hand to in front of the right shoulder, palm down. Turn the torso slightly rightward and look at the left hand. (image 2.160)

ACTION 2: Advance the left foot and bend the knees to sit down into a half horse stance. Brace forward and up with the left arm rounded, palm forward and thumb down at head height, blocking up and across. Push forcefully forward to chest height with the right hand, palm forward and thumb up. Push the right hand forward past the left elbow. Press the head up, tuck in the chin, and look forward. (image 2.161)

**Pointers**

- Coordinate the circling of the hands with the withdrawing step. Coordinate the pushing brace of the hands with the advancing step.
- The hands must draw a circle and use a circular power. Use the body to get power to the hands. In the final position the torso should lean upwards slightly.

### 30.    Closing Move           shòu shì              收势

ACTION 1: Withdraw the left foot to in front of the right foot, touching the toes down. Clench the right hand and pull it back to the belly, then drill the right fist up by the sternum and forward to nose height, ulnar edge turned up. Turn the left hand over and clench it, covering and pressing down as it pulls back to the belly, clenching it. Look at the right hand. (image 2.162)

ACTION 2: Advance the left foot and shift the right foot slightly to sit into a *santi* stance. Drill the left fist out past the sternum to the right elbow then unclench the hands and split forward with the left hand while pulling the right hand back to the belly. Press the head up and look past the left hand. (image 2.163)

ACTION 3: Without moving the feet, clench the fists and pull them back to the belly. Press the head up and look forward (image 2.164)

CHAPTER TWO: THE EIGHT SKILLS    185

ACTION 4: Shift forward and bring the right foot up to the left foot, keeping the knees bent. Unclench the hands and lift them at the sides, palms up, to shoulder height. Then bend the elbows to bring the hands to the front, palms down and fingers facing each other. Look forward. (images 2.165, 2.166, and 2.167)

ACTION 5: Press the hands down in front of the belly and stand up to attention, letting the hands hang down to the sides. Look forward. The form is now finished. (image 2.168)

## Pointers

- Bring the feet together as the hands rise together.
- Stand to attention as the hands press down.

  The closing movement must be continuous, steady, and stable, with full spirit and intent, and a serious mien.

CHAPTER THREE

# PARTNER FORM

# PROTECT THE BODY

安身炮

### Introduction To Protect The Body, *Anshen Pao*

*Anshenpao*, the Protect The Body partner form, is one of the outstanding classic partner forms of Xingyiquan, and as such is very popular and widespread. Different branches and localities of Xingyi show only small differences. It exemplifies the fighting characteristics and flavour of Xingyi, with its well-organized path, its smoothly flowing movements, its realistic attack and defense, and its practical applicability. The classics say that this form involves the whole of the Xingyi system.

The name 'protect the body' probably comes from its practical nature, since there are an abundance of self defense moves within the form. If you practise it often you can develop a smooth and natural fighting ability, or the ability to ' *an shen* ' – keep yourself safe.

Partners A and B each do twenty one attacking and defending actions, so that each has a total of forty two actions. Since partners A and B trade places, each learns and practises both attack and defense. All five element techniques are here, as are some animal models such as monkey, snake, and sparrow hawk. There are also some extra moves – such as *hook to the ear, steal a punch, sparrow hawk grabs a shoulder, lead along a sheep, intercept to right and left,* and *cut to the neck.* Split and drive occur the most often ( *cut to the neck* counts as a split), partners A and B both use split nineteen times, and drive eight times. There is a good variety of split techniques such as *advance split, retreat split, dodging split, reverse stance split,* and *cut to the neck.*

You can see Xingyiquan's close range fighting and fast straight line attacking methods clearly in this form. The first and second thirds of the form show the main targets of attack: the head, neck, ribs, solar plexus and groin. These points are the weak points, as the classics say, "when going high, go for the throat, when going low, go for the groin, when going for the centre, go for the ribs." You can use a smaller force to greater effect when hitting these weak points. If you use greater force then you can incapacitate your opponent.

## 188 PROTECT THE BODY, ANSHEN PAO

The protect the body partner form has the following characteristics:

- It takes care of everything at once – attack and defense are simultaneous. The defensive action is an attack, and an attack contains a defensive action. This is typical of Xingyi methods. For example, the advancing block and punch of the cannon punch, the split within the lead back, the driving punch that flows directly from the double intercept, and sparrow hawk grabs the shoulder.
- The techniques flow well and are practical. The short sequences of hand techniques are exceptional. The power is very smooth and tightly knit, the movements make sense, are practical, and in keeping with the principles of combat. There are some very nice sequences in the form, like *intercept and punch, hook to the ear and steal a punch, pull left knock right and punch, step forward slap and reverse pull, brush and shop, pull and cross kick to split,* and *monkey pulls the rope.* These applications can be taken out of the form and practised as individual sequences, alternating right and left, in practical sparring drills. When these short drills have been practised repeatedly until their use becomes a natural, instinctive reaction, then they can be used in a fight. Short combinations drills can improve your combat ability considerably.
- You freely advance and retreat, quickly and accurately. Both A and B show the characteristic Xingyi footwork: To advance, first advance the lead foot, then you must follow in with the rear foot. To retreat, first retreat the rear foot, then you must withdraw the lead foot."
- This footwork is quick and agile. When you advance, everything advances, and when you retreat, everything retreats. This keeps the body stable and well balanced. If you look at the footwork of both sides of the form, this characteristic is very clear. Both advance and retreat very naturally, advancing with a follow up step, and retreating with a withdrawing step, so that the whole body moves forward or backward.
- Attack and defense follow the rules of Xingyi, and the moves are well knit. All techniques show the characteristics and flavour of Xingyi. The lines of power, the path that the moves take, all follow the characteristic fighting principles of Xingyi. You protect the centre and attack the centre, almost always attacking the midline. The moves connect together so smoothly that attack and defense are tightly knit, which shows Xingyi's spirit of "chasing the wind and chasing the moon without slackening".

To sum up, the protect the body partner form is one of the most important forms in the Xingyi system. It has abundant content, tightly knit techniques, well-organized attack and defense, remarkable flavour, and is highly practical.

# CHAPTER THREE: PARTNER FORM

## NAMES OF THE MOVEMENTS

1. A: Advance Right Driving Punch
   B: Retreat, Left Press Down, Right Driving Punch
2. A: Step Forward, Left Split
   B: Left Aligned Stance Cannon Punch
3. A: Dodging Right Split
   B: Dodging Right Split
4. A: Double Intercept to the Left
   B: Stationary Left Cut to the Neck
5. A: Double Intercept to the Right, Right Driving Punch
   B: Withdraw, Pull, Knock Aside and Hit
6. A: Monkey Pulls the Rope
   B: Retreat, Right Drill
7. A: Step Forward, Right Cannon Punch
   B: Retreat, Left Split
8. A: Step Forward, Right Hook to the Ear
   B: Withdraw, Left Drill
9. A: Advance and Steal a Hit
   B: Changeover Step, Slap to Knock Aside and Draw Out
10. A: Changeover Step Left Split
    B: Pull and Grab the Head
11. A: Step Forward, Snake
    B: Retreat, Left Cut to the Neck
12. A: Left and Right Cut to the Neck
    B: Right Drill, Left Driving Punch
13. A: Ape Pulls the Rope
    B: Retreat, Right Drill
14. A: Step Forward, Pull Back, Right Cut to the Neck
    B: Withdraw, Double Intercept to the Left
15. A: Left Cut to the Neck
    B: Double Intercept to the Right, Right Driving Punch
16. A: Pull Back, Crossing Kick, Step Forward, Right Split
    B: Retreat, Left Crosscut

## 190  PROTECT THE BODY, *ANSHEN PAO*

17. A: Step Forward, Left Scoop Up, Right Split
    B: Grab the Shoulder with the Left Hand (Sparrow Hawk Grabs the Shoulder)
18. A: Brush Aside, Right Split
    B: Left Hooking Block, Right Cut to the Neck
19. A: Double Intercept to the Left
    B: Left Cut to the Neck
20. A: Double Intercept to the Right, Right Driving Punch
    B: Retreat, Left Press Down
21. A: Advance, Right Driving Punch
    B: Retreat, Left Press Down, Right Driving Punch

**Description of the movements**

Partner A is in the 'attacker' in dark uniform on the left, partner B is the 'counter-attacker' in the light uniform on the right. Partner A starts facing south, and partner B starts facing north. During the first section of the form, partner A will generally start and partner B will react. In general, but not always, partner A will attack with forward moving steps and partner B will defend with retreating steps.

In general, for each move the first action and image describe partner A's attack, with partner B not reacting. The second action and image describe partner B's defensive reaction with partner A not reacting. If necessary, a third action and image describe partner B's counter-attack with partner A not reacting.

**Opening and *Santishi***          sāntǐshì          三体势

ACTION 1: Partners A and B stand about three to four steps away from each other, presenting their sides to each other. They stand properly to attention to show they are ready. (image 3.1)

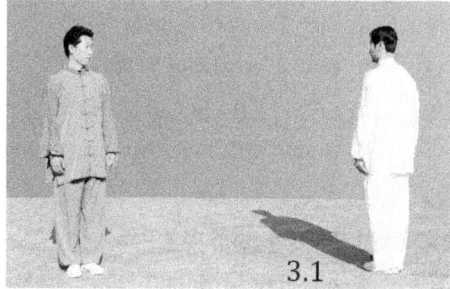

**Pointers**

  o  Hold the head straight and tuck in the jaw. Press the head up, keep the lower back flat, settle the shoulders, and hang the hands naturally at the sides. Keep a calm expression, empty the mind of extraneous thoughts, settle the *qi* to the *dantian*, and focus on the task at hand. Prepare fully for the partner practice.

ACTION 2: Partners A and B move together, raising the hands to the sides to shoulder height, with the elbows bent. They then bring the hands together in front of the face, and press down to the belly. While doing this, they sink to a 120 degree bend in the knees. (image 3.2)

ACTION 3: Partners A and B both turn ninety degrees and twist the right fist up to the solar plexus, then drill it forward to nose height. (image 3.3)

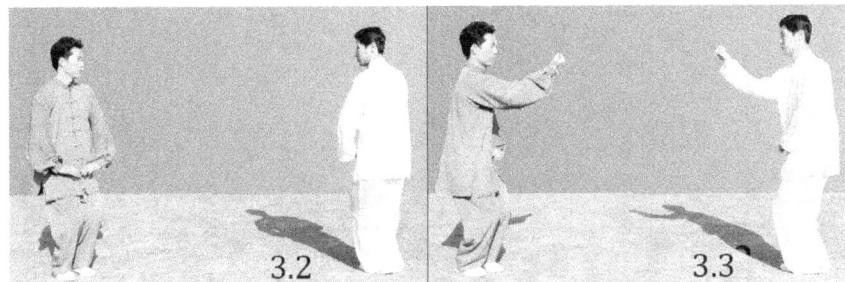

ACTION 4: Partners A and B both step the left foot forward without moving the right foot. At this time, they unclench the left hand and bring it along the right forearm to split forward, pulling the right hand back to the belly. They look in the direction of the left hand, and settle into a *santishi*. (image 3.4)

**Pointers**

- Partners A and B must step forward into the *santishi* at exactly the same time and at the same speed – all movement occurs simultaneously. The on guard stance should be taken quickly and with power.

1. **A: Advance Right Driving Punch**

    jìnbù yòu bēngquán          进步右崩拳

    **B: Retreat, Left Press Down, Right Driving Punch**

    tuìbù zuǒ àn yòu bēngquán   退步左按右崩拳

ACTION 1: Partner A advances the left foot forward and follows in the right foot to behind the left heel, keeping the weight on the right leg. Partner A slaps B's left hand down with the left hand and throws a driving punch towards B's solar plexus with the right fist. (image 3.5)

## 192   PROTECT THE BODY, *ANSHEN PAO*

ACTION 2: Partner B retreats the right foot a half-step then withdraws the left foot a half- step, pressing the left palm down on A's right fist. Partner B controls and presses the arm down forward along the line of attack, making A miss the target. (image 3.6)

ACTION 3: Partner B advances the left foot a half-step and follows in the right foot a half- step, throwing a driving punch towards A's solar plexus. Partner B looks at A. (image 3.7)

**Pointers**

- When doing the driving punch, the forward hand should control the opponent by slapping his hand away or grabbing it. The punch should be fast and strong, driving towards the solar plexus. When stepping forward, thrust strongly from the rear foot and charge forward with the lead foot. The punch is timed with the landing of the foot, and should have one-inch power.
- Partner A should adjust the size of the step when he advances, according to how far away they are in the *santishi*. If they are far away then partner A should take a big step in, and if they are close then A should advance just a little. If they are too far away for one step to enter, then A may take a step forward with the right foot and then advance with the left. The step must bring partner A close enough to hit with the driving punch. When doing partner forms, it is important to get the spacing right – the punch should touch the partner.

## CHAPTER THREE: PARTNER FORM    193

- o    Partner B must retreat and withdraw the feet quickly, getting out of the way as A enters. In actual application B would hook and grab the punch, but in a partner form should just press down and keep it out of the way.
- o    Partners A and B need to coordinate the advancing and retreating so that they move smoothly together. They should not actually hit each other with force, but neither should they do empty and useless techniques. The cooperation should be tight, the techniques correct, the attack and defense appropriate, and the intentions true to life.[12]

2.  **A: Step Forward, Left Split**    shàngbù zuǒ pīquán    上步左劈拳

    **B: Left Aligned Stance Cannon Punch**

    zuǒ shùnbù pàoquán    左顺步炮拳

ACTION 1: Partner A withdraws the right foot a half-step then withdraws the left foot. Partner A first brings back the right fist, then drills it up underneath B's right fist, and then unclenches the right hand and pulls B's hand down and back. Partner A prepares his left hand at the chest, looking at B's right fist. Partner A then advances the left foot a half-step and does a split towards B's face with the left hand. Partner A looks at B. (image 3.8)

ACTION 2: Partner B retreats the right foot and withdraws the left foot, bringing the right fist inside A's left arm to drill up, hooking up to the right ear, and moving the left fist up to the chest. Partner B advances the left foot a half-step and turns the left fist eye up, punching to A's solar plexus with the punching arm slightly bent. Partner B looks at A. (image 3.9)

---

[12] Editor's note: Always attack to the required height so that the defensive response is realistic. Here, for example, if partner B punches too low, then partner A's counter would not make sense.

## 194 PROTECT THE BODY, *ANSHEN PAO*

**Pointers**

- To apply split, first drill the rear hand up to deflect, and then turn and unclench it, circling and coiling around the attacking limb to hook and pull. The foot should move in quickly and the lead hand strike the opponent's face. When doing a partner form, the hooking hand should not grab, just be aware of the possibility. When striking to B's face, A should have a point of focus, to avoid accidentally hitting B if B defends poorly.

- The *aligned stance cannon punch* is also called *sparrow hawk enters the woods*. When using it, the right fist drills up and deflects the attack. The body needs to tuck in as the fist rises, then the left foot must step forward quickly and the body turn to present the side, aiming to enter the opponent's groin area. The left punch is fierce and extended with good body action. When doing a partner form B should aim at A's solar plexus, but with a controlled focus. Also, B should not take too big a step forward, but keep a certain distance.

3. **A: Dodging Right Split**     yáoshēn yòu pīquán     摇身右劈拳

   **B: Dodging Right Split**     yáoshēn yòu pīquán     摇身右劈拳

ACTION 1: Partner A first withdraws the left foot, then takes a circling hook-out step to the right – the foot circles forward a half-step with the foot turned slightly out. Partner A drills the left hand up underneath B's left fist to knock it away, then pull down. A looks at the left hand. Partner A then steps the right foot forward and chops B's face with the right hand, looking at B. (image 3.10)

ACTION 2: Partner B retreats the right foot a half-step and brings the left fist back. Partner B then withdraws the left foot, then circles it forward a half-step to the right with the foot turned out. B drills the left hand up and turns it to hit A's right hand to knock it away to the left, looking at the left hand. Partner B then steps the right foot forward and chops A's face with the right hand. (image 3.11)

3.10

3.11

# CHAPTER THREE: PARTNER FORM

**Pointers**

- Partner A should first withdraw the left foot, and then circle it to advance. Pay attention to the body technique and body shape to first move back then advance. The body should move with the foot, dodging slightly as the foot circles – the backwards countermovement prepares for a smooth forward movement.
- Partner B should first retreat the right foot, withdraw the left foot, and then immediately circle the left foot to advance. The retreat and withdrawal is a dodging action to readjust positioning in order to follow up with an advance and attack.
- When A and B strike to the face they should stop the hand just before it reaches the face, to avoid unwanted accidents.

4. **A: Double Intercept to the Left**    zuǒ shuāng jiéshǒu    左双截手

   **B: Stationary Left Cut to the Neck**    yuánbù yòu qiēbō    原步右切脖

ACTION 1: Partner A shifts back mostly onto the left leg. A clenches both hands and bends both elbows to place the forearms vertical – the right fist in front with the fist heart facing in, and left fist behind with the fist heart facing out. Partner A connects both forearms on the inside of B's right arm, to intercept horizontally to the left. Partner A's fists are at nose height, and he looks at B. (image 3.12)

ACTION 2: Partner B, without moving the feet, turns the left palm up and slices towards the right side of A's neck with the palm edge, arm slightly bent. Partner B pulls the right hand back to the belly and looks at A. (image 3.13)

3.12    3.13

**Pointers**

- The double intercept is a technique that uses both forearms to knock an attack aside horizontally. The right forearm rotates palm towards thumb so that the ulnar bone side is the point of contact, either on the forearm or the upper arm of the opponent. The power comes from the lower back and waist, which draw the shoulders and elbows across. The lower back

## 196  PROTECT THE BODY, *ANSHEN PAO*

should be relaxed and the buttocks should settle down.

o  The cut to the neck is a horizontal strike that goes for the carotid artery. In a partner form you should focus the hit and not use hard power or really hit, to avoid unwanted accidents.

5. **A: Double Intercept to the Right, Right Driving Punch**

yòu shuāngjié yòu bēngquán 右双截右崩拳

**B: Withdraw, Pull, Knock Aside and Hit**   chèbù lā bō dǎ   撤步拉拨打

ACTION 1: Partner A withdraws the right foot a half-step and intercepts to the right with both fists – the left arm forward and the right fist behind – knocking B's left forearm towards the right. Partner A looks at B. (image 3.14)

ACTION 2: Partner A advances the right foot a half-step and drives a right punch towards B's solar plexus. The fist eye is up and the arm slightly bent. Partner A pulls the left fist back to the side of the waist and looks at B. (image 3.15)

ACTION 3: Partner B retreats the left foot a half-step and withdraws the right foot, shifting back. B turns the right palm to face right and stretches open the web of the palm, extending to slide along the inside of A's forearm. (image 3.16)

## CHAPTER THREE: PARTNER FORM 197

ACTION 4: Partner B extends the left fist, with the elbow bent, up inside A's fist and knocks it away to the left while pressing it down, bringing the fist back towards the left waist. Partner B advances the right foot a half-step and drives a right punch towards A's solar plexus. (image 3.17)

3.17

### Pointers

- The double intercept / driving punch combination that repeats in this form is a particularly useful technique. It is compact, flows smoothly and is readily used. When actually using it, be sure to advance for the punch to hit harder. When doing it in the partner form, use the intercept technique to get the feel for the waist power. Defend yourself with just as much force as necessary, and do the driving punch with a focal point.

- Partner B should do the pull, knock aside, and hit in one continuous coordinated action, quickly and smoothly, hands and feet working together. Partners A and B must cooperate closely to coordinate appropriate speed, timing, and distance.

6. **A: Monkey Pulls the Rope**  hóu dáo shéng    猴捯绳

   **B: Retreat, Right Drill**  tuìbù yòu zuānquán   退步右钻拳

ACTION 1: Partner A withdraws the right foot a half-step and shifts back to the left leg. Partner A unclenches both hands with the palms down. Partner A places the right hand on B's right forearm and draws it down and back. Partner A does the same action with the left hand, timed slightly after the right hand, so that both hands are controlling B's arm. (image 3.18)

ACTION 2: Partner A advances the right foot a half-step and strikes towards B's face with the right palm, looking at B. (image 3.19)

3.18

ACTION 3: Partner B retreats the left foot and withdraws the right foot a half-step, shifting back. Partner B brings back the right fist then drills it out along the outside of A's right hand towards the nose. Partner B looks at the right fist. (image 3.20)

3.19

3.20

**Pointers**

- Monkey pulls the rope should be done with both hands moving continuously and quickly, with no pause at all [like a monkey pulling hand over hand on a rope]. In the partner form, do not really grab and pull – just slap. When A advances the right palm he should stop as he approaches B's face.

- Partner B must retreat the left foot quickly then withdraw the right foot immediately. Partner B should drill the fist up as the foot withdraws, with fully integrated power.

**7. A: Step Forward, Right Cannon Punch**

    shàngbù yòu pàoquán  上步右炮拳

**B: Retreat, Left Split**    tuìbù zuǒ pīquán  退步左劈拳

ACTION 1: Partner A takes a big step forward with the left foot and follows in a half-step with the right foot, clenching both hands. Partner A extends the left fist under B's right forearm, then bends the elbow and drills the fist up and forward. Partner A first brings the right fist in, then punches hard towards B's solar plexus. The fist surface is the contact point, the fist eye is up, the arm is slightly bent, the torso leans slightly into the punch, and the eyes look at B. (image 3.21)

3.21

ACTION 2: Partner B retreats the right foot back and withdraws the left foot a half-step, shifting back and bringing the right fist back beside the waist. Partner B lifts the left hand in front of the left shoulder and chops forward and down to take A's fist down. Partner B looks at the left hand. (image 3.22)

**Pointers**

- When actually using the cannon punch, the step must be fast and the body must charge forward. One hand slices up and turns to deflect while the other hand protects the centre with the elbow. The punch comes from the turn of the body, driving down the centre line to the opponent's solar plexus. It must be fierce and penetrating.

- In the partner form, A must be careful with his partner when doing the cannon punch. He must not hit the solar plexus, but he can hit the large muscled area on the chest. To avoid unwanted injury A may first step forward with the deflection, wait until B has retreated, and then punch,

- When B does the retreat step he turns his body sideways to avoid A's attacking force. Partner B should cover with the left elbow and chop down with the palm so that A's punch does not connect. This is the way to break the cannon punch.

- In the partner form the partners need to cooperate with their footwork to get the timing and spacing right.

8.  **A: Step Forward, Right Hook to the Ear**　　　　shàngbù yòu guàn'ěr　　上步右贯耳

    **B: Withdraw, Left Drill**　　chèbù zuǒ zuānquán　　撤步左钻拳

ACTION 1: Partner A steps the right foot forward to the outside of B's left foot, then follows in with the left foot. Partner A unclenches the left hand and extends it to B's wrist with the palm down to cover, press down, grab and pull, drawing B's hand down to the left, looking at the left hand. Partner A brings the right fist back, rotates the palm away from the thumb, then swings it right and forward in an arc

## 200    PROTECT THE BODY, ANSHEN PAO

with the fist eye inward, to punch B's ears with the knuckle edge of the fist. Partner A looks at his right fist. (image 3.23)

ACTION 2: Partner B retreats the right foot to the right and withdraws the left foot a half- step, shifting back and drilling the left fist up along the inside of A's right forearm. This is a slight crosscut to the left. Partner B looks at his left fist. (image 3.24)

### Pointers

- The actual application is a grab and pull to draw the opponent's hand down. In a partner form, one should just slap down. Also, when striking the ear, one should stop short of the ear. One should not use the full force of the back to swing the arm forcefully to hit the ear.

- Partner B needs to do the retreat and withdraw footwork quickly and shift the weight back quickly. Partner B's upward drill should have a bit of crossing power in it.

- The partners need to work out a mutual understanding to coordinate the advancing and retreating techniques.

**9. A: Advance and Steal a Hit**           jìnbù tōu dǎ         进步偷打

   **B: Changeover Step, Slap, Check, Punch**   huànbù pāi bō dǎ 换步拍拨打

ACTION 1: Partner A advances the right foot a half-step and extends the left hand to slap B's left fist. Partner A unclenches the right hand, bringing it back to the chest in preparation for the hit. Partner A looks at the left hand. (image 3.25)

ACTION 2: Partner A strikes out at B's face with the right hand, palm facing forward, bringing the left hand back to the chest, and looking at the right hand. (image 3.26)

ACTION 3: Partner B withdraws the left foot to inside the right foot and lands it, shifting weight to the left foot and lifting the right hand with the palm facing left to slap A's right forearm towards the left. Partner B looks at the right hand. (image 3.27)

ACTION 4: Partner B bends the left arm and slides it up inside A's arm, extending it and hooking it back to brush aside to the left. Partner B looks at the left hand. Partner B advances the right foot without moving the left foot and slaps A's face with the back of the right hand, bracing out with the left hand to develop more power. Partner B braces both arms, contains the chest and opens the upper back. Partner B looks at A. (image 3.28)

**Pointers**

- Partner A's stolen hit is the right hand chopping the opponent's face while the left hand deals with the opponent's left hand. The left hand has a covering, pressing down, pulling back and down power, and the right hand pounces out in an arcing move. The hands move forward and back in one integrated action. The right hand should strike out exactly as the right foot steps forward. When doing a partner form the striking hand needs to have a focal point. Partner A should also just slap B's hand down to the right instead of grabbing and pulling back, so that B can continue on with the next action.

- Partner B should withdraw the left foot and slap across with the right hand to the left at the same time. After B withdraws the left foot he must shift immediately to the left foot. Partner B should advance the right foot and do the backhand strike with the right hand while bracing out with the left hand, all at the same time, with fully integrated power. B must not use full power to hit A's face, the strike must have a focal point.

## 10. A: Changeover Step, Left Split    huànbù zuǒpī    换步左劈

### B: Pull and Grab the Head    lǔshǒu zhuā tóu    捋手抓头

ACTION 1: Partner A withdraws the right foot to inside the left foot and shifts to the right leg, while bringing the right hand back to the belly, clenching it, then drilling it up along the outside of B's right arm. This breaks B's backhand strike. Partner A prepares the left hand at the chest and looks at the right fist. (image 3.29)

ACTION 2: Partner A advances the left foot while unclenching the right hand and turning the palm down to grab and pull B's right forearm. Partner A chops towards B's face with the left palm and pulls the right hand down to the belly. Partner A looks at B. (image 3.30)

ACTION 3: Partner B retreats the left foot and withdraws the right foot a half-step, bending the right arm. Partner B swings the right arm up to the right and circles it to bring it in front of the chest to break A's left split. Partner B brings the left hand forward and right to grab and pull A's left arm. Partner B looks at A's left hand. (image 3.31)

ACTION 4: Partner B advances the right foot a half-step and pulls the left hand back to the belly, striking A's head with the right hand with the palm facing forward. Partner B looks at his right hand. (image 3.32)

**Pointers**

- Partner A should withdraw the right foot and drill the right fist at the same time, moving quickly. The drilling fist must contain a bracing forward power. Partner A should step the left foot forward, chop with the left hand and pull back with the right hand all at the same time. In a partner form the pulling hand should not grab and hold on, but just indicate the intent. The changeover step must be done quickly.

- Partner B should coordinate the two hands – one forward and one back, one up and one down – moving simultaneously. In a partner form one should not actually grab. The footwork and hand techniques must be coordinated and move together.

11. **A: Step Forward, Snake**  shàngbù shéxíng  上步蛇形

    **B: Retreat, Left Cut to the Neck**  tuìbù zuǒ qiēbō  退步左切脖

ACTION 1: Partner A first withdraws the left foot a half-step, bringing back the left hand to drill up inside B's right forearm. Partner A unclenches the left hand and turns it to grab B's right wrist, pulling it back to the head and preparing the right hand at the belly. Partner A looks at B's right hand. (image 3.33)

ACTION 2: Partner A steps the right foot into B's groin and follows in a half-step with the left foot, dropping the stance a bit. While doing this, A forcefully slices up into B's groin with the backhand, continuing to pull up and back with the left hand. Partner A looks at B. (image 3.34)

## 204   PROTECT THE BODY, *ANSHEN PAO*

ACTION 3: Partner B retreats the left foot a half-step, retreats the right foot a big step to the rear, and withdraws the left foot another half-step. Partner B rotates the right hand palm away from the thumb so the palm faces right, fingers down, and slides it along the outside of A's right arm, hooking it back to the right hip. Partner B turns the left palm up and strikes to A's neck. Partner B looks at A. (image 3.35)

**Pointers**

- The main technique of the snake tehcnique is the slice to the groin. The application is that the upper hand pulls back to open up the opponent while the lower hand slices up with a straight arm as the footwork moves in. The footwork should take over the opponents groin area as if you were going to do a shoulder strike. The key lies in entering the footwork to get the body as close as possible, so the footwork needs to be agile and quick. In a partner form you do not grab and hold on, and you must be sure to focus the groin strike to not to hit your partner's groin. This stance is relatively low.

- Partner B must retreat quickly and shift well back. The right hand needs to be accurate with the hook and deflection. When B retreats the right foot to the rear the body must turn sideways so that A's groin slice misses its target. When B slices to the neck he should use a twisting power in the body. Be sure to have a focal point, and stop before hitting your partner's neck.

**12. A: Left and Right Cut to the Neck**   zuǒ yòu qiēbō   左右切脖

**B: Right Drill, Left Driving Punch**  yòu zuān zuǒ bēngquán 右钻左崩拳

ACTION 1: Partner A shifts back without moving the feet, shifting almost completely back to the left leg. Partner A bends the right elbow and hooks back by the right ear to defend against B's neck cut. While doing this, A turns the left palm up and cuts horizontally to B's neck. Partner A looks at B. (image 3.36)

ACTION 2: Partner B drills the right fist up along the inside of A's left arm to knock it horizontally to the right. (image 3.37)

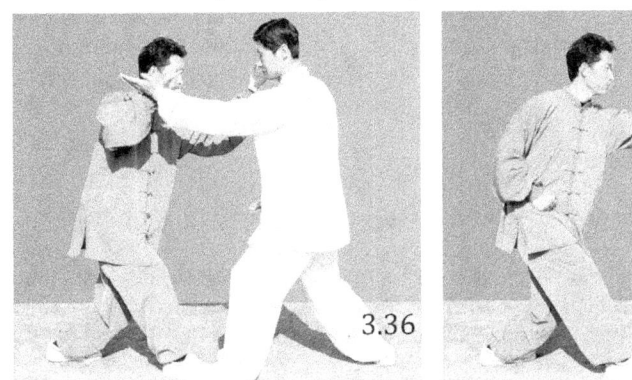

ACTION 3: Partner A turns the right palm up and cuts horizontally to B's neck. Partner A looks at B. (image 3.38)

ACTION 4: Partner B brings the left hand back to the left waist and unclenches the right hand, bringing it along the inside of A's right arm to slap to the left. Partner B advances the left foot a half- step without moving the right foot, and turns the body rightward, forming a half horse stance. Partner B does a left driving punch to A's right ribs, fist eye up, and brings the right hand back to the belly. Partner B looks at the left fist. (image 3.39)

**Pointers**

- Partner A should do two continuous cuts to the neck. When doing the cuts, the arms should stay slightly bent and the power should come from the turning of the waist and shoulders. The palms swing forward, cutting diagonally down. The elbows should stay settled. The cuts should have a forward subduing power. In a partner form you should not hit with power, just place the palms at the side of the partner's neck.

## PROTECT THE BODY, *ANSHEN PAO*

- o  Partner B needs to do two continuous deflections with the right hand, to the right and left. When slapping leftward, he should slide leftward and back along A's right arm. The left foot advance and left driving punch are simultaneous, and the body should twist rightward to increase the power of the punch. In a partner form the punch should be focused near the ribs. Be sure to sit down into the punch.

**13. A: Ape Pulls the Rope**     yuánhóu dáo shéng     猿猴捯绳

**B: Retreat, Right Drill**     tuìbù zuānquán     退步钻拳

ACTION 1: Partner A withdraws the right foot back a bit and turns the right palm down to slide along the top of B's arm, pulling it down and back to in front of the chest. Partner A also turns the left palm down and slides it along the top of B's left arm, pulling it down. Partner A looks at B. (image 3.40)

ACTION 2: Partner A advances the right foot a half-step and follows in a bit with the left foot, striking to B's face with the right hand, palm forward, fingers up. Partner A looks at B. (image 3.41)

ACTION 3: Partner B retreats the left foot to the rear and withdraws the right foot a half-step, drilling the right fist along the outside of A's right forearm to deflect A's right strike. Partner B brings the left fist back to the belly and looks at A. (image 3.42)

### Pointers

- o  Points to consider are the same as in movement 6.

## CHAPTER THREE: PARTNER FORM    207

**14. A: Step Forward, Pull Back, Right Cut to the Neck**

shàngbù lǚshǒu yòu qiēbō    上步捋手右切脖

**B: Withdraw, Double Intercept to the Left**

chèbù zuǒ shuāng jiéshǒu    撤步左双截手

ACTION 1: Partner A advances the right foot a half-step and drills the left fist up along the inside of B's right arm. Partner A unclenches the left hand and turns it palm down to hook onto and pull B's hand down to the left. Partner A steps the left foot forward and turns the right palm up to cut forcefully towards B's neck, the arm slightly bent. (image 3.43)

ACTION 2: Partner B retreats the left foot to the rear and withdraws the right foot a half-step, shifting back. Partner B clenches both fists, bends and drops the elbows to place the forearms vertically. The right fist is forward with the fist heart turned in, and the left fist is behind with the fist heart turned out. Partner B does a horizontal intercept to the left with both fists on A's right forearm, fists at nose height. Partner B looks at A's right hand. (image 3.44)

**Pointers**

- When A does the drill and grab he should not actually grab during a partner form, but should just knock the hand aside to allow his partner to continue with the next action. The step forward is timed with the neck cut, and be sure to focus the strike. When actually using this strike, the foot should step forward behind the opponent's foot so that he cannot retreat and get away. In a partner form you need to wait until the partner has retreated, then step forward.

- Partner B should retreat quickly and with a big step. After retreating, he should quickly withdraw the other foot. The intercepting action should also have forward leading power.

## 15. A: Left Cut to the Neck   zuǒ qiēbō   左切脖
### B: Double Intercept to the Right, Right Driving Punch
yòu shuāngjié yòu bēngquán   右双截右崩拳

ACTION 1: Partner A does not move the feet yet, and turns the left palm up to cut towards B's neck with the palm edge. Partner A looks at B. (image 3.45)

ACTION 2: Partner B, after intercepting to the left, quickly turns rightward and withdraws the right foot slightly, turning both fists to intercept A's left forearm to the right. Partner B's left fist is forward with the fist heart turned in. (image 3.46)

ACTION 3: Partner B lowers the right fist lowers to the right waist. Partner B advances the right foot a half-step and punches to A's solar plexus with the right fist, pulling the left fist back to the belly. Partner B looks at A. (image 3.47)

### Pointers

- Partner A should do the two neck cuts continuously without hesitation.
- Partner B should do the two intercepting actions continuously, being sure to defend strongly. After taking A across to the right, B should quickly do the driving punch.
- The partners should cooperate closely so that the actions appear and feel realistic.

## 16. A: Pull Back, Crossing Kick, Step Forward, Right Split

lǔshǒu héngtī shàngbù yòu pī      捋手横踢上步右劈

**B: Retreat, Left Crosscut**   tuìbù zuǒ héngquán     退步左横拳

ACTION 1: Partner A shifts back to the right leg and slides the left hand outside B's right arm to pull down and to the right. Partner A rotates the right palm away from the thumb in front of the chest to grab B's right wrist. Partner A grabs and pulls with both hands down to the right, pressing the head up and looking at B. (image 3.48)

ACTION 2: Partner A turns the right foot out and does a crossing kick to B's knee, keeping the grip on B's arm. (image 3.49)

ACTION 3: Partner A lands the right foot forward and steps the left foot forward, chopping the right hand to B's face, palm forward. (image 3.50)

ACTION 4: Partner B retreats the left foot a half-step then retreats the right foot a step, to avoid A's kick. Partner B then withdraws the left foot a half-step and drills the right fist up along the outside

of A's right forearm, crossing it to the right, fist centre up. Partner B pulls the left fist back to the belly, shifts most weight to the left leg and looks at A. (image 3.51)

**Pointers**

- When A uses both hands to draw B's right wrist and shifts back, this is called "lead the sheep while going along ". Drawing someone in along the line of their stance causes them to lose balance forward. In a partner form one should not grab and pull, but just defend and then attack.

- The target for the crossing kick is the opponent's knee. When actually using this technique, first pull back then kick, still holding on, so that the opponent cannot step away. In a partner form you should make sure your partner has stepped away before kicking. You must time this carefully and cooperate tightly to avoid injury. B must retreat quickly, shift back quickly, and coordinate well with A.[13]

### 17. A: Step Forward, Left Scoop Up, Right Split

shàngbù zuǒ tiǎo yòu pī　　上步左挑右劈

**B: Grab the Shoulder with the Left Hand**

zuǒ shǒu zhuā jiān　　左手抓肩

ACTION 1: Partner A advances the left foot a half-step and follows up with the right foot, clenching the left fist with the fist heart up and scooping up under B's right arm. Partner A then unclenches the left hand and turns the palm out to pull B's right arm towards the left. Partner A chops to B's face with the right hand, looking at B. (image 3.52)

---

[13] Editor's note: Partner A can help B get away by pushing partner B's arm forward. If partner B stiffens his arm, this push will send him back. The cooperation is hardly noticeable to an audience if done smoothly.

ACTION 2: Partner B retreats the right foot a half-step and withdraws the left foot. Partner B turns the left thumb down and the fingers up, stretching the thumb to forefinger web widely. Partner B shifts slightly to the right and turns to forcefully brace on A's right shoulder. Partner B looks at his left hand. (image 3.53)

**Pointers**

- When doing a partner form A should not grab the arm after doing the scoop up. Do not move the feet yet when scooping up. Advance the left foot a half-step and follow in with the right foot when doing the chop.

- Partner B should first retreat then brace on A's shoulder, to prevent A's arm from landing the chop. This move is traditionally called "sparrow hawk grabs the shoulder".

18. **A: Brush Aside, Right Split**  lōushǒu yòu pī  搂手右劈

    **B: Left Hooking Block, Right Cut to the Neck**

    zuǒ guà yòu qiēbō  左挂右切脖

ACTION 1: Partner A withdraws the left foot then the right foot slightly and turns the left palm to face right, fingers up, to push B's left hand to the right. Partner A turns the right palm down and hooks the right wrist onto B's left elbow to brush it out to the right. Partner A looks at B. (image 3.54)

ACTION 2: Partner A advances the right foot a half-step and turns the right palm forward to slap towards B's face. Partner A looks at B. (image 3.55)

## 212  PROTECT THE BODY, *ANSHEN PAO*

ACTION 3: Partner B retreats the right foot a half-step and withdraws the left foot, bending the left elbow. Partner B turns and lifts the left hand inside A's right arm to hook it back towards his left ear. B turns the right palm up and cuts towards A's neck. Partner B looks at A. (image 3.56)

**Pointers**

- Partner A coordinates three actions together: the right foot withdraws slightly, the left hand knocks aside to the right, and the right hand brushes down and out. The brush aside should use a cold, heavy, shaking power.

- Partner B coordinates two actions together: the right foot advances and the right hand slaps forward. He should settle the elbow and wrist for the strike.

- Partner B should first retreat the right foot. He should withdraw the left foot when hooking the left hand. He should turn the body and extend the shoulder to chop the neck. In a partner form all strikes should have fixed focal points to avoid unwanted injury.

19. **A: Double Intercept to the Left**   zuǒ shuāng jiéshǒu   左双截手

    **B: Left Cut to the Neck**   zuǒ qiēbó   左切脖

ACTION 1: Partner A clenches both fists and bends the elbows to put the forearms vertical. He uses both arms inside B's right arm to intercept horizontally to the left. The right fist is forward with the fist heart in and the left fist is back with the fist heart out. The feet do not move, and A looks at B's right hand. (image 3.57)

ACTION 2: Partner B does not move the feet, and turns the left palm up to chop towards A's neck, bringing the right hand back to the belly. The left arm is slightly bent. Partner B looks at A. (image 3.58, partner A already doing the double intercept)

3.58

**Pointers**

- The intercept and cut are the same as done previously in move 4.

**20. A: Double Intercept to the Right, Right Driving Punch**
yòu shuāng jiéshǒu yòu bēngquán     右双截手右崩拳

**B: Retreat, Left Press Down**    tuìbù zuǒ àn    退步左按

ACTION 1: Partner A withdraws the right foot back slightly and hits across to the right with the left forearm forward and the right fist back, inside B's left forearm, intercepting across to the right, looking at B (see image 3.58). Partner A advances the right foot a half-step and launches a driving punch with the right fist towards B's solar plexus. The fist eye is up and the arm slightly bent. A pulls the left fist back to the side while punching. Partner A looks at B. (image 3.59)

ACTION 2: Partner B retreats the right foot and withdraws the left foot to just in front of the right foot. Partner B turns the left palm down and crossways and presses down on A's right fist. B brings the right hand back to the belly and looks at A's right fist. (image 3.60)

3.59

3.60

**Pointers**

- The intercept and driving punch are the same as done previously in move 5.

214  PROTECT THE BODY, *ANSHEN PAO*

- o  Partner B must retreat and withdraw quickly. The palm press must be timed just right to catch the oncoming fist.

**21. A: Advance, Right Driving Punch**   jìnbù yòu bēngquán   进步右崩拳

  **B: Retreat, Left Press Down, Right Driving Punch**
  tuìbù zuǒ àn yòu bēngquán   退步左按右崩拳

This move is the same as move 1, but partners A and B have just traded places. The white uniform is now partner A and the dark uniform is now partner B. (image 3.61)

- The first twenty moves are the first section of the form. From move 21 on is the second section. The form repeats going back, and partners A and B trade sides in the second section. Both partners learn both sides, taking turns being the initiator and the defender. This makes the form more interesting and involves learning and mastering more techniques.

- On getting to the end of a section, you could also change places and repeat the same side. To do this you need to stop and change places at the end of the section so that you return to the starting point.

- Editor's note: Prior to closing, Partner B can signal the desire to stop by pressing down and controlling a bit longer in movement 20, and not punching. Similarly, partner A can press and control in movement 2, when he has just become side B.

## 22. Closing Move  shōu shì  收势

ACTION 1: Partners A and B both retreat the right foot back a big step and shift back, putting most weight on the right leg. (image 3.62)

They then withdraw the left foot to touch the toes down in front of the right foot. Partners A and B both bring the right fist back to the belly, then drill it up past the solar plexus to nose height, the ulnar side twisted up. They press their heads up and look at their right fists. The left fist stays in front of the belly. (image 3.63)

ACTION 2: Partners A and B both advance the left foot a half-step without moving the right foot, to sit into a *santi* stance. Both unclench the hands and do a left split, pulling the right hand back to the belly. Both press the head up and look at the left hand. (image 3.64)

## 216  PROTECT THE BODY, *ANSHEN PAO*

ACTION 3: Partners A and B both withdraw the left foot to place the feet together. Both pull the left hand back to the belly and clench it, standing steadily with the legs slightly bent. Both then lift the palms up beside the body to shoulder height, then bend the elbows to bring the hands together in front of the face, then press with palms down in front of the belly. Both stand up and allow the hands to hang naturally at the sides. Both look forward, and the closing of the form is completed. (images 3.65, 3.66)

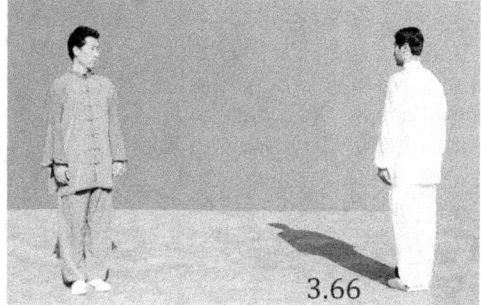

**Pointers**

- Partners A and B do the closing together, moving in unison. When both partners retreat the right foot a big step this should be as big as possible. Be sure to keep balance when moving back, and keep the whole movement together.

CHAPTER FOUR

# DISCUSSIONS ON THEORY AND TEACHING

## BREATHING FOR POWER

All Xingyi techniques are done as integrated movements. The hands initiate and land the technique; the legs stride forward with a thrust backward; the power gathers then launches; and the breath flows in then out. Breathing in Xingyi is 'positional breathing,' in which the techniques incorporate the breathing. The classic texts say; "to attain adequate power you must first attain complete breath," and "techniques have form and the strength of the breath has no form. Techniques must gain strength from the breath." You must focus on synchronizing breathing and movements. This type of breathing improves the body's ability to take a hit, helps apply power, and increases the speed of explosive power.

Each technique uses a full breathing cycle.

- Inhale to store power with a long deep breath, exhale to launch power with a short powerful breath. "Inhale long and exhale short" is a characteristic of the synchronized breath and action of Xingyi. This makes the power integrated and the strength full.

- When breathing out, do not simply exhale all of the breath that you inhaled. Instead, as you deliver force, exhale a portion of your breath then suddenly stop, tightening the *dantian* area of your abdomen to brace your whole body, delivering a whole body power.

- The general rule is: inhale when the limbs are circling and when the body technique is folding or closing in; exhale when the limbs are extending or applying power and when the body is turning or opening up. More simply: inhale when the lead hand and foot move and exhale when the rear foot and fist come through to apply power. Contain the breath, that is, breathe neither in nor out when readying.

- Breathe naturally during non-forceful movements.

Positional breathing technique is the main method used during the obvious power stage of 'training spirit to change energy and change sinews'. This is also the main method used to gain whole body power. You must also understand that you use exhalation to assist the action of delivering power; you are not "exhaling power." In other words, you need to breathe out in order to deliver a powerful hit, but the breath is not the power itself (obviously, you can breathe out without delivering power).

Breathing is greatly affected by the speed of movement. It is easy to regulate breathing while moving slowly, but more difficult when moving quickly. When training Xingyi the movements should not be done too quickly; they should not 'flow like the current of a river' as do the movements of Longfist. Xingyi uses a rhythmic alternation of action and stillness that emphasizes whole body power. To develop the whole body power it is essential to work on the proper co-ordination of breath and power.

At the beginning a student should breathe naturally without much thought to breathing. You should pay attention to learning the proper movements and gaining a basic command of the requirements of the movements. You should not try too hard to coordinate breathing with actions. The first thing to do is learn the movements, master the lines, directions, angles and synchronization of all the body segments, and to work on integrated power. Breathe naturally, just keeping breathing smooth with the actions. Once the actions have been grasped then you may start to pay more attention to using breath together with the movement.

Xingyi uses reverse abdominal breathing, which is the natural way to put power into a movement. Raise the diaphragm and bring in the abdomen as you inhale, lower the diaphragm and round the abdomen as you exhale. This keeps power in the *dantian* area and allows you to launch power to wherever it is needed.

The general principle to apply to breathing is: control your body with your mind; control your breath with your body. But, once you've reached a high level, then "you can use your *qi* anytime, following your inclination; hit hard or enter hard without impediment."

# A DISCUSSION OF THE FIVE ELEMENTS IN XINGYIQUAN

## UNDERSTANDING THE RELATIONSHIP BETWEEN THE FIVE ELEMENT TECHNIQUES AND THE FIVE INTERNAL ORGANS

### How the five elements relate to the internal organs

The five elemental techniques of Xingyiquan are traditionally called metal, wood, water, fire and earth. Is it scientific and logical to name them in this way? The theory of the five elements sums up the martial techniques; it uses the mutual creation and mutual control cycles of the five elements to direct martial techniques. This shows the close connection between martial arts and ancient Chinese philosophical thought. From today's scientific point of view, it is a little sweeping and crude to interpret everything according to the five elements theory, but this ancient methodology and worldview is still able to guide us and deepen our understanding of Xingyyiquan.

The theory of the five elements made traditional Chinese medical theory more comprehensive and more rational. The five elements are used to explain the interplay of mutual harmony and harm between the five internal organs. Their

## CHAPTER FOUR: THEORY AND TEACHING

connections are described in terms of physiological functions and pathological changes, which explain the connection of the body to the outside environment[14] and guide diagnosis and treatment.

The relationships between the five elements and the five internal organs are:

- Metal relates to the Lung.[15] The Lung rules $qi$[16] and manages respiration. It rules the exterior of the body, which means the skin and body hair. It rules descending and liquefying. The Lung moves and adjusts the water channels. It opens to the nose.
- Wood relates to the Liver. The Liver rules flowing and spreading of $qi$ and blood, and governs the storage of blood. The Liver governs the tendons and is manifest in the nails. It opens to the eyes.
- Water relates to the Kidney. The Kidney stores the essence, and rules the body's development and reproduction. It governs fluids, the grasping of $qi$, governs the bones, produces marrow, and goes through to the brain. It manifests in the hair. It opens to the ears.
- Fire relates to the Heart. The Heart rules the blood and vessels. It is manifest in the face. It governs the spirit and the will. It opens to the tongue.
- Earth relates to the Spleen. The Spleen rules transformation and transportation [of raw materials of food and liquids for production of $qi$ and blood]. It governs the muscles, flesh, the four limbs, and blood. It manifests in the lips. It opens to the mouth.

### How the five techniques relate to the five internal organs through $qi$

Each of the internal organs governs something specific according to the traditional Chinese medical system, but I feel that [for the martial artist] something else is more important – the five visceral $qi$. Chinese medical theory says that the $qi$ of each of the five internal organs has a close connection to the activity of the spirit and will. The relationship of exterior and interior each influences and assists the other:

---

[14] Editor's note: The external correspondences are: metal – dryness, wood – wind, water – cold, fire – heat, and earth – damp. This is one step beyond where martial techniques are likely to relate to the five elements.

[15] Translator's note: Chinese medical theory does not see the five internal organs – Heart, Liver, Spleen, Lung, and Kidney – as the anatomical organs as understood in Western medical theory. The Chinese terms are the energetic functions of the organ, which include the physical organ and its associated organs, sensory organs, channels, tissues, and emotions. It is standard to write them with a capital letter to indicate the Chinese meaning, and in small letters to indicate the Western meaning.

[16] Translator's note: both the natural air '$qi$' and the '$qi$' of the body.

- The Lung contains the corporeal soul, the Liver contains the ethereal soul, the Kidney contains the will, the Heart contains the spirit, and the Spleen contains the cognitive mind.

Whether or not the five internal organs are functioning properly, whether they are strong or weak, directly affects the activity of these five aspects of consciousness or senses. And the opposite is also true – changes in the corporeal soul, the ethereal soul, the will, the spirit, and the cognitive mind can also influence the normal functioning of the five internal organs. The internal – the five internal organs – is the foundation, the root. The external – the five senses – is what is apparent, the outward manifestation. The Chinese medical system says that the outward manifestation and the root affect each other, but that the root is the ruler.

Sun Lutang stated the relationship between the five techniques, five elements, and five internal organs and their *qi* in his Study of Xingyiquan:

"Train the five fists externally to develop the five internal organs internally.

Split is like an axe. It correlates to metal and the Lung. When split's power is smooth then the Lung's *qi* is harmonious; when its power is awkward then the Lung's qi is perverse.[17]

Drill is like lightning. It correlates to water and the Kidney. When drill's power is smooth then the Kidney's *qi* is sufficient.

Drive is like an arrow. It correlates to wood and the Liver. When drive's power is smooth then the Liver's *qi* flows smoothly. When its power is contrary then the Liver's *qi* is damaged.

Cannon is like explosives. It correlates to fire and the Heart. When cannon's *qi* is harmonious then the Heart is carefree. When its *qi* is contrary then the Heart is clouded.[18]

Crosscut is like a cannonball. It correlates to the earth and the Spleen. When it is round then its nature is solid. When crosscut's *qi* is smooth then the Liver and stomach are harmonious. When it is contrary then the Spleen is empty and the stomach weak, and then all five internal organs lose their ability to work harmoniously together.[19]

---

[17] Translator's note: 'perverse' means that the *qi* flows in the opposite direction to normal. Smooth Lung *qi* flows upward, so perverse flow is downward.

[18] Translator's note: In both the physical and emotional sense.

[19] Editor's note: Just as crosscut is a pivotal technique, the Spleen and stomach are pivotal organs. When they are healthy then all other organs benefit. When they are weak then all other organs eventually suffer.

When the techniques are smooth then the internal five elements are harmonious and *qi* flows smoothly within the channels. When the techniques are awkward then the *qi* becomes blocked."

Techniques being 'smooth' or 'awkward' refers to whether or not the movements are coordinated, and how this relates to whether the *qi* flow of the internal organs is unimpeded, blocked or perverse, which in turn affects the health of the organs. When a technique is 'smooth' then the movement is coordinated and the power flows well, and that is good for the internal organs. This is obvious. The opposite is also true – when a technique is poorly done, the movement is uncoordinated and the power is stiff and awkward, and this is not good for the internal organs. But should one say that the techniques harm the internal organs so specifically as in the following phrases?

"When the technique of split is awkward then the Lung's *qi* is perverse.

When the technique of drive is awkward then this harms the Liver.

When the technique of drill is awkward then it creates a crossing strength which makes the Kidney empty and the *qi* perverse.

When the technique of cannon is awkward then the limbs hang flaccidly, the Heart's *qi* is perverse, and all the channels are blocked.

When the technique of crosscut is awkward then the *qi* is overexerted and the strength is harsh, harming the Spleen."

This harm to the internal organs is a bit exaggerated, and puts undue emphasis on the damage that the techniques can do to the internal organs. You should simply say that if the techniques are not smooth and coordinated then this does not help the regulation of the internal organs, and that is enough. Looking at it from another angle, the old masters were emphasizing to their students that it was important to train the five techniques until they became correct and had smooth power flow. Only when the techniques are correct and the power flow is smooth can you achieve the goal of regulating the internal organs. This serves to emphasize the importance of the basic techniques and foundation postures.

**How the five techniques relate to the internal organs through their nature**

There is another way of matching the five techniques to the five internal organs. The outer appearance can relate to the outer manifestation of the organs. The classics often say:

"The Lung moves like the sound of thunder.

The Liver moves like a flying arrow.

The Kidney moves as fast as the wind.

The Heart moves like a blazing fire.

The Spleen moves in strong attacking force."

## How the five techniques relate to the internal organs through the meridian system

The five techniques are also related to the five internal organs by means of the meridian system, or the energy lines throughout the body. The meridians and collaterals are the pathways that circulate to interconnect the organs and internal organs, and connect them with the extremities of the body. They connect the interior and exterior of the body, the surface and the deep, the upper part and lower parts of the body, circulate the *qi* and the blood, and nourish the body. There is nowhere the meridian system does not reach, nowhere that is not connected. The term meridian system is a collective term for the meridian channels and the collateral vessels. The meridian channels are the trunks that travel longitudinally, the collateral vessels are the branches that wrap around the body. There are twelve meridians directly related to the various internal organs, as well as several extraordinary vessels.

The connection between the meridians and the internal organs is roughly thus:[20]

The Lung meridian (the hand greater *yin*) originates in the lung area and, after running down internally to the large intestine, then back up to the throat, emerges to the surface at the *Zhongfu* acupoint [Lu1; the lateral aspect of the chest, then along the medial aspect of the upper arm], through *Chize* [Lu5], *Kongzui* [Lu6], *Liuque* [Lu7], and *Yuji* [Lu10] to *Shaoshang* [Lu11; the radial side tip of the thumb].

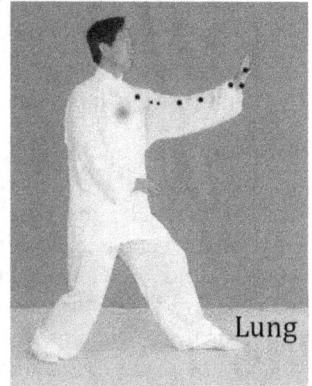
Lung

---

[20] Editor's note: This is a very rough description of the meridians. I have added clarification, and did not always indicate where is my voice and where is the authors. I also plotted the points on the photos as best I could in the position relating to each internal organ. There are many books available that go into the meridians in much more detail. Please note that 1) I drew points that are inside the body just to give an idea of the lines, and 2) I drew only on the side most visible in the photos – the meridians are bilateral.

The Heart meridian (the hand lesser *yin*) originates in the heart, emerges to the surface through the *Jiquan* acupoint [Ht1; in the armpit], and the external branch runs out the midline of the inner arm, elbow and forearm through *Shaohai* [Ht3], *Lingdao* [Ht4], *Shenmen* [Ht7], and *Shaofu* [Ht8] to *Shaochong* [Ht9; the inside tip of the little finger].

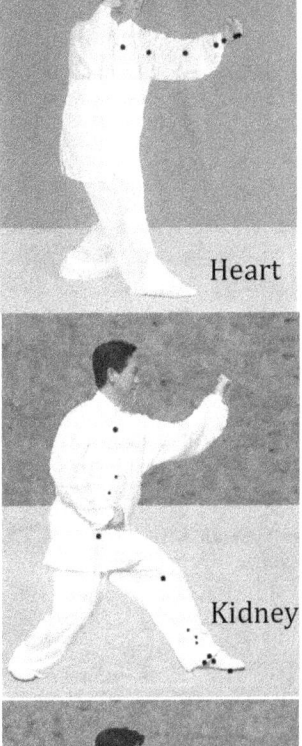

Heart

The Kidney meridian (the foot lesser *yin*) originates in the *Yongquan* acupoint [Ki1] on the sole of the foot, emerges to the surface through the *Rangu* [Ki2; at the arch of the foot], and ascends the medial side of the leg through *Taixi* [Ki3], *Zhaohai* [Ki6], *Yingu* [Ki10], penetrates the body at the base of the spine, and continues up the body to the *S h u f u* [Ki27].

Kidney

The Liver meridian (the foot terminal *yin*) originates in the *Dadun* acupoint [Liv1] on top of the big toe, and emerges to the surface through the *Xingjian* [Liv2], *Taichong* [Liv3], ascends the medial side of the leg through *Zhongdu* [Liv6], *Xiguan* [Liv7], *Ququan* [Liv8], *Wuli* [Liv10; penetrates the body in the lower abdomen, continues up] *Zhangmen* [Liv13], and connects to the Liver and gall bladder at *Qimen* [Liv14]

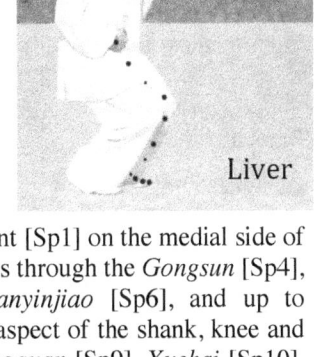

Liver

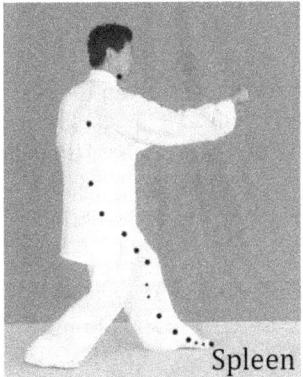

Spleen

The Spleen meridian (the foot great *yin*) originates in the *Yinbai* acupoint [Sp1] on the medial side of the big toe, circulates through the *Gongsun* [Sp4], *Shangqiu* [Sp5], *Sanyinjiao* [Sp6], and up to through the medial aspect of the shank, knee and thigh through *Yinlingquan* [Sp9], *Xuehai* [Sp10], *Jimen* [Sp11], enters the abdominal cavity and moves up inside the body, emerging at *Xiongxiang* [Sp19], to *Dabao* [Sp21].

## Developing The Relationship Between The Five Techniques And The Five Internal Organs

Everyone risks falling ill at some point in their lives, martial artists included. Martial artists must strengthen their bodies to nurture their health and prevent illness. In ancient times, martial artists already knew quite well that the body is the vehicle for trained deep martial skill [ *gong* ]. There is a direct relationship between the level of deep skill and the strength or weakness of the body, both internal and external. There is no way that high level martial skill can be put to good use if it is not based on a healthy solid body. Before firearms, the main purpose for martial arts training was combat. An unknown martial artist could advance socially once he became skilled through hard training. On gaining a reputation, one needed to maintain it in order to earn a living as a bodyguard, security guard, or teacher. But once a master became famous he would meet many challengers; "a person fears becoming famous, a pig fears getting fat." A martial artist would have to condition his body regularly to remain combat fit and successful, because if he lost a fight all his years of hard work would come to nothing. For this reason martial artists put great store in a healthy and strong body. The Chinese medical system gave a readymade body of theory and practical experience in diagnosis and treatment to nurture health. Xingyi masters took the theory concerning the internal organs into their martial system, as well as absorbing some Daoist cultivation methods. Old Xingyiquan classics say:

> "Strengthen your root internally, strengthen your body externally. The internal is the way to nourish health, the external is the way to move.
>
> If you have the internal but not the external then you cannot succeed at martial arts, if you have the external but not the internal then you cannot succeed at deep trained skill.
>
> The five internal elements must be united, the five external elements must flow smoothly."

Both medical theory and Daoist cultivation techniques emphasize that training must include both the internal and the external. This is why Xingyi masters drew a correlation between the five internal organs and the five techniques in Xingyiquan.

The inter-relationship of mutual creation and control of the five techniques [A] is explained by the five elements [B]. The interrelations of the physiological functions and conditions of the five internal organs [C] are also explained through the interrelationship of the five elements [B]. So, with the reasoning "if A=B and B=C, then A=C," the five techniques were related with the five internal organs. There is a certain analytic logic at work here.

The power of each of the five techniques combines to form the whole system – each different power complements the others, so each is necessary to the system. The five internal organs are also an integrated unit. Each organ is necessary to the body. Chinese medical theory believes that if any one organ is unbalanced or develops a problem then this can affect all the other organs and the whole system. Each organ is a vital part of life, something that the whole cannot do without. As described above, each has its own *qi* and each type of *qi* interacts with and blends with the others. The internal organs are connected by their *qi*, a different *qi* for each connection between them, and the whole this forms an integrated and interacting unit. The *qi* of the five internal organs have a tight connection with the vitality of the person. These five kinds of vitality and expression are the outer manifestation of the fullness of the internal organs, that is, the manifestation of the *qi* of each internal organ. Nurturing the internal organs through training the techniques promotes the health of the whole system.

## Using the meridian connections of the five techniques to strengthen the internal organs

The ability to connect the five techniques and the five internal organs came about after the Xingyi masters built up a certain level of skill. They directed their thoughts to move their *qi* to further build a strong and healthy body. That is, they led their internal environment with their external movements, with an internal training method of connecting movements with the internal organs. Of course, at the beginning stages of training obvious power there is no way to make this kind of connection, or to kinesthetically feel the hidden meaning of internal training. This kind of training can be used only after one attains the hidden power stage of training, after one has developed a kinesthetic awareness and a feeling of *qi*.

The five elemental techniques and the five internal organs can, under the direction of the mind, be connected through the pathways of the meridians.

- Seek to feel the body and *qi*, under the conditions of a quiet heart and spirit, a relaxed mind and body, slow and steady breathing, and slow practice. This feeling of *qi* comes naturally when the body is healthy and the skill is deeply trained, while one is doing relaxed and soft movements.

- Once the feeling of *qi* is achieved, move the *qi* along the meridians to the five internal organs by using the movements of the five techniques. Lead the *qi* with the techniques by using the mind to lead the internal *qi* along the meridians to reach the internal organs.

- Over a long period of time one can gradually develop a thoroughfare for the *qi* to circulate through the meridians. This thoroughfare becomes more open and clear the more it is used, so that eventually the five elemental techniques are connected to the five internal organs.

The higher the level of practice and the deeper the achieved skill, the more coordinated the functions of the internal organs can become with the actions. This causes the actions of the internal organs to adjust to the needs of the physical actions, which in turn enables the internal organs to support the actions. This develops a strong and healthy body and creates a good environment for the further development of martial skills.

- If you want to treat illness or to rehabilitate from injury, then that is another emphasis in training. Pick one or two techniques that apply to your specific condition to use as supplemental therapy. The emphasis in the mind differs, and is more specific to strengthening the ailing organ.

**Using the *qi* of the internal organs to strengthen the organs and the power of the five techniques**

As shown above, the relationship between the five techniques and the five internal organs is one of *qi*. The five techniques are five internal powers and five external movements. The five internal organs are five internal *qi* and five external vitalities. When training the five techniques, you train the five powers to experience and show the five vitalities. In this way you can connect with the five internal organs and regulate their *qi*, feel the responses of the internal organs' *qi* and feel the connection between the five techniques and the five internal organs.

- Perform the techniques as a *qigong* practice: calm the heart and collect your thoughts, relax the whole body, do the movements slowly, breathe deeply and long, and keep the power full.
- This enables you to experientially feel the connections [not in the imagination, but in reality]. Seek out the different vitalities of each technique, and feel the *qi* of each organ connecting. After a long time you will certainly feel something.

This type of training of course, can only be done once the five techniques are extremely well mastered, coordinated, and integrated into the body and brain. The mind no longer needs to pay full attention to the performance of the techniques and can fully concentrate on the essence and connection of the techniques to the internal organs. One uses the external to lead the internal, uses the mind to lead the *qi*, and connects the action to the *qi*. This builds a healthy and strong body, which in turn improves combat effectiveness.

The connection between the five techniques and the five internal organs may be explained to beginners to show that this viewpoint and this way of training exists, but a teacher should not explain the exact relationship and training method too early. Someone who has not reached the appropriate level of skill and understanding of Chinese medical theory and meridian theory cannot understand the training yet. The connection between the five techniques and the five internal organs is a bond that is gradually built up after a long period of training martial movements under the direction of the mind.

# A DISCUSSION OF THE SIX MODELS FOR THE BODY IN XINGYIQUAN

Traditional Xingyiquan theory describes six models that the body must copy: chicken legs, dragon torso, bear shoulder girdle, eagle claw, 'tiger leopard head,' and thunder sound. The six models should inform all actions and postures of Xingyiquan.[21] Various opinions have been expressed on these within the Xinyiquan and Xingyiquan worlds.[22] Sun Lutang, in his Study of Xingyiquan, was the first to discuss the 'four likenesses.' He said "Chicken legs have the shape of standing on one leg. Dragon torso is the form of having three folds. Bear shoulders is the power of standing upright. 'Tiger holds the head' is the form of the hands embracing like a tiger leaving its den." The book Explanation of Xingyiquan that followed also held this view, and most subsequent authors developed this same idea.

But the six models for the body should be understood to describe the overall picture, not individual techniques. We should analyze the six models as a whole, as they describe the character of Xingyiquan movements using the characteristics of animals. The six models are descriptive images for the hands, eyes, bodywork, legs, spirit, *qi*, strength, and deep achieved skill of Xingyiquan. They describe the requirements to help people find the feeling and achieve the spirit for themselves. This method is customarily used in Chinese martial arts as it is a traditional mode of thinking for the Chinese. For example, in Baguazhang they say 'dragon steps, monkey likeness, tiger sits, eagle wheels,' and in Taijiquan 'one body makes five bows.' These are images that help us understand and remember more deeply. Using this imagery during practice can help you analyse, imagine, reproduce and finally teach yourself through experience, more quickly understanding the requirements of the movements and the characteristics of the skills.

### CHICKEN LEGS

Chicken legs means that the footwork of Xingiquan is fast and stable, moving suddenly and stopping steadily. Of course, describing the footwork only as chicken legs is not enough, so there is also the phrase "the skill of striking." The description of chicken legs also reminds you to try to set the legs solidly into the ground.

---

[21] Author's note: Or the four likenesses. Some texts speak of four likenesses of the body: 'chicken legs, dragon trunk, bear shoulders, and tiger leopard head.'

[22] Author's note: The old masters passed on their knowledge orally, so there were few written records, and the poems and materials passed on by the old masters are all drawn from the oral teachings by previous generations. There are many different accents and dialects in the different regions of China, so when the written word was put down, often there is a word that is pronounced the same but is written with a different character. There have also been errors made in copying texts.

## DRAGON TORSO

Dragon torso refers to bodywork. We can understand the 'three folds' of the dragon's body because, although a dragon is an imaginary magical animal, everyone has seen the performance of a dragon dance. The dragon's body is light and long, it flexes and extends, it can bend and move freely at will. Xingyiquan elders took the metaphor of the dragon's free body movements to describe how freely the human body should move. This is brilliant and apt imagery. Bodywork is the technique of moving the trunk, which includes the 'swallowing and spitting' of the chest, the twisting and turning of the waist, and the opening up and closing in of the chest and back.

## BEAR SHOULDERS

Bear shoulders describes how the shoulder girdle area is released and settled. The shoulder girdle includes the shoulders and upper arms, the deltoid area, and the shoulder blades. When this area is released and settled like a bear then movement can be agile and power can be launched. If you look at a bear, its forelegs and shoulders are always very loose. Xingyiquan requires that the shoulders be relaxed, so describing this as bear shoulders is very apt. The classics also say: "bear shoulders is the power of holding the neck upright." This 'power of holding the neck upright' refers to the neck of the bear. Holding the neck upright helps you to release the shoulder girdle, and relaxing the shoulders helps you to hold the neck upright.

## EAGLE CLAW

Eagle claw describes the hand shape and hand techniques of Xingyiquan. The hand shape of Xingyiquan is: the five fingers slightly bent and curving in, the palm curving in and the web of the palm spread. Although the hand shape is not held exactly in an 'eagle claw,' it does have the spirit of the grasping of the eagle claw at all times. "Don't try to imitate, but to borrow the right meaning." The meaning is quite broad and is just a model, and includes the power and the application. Freely imitate the whole range of meaning of eagle claw to deepen your understanding of the requirements and characteristics of Xingyiquan and better show it's flavour.

## TIGER LEOPARD HEAD OR TIGER HOLD HEAD

The term 'tiger leopard head' 虎豹头 is written as 'tiger holds head' 虎抱头 in some texts. There are a variety of opinions over what the tiger leopard head means. Most respect the opinion of the classics, "tiger leopard head means the two hands embracing like a fierce tiger coming out of its den," or "tiger hold head refers to how the tiger protects its head with its front legs when it comes out of its den." It has also been explained as "the hands in front hold the position of protecting the neck." I think that this sort of explanation is incorrect, and clearly not what the elders originally meant. It is incorrect to see 'tiger leopard head' or 'tiger hold head' as specific techniques. Within the six models for Xingyiquan, the tiger leopard head is an image that refers to the spirit and mien of the head and eyes.

'Tiger leopard head' is the head of a tiger or a leopard, and 'tiger hold head' is the tiger holding up its head. You should have the same spirit showing in your eyes as a tiger or leopard, your stare should shoot at an opponent, making him too fearful to face you. Showing the spirit of a tiger or leopard causes an opponent to lose confidence and lose to you.

### THUNDER SOUND

Thunder sound refers to the sound that you make when you emit power, which is a deep sound like thunder. You use your sound to assist your action, getting more spirit and power. Just as the sound of thunder rolls on, your power is not broken. A lightning flash is followed by a thunderclap, so swift that it is too late to cover the ears. The practice of using sound when launching power has fallen into disuse in Xingyiquan. Although the thunder sound is little used during practice, it should be used appropriately in fighting to put fear into your opponent. It puts more *qi* into your strength, increases your hitting power, and increases your ability to take hits. Thunder sound describes both your sound and your mien.

### SUMMATION

The six models for the body use the imagery of animals to explain principles that apply to the whole body. Chicken, dragon, bear, eagle, tiger, and thunder explain the handwork, eye movement, body action and footwork of Xingyiquan. This is an overall concept, not a specific technical description – you should follow the six models in every stance and every action, in the hands, eyes, body, footwork, essence, spirit, *qi*, strength, and skill.

Xingyiquan imitates shape to some extent, but more important is the intent and the spirit. "Do not seek to imitate, but seek to find the essence." Xingyiquan is not an imitative style, it is a style that emphasizes intent. Moreover, within the range of imitation one should use the hands, eyes, body and footwork, the essence and spirit, the *qi* and the strength as an integrated whole to show the martial intent and the imposing nature of Xingyiquan.

# A DISCUSSION OF THE THREE LEVELS OF XINGYIQUAN

## CLEAR, HIDDEN, AND TRANSFORMED POWER

The three levels of Xingyi were first written up by Sun Lutang, who said, "Xingyiquan has three levels of theory, three stages of deep skill, and three types of training". Sun referred to Guo Yunsheng's talk on Xingyiquan to introduce, define and explain these three levels, but actually they represented his own ideas. They were the culmination of Sun's many years of research and collection of materials, study of theory, his own thought on Xingyiquan, and his knowledge of Daoist internal training theories. Indeed, the stages were not created by martial artists, but were borrowed from Daoist thought and training methods – Daoist thought, spirit, theory, and training methods have long influenced and permeated Xingyiquan theory and methods. They have become a part of the Xingyiquan system, which further developed and improved its theoretical foundation.

As to the three levels of deep skill, the first is to change the bones, the second is to changes the tendons, and the third is to wash the marrow. Sun Lutang said, "Master Da Mo passed on two classics, the tendon changing and the marrow washing. Study them to strengthen your body. This should be the first goal of the beginning student. In the later Song dynasty, Yue Wumu expanded on the two classics by developing the three classics; bone changing, tendon changing, and marrow washing. The three classics were incorporated into martial arts theory." Although Sun Lutang quoted Yue Fei and Guo Yunsheng, this is not historically verifiable. Probably Sun Lutang developed them himself and used the names of Yue Fei and Guo Yunsheng to authenticate his ideas. The theory behind these three levels of theory, three stages of deep training, and three methods of training made Xingyiquan's training more systematic and linked it to ancient culture.

The three training methods, clear, hidden, and transformed power were not clearly defined by previous generations of masters and are difficult for a modern beginner to understand. The three levels of theory are meant to describe three layers and types of training power. The three stages of deep skill are three stages of training. Each one has a specific goal and uses specific methods.

Xingyiquan's theory of clear, hidden, and transformed power has been applied by other martial arts styles. They are not only three types of training and three types of power, but also describe how someone advances and changes gradually from a low level to a high level of skill. During this process each stage is not clearly separated from the other, but there is a gradual accumulation of changes. Once someone reaches a certain level this creates the conditions to pass to the next level.

The following table breaks down the three levels of theory, three stages of skill, and three types of training to a chart. This is presented to give a basis for analysis. Some categories explain the overall picture, some categories give a partial analysis, and some just emphasize a certain aspect. Please use the chart to help you understand and get a feel for the requirements and characteristics of the three stages.

| CATEGORIES | LEVEL ONE | LEVEL TWO | LEVEL THREE |
|---|---|---|---|
| stage | beginner | intermediate | advanced |
| principle of the level | train essence to transform *qi* | train *qi* to transform spirit | train spirit to return to emptiness |
| power application | clear, obvious | hidden | transformed |
| compared to school | primary and high school | university | specialist, teacher |
| relative to theory | most difficult work stage | necessary road to become skilled | highest stage of martial study |
| relative to changing the body | change bones | change tendons | wash marrow |
| relative to martial and Daoist skill | martial skill | Daoist skill | martial and Daoist combined |
| function and goal | train to build foundation, strengthen the body | train to expand the membranes, to develop the tendons | train to cleanse the inside to emptiness, lighten the body |
| training the body | train the muscles and willpower | discipline the spirit | combine heaven and man |
| characteristic power | whole body power | internal power | soft and dissolving |
| goal of power in attack | explode | penetrate | adhere |
| basics and internal training mix | emphasis on basics and applications | emphasis on applications and internal power | applications secondary |
| what is changing | change power | change the physical makeup | emphasis on internal power, change the energy's makeup |

| CATEGORIES | LEVEL ONE | LEVEL TWO | LEVEL THREE |
| --- | --- | --- | --- |
| what is being disciplined | muscles | mind | spirit |
| what capability is being developed | train to become self capable | train to become instinctive | train to have concealed potential |
| training of internal and external | use the external to develop the internal | use the internal to develop the external | no division between internal and external |
| emphasis in each stage | train shape and structure | train intent | train spirit |
| motor control of the brain | extensive | differentiated | natural |
| intentional control of the mind | fully intentional | low control | natural |
| speed used | fast | slow | fast and slow intermingle |
| three internal combinations | strength and *qi* | *qi* and mind | mind and spirit |
| what to strength to remove | remove brute strength | remove hard strength | power is smooth and flowing |
| type of power | hard and forceful | soft and smooth | hard and soft together |
| movement requirements | strictly in accordance to rules | in accordance to rules | naturally will fit patterns |
| positions | expansive | compact | round and full |
| power to train | train whole body power, seek hardness | train relaxed power, seek softness | train agility, seek high skill |
| speed to train | seek integration in speed | seek lengthening in slowness | fast and slow blend naturally |

| CATEGORIES | LEVEL ONE | LEVEL TWO | LEVEL THREE |
|---|---|---|---|
| attitude | body upright and *qi* strong | take care of all directions | spirit rounded and lively |
| qualities manifested in movements | rise and fall as a unit | power rounded, mind farseeing | spirit and mind fully connected |
| use | have shape and image | have name, have shape, but leave no trace | no shape, no image, no sound |
| control of power | can release whole body power | can accept and control | can use naturally |
| combative use | emphasize attack | emphasize control | emphasize diffusion |
| foot landing | has sound | no sound | hear the sound of thunder although there is no sound |
| power applied from | hands | elbows | body core |
| coordination of *qi* in the *dantian* during power release | settle *qi* to *dantian* | gather *qi* in *dantian* | move *qi* in *dantian* |
| big heavenly circuit and *dantian* | strengthen *dantian* | train whole heavenly circuit | move through whole heavenly circuit |
| *qi* and mind connection | urge the strength with the *qi* | lead the *qi* with the mind | no mind, no *qi* |
| use of *qi* | use strength to lead *qi* | use *qi* to nourish the spirit | use spirit to control *qi* |
| the *dantian* being trained | lower *dantian* | middle *dantian* | upper *dantian* |

| breathing | control breath, shows form outside | controlled breath, shows form inside | embryo breath, shows no form |
|---|---|---|---|
| length of breath | inhale long, exhale short; short and powerful | inhale and exhale long; controlled and soft, lead short to draw long | long and short as needed; gentle, level, deep, long |
| breathing requirement | controlled | coordinated | natural |

# TEACHING METHODOLOGY

## DISCUSSION OF POWER

Both teacher and player need to understand the difference between power and strength, or force. The power (*jin*) spoken of in martial arts is far removed from the strength (*li*) spoken of in daily life. Strength (*li*) refers to the amount of strength or force a person has. This includes the physical ability or fitness and the strength of contraction of the muscles. Power (*jin*) in martial arts refers to a combination of repeatedly trained skills added to the muscular force trained in these skills. Power is integrated body strength created by the intentional coordination of muscular contraction plus the orderly synchronization called for to perform specific skills. For this reason, each specific power needs to be trained for each specific skill. Power is developed gradually with repeated practice of proper technique.[23]

---

[23] Editor's note: Simply put, power is strength that has been harnessed and trained until actions can be done in a relaxed and smooth way with the same force output.

# TEACHING PROGRESSIONS

1. First teach post standing in each position to teach students the proper hand and body placement, shapes, and angles. This reinforces their self-awareness so that the correct position becomes habitual sooner than if they only practised moving techniques. Post standing teaches the amount of flex in the legs, the position of the feet and knees, the angles of the body, the exact flex of the arms and the forward press of the hands. The students first need to find the correct outer appearance, then train the intent, energy and power and put that into the stance. This will speed up mastery of the technique. The teacher must explain the most essential points and make sure every body segment is in the correct position. Correct the students when they are post standing. If mistakes are corrected in a timely fashion the students will form correct habits.

2. Have students practise stationary alternation of the hand techniques without moving their feet. Do not have them apply power for this practice, but concentrate on the line of action, proper height and angles of the hands and arms, and focus on the requirements and movement standards.

3. Have the students perform the full movement slowly. Keep the movement slow and stop for a while in every set position, for every single movement. This training method helps to fine-tune the movement, helps master the lines and movement patterns of each body segment, and gradually develops a conditioned reflex, serving to make the movement more coordinated. This is simply a training method however, and once the movement has been mastered it should be sped up and trained at regular speed.

4. In group practice, have the students do the movements in unison on command. On the count of one take the half-step advance and do the first hand actions. On the count of two step forward and hit. Carry on the practice according to the size of the training area.

To use *standard drill* as an example, on 'one' advance the lead foot a half-step, lift the rear foot and press down the lead hand. On 'two' step the rear foot through, follow in with the other foot, drill the rear hand forward and up and pull the lead hand back to the belly.

## SAMPLE TEACHING PROGRESSION OVER THREE YEARS

1. Post standing (in the old days, this would last the full three years before going on to anything else).

2. Part training (first for split, then more quickly for the other four).

3. Slow and soft whole training (first for split, then more quickly for the other four).

4. Body technique within the techniques.

5. Pounding post standing.

6. Five elements connected form.

7. Partner forms.

8. Applications.

**TEACHING PROGRESSION WITHIN THE FIVE PHASES**

DRILL: Drill should be learned after split. Many teachers teach drive after split because of the five element controlling order 'metal controlling wood' but I teach drill after split, using the creation order 'metal creates water.' Drill uses the same footwork as split, so teaching it after split reinforces the most basic footwork of Xingyi.

DRIVE: When teaching drive, the *back leg hit drive* should be learned first, then the *lead leg hit drive,* then the variation *reverse stance (alternating) drive.* There are many different ways of doing drive but they all involve the basic idea that the arm extends into a straight punch. The various punches look quite similar, but their intent will differ – some hook and hit, some press and hit, some block out and hit, some drop the wrist and hit. Some do a punch for each step, some do a punch for two steps, and some do two punches for each step. If the basic power of the straight punch has not been found, the variations will not be well done.

# TEACHING SUGGESTIONS[24]

- All five of the basic techniques have different positions and power applications, and different requirements for body position, hand form and stance. So you must always start out with post standing for each to form an initial model of the position. This helps the student gain a basic understanding of the structure and action.

- The teacher must correct mistakes as soon as they occur, and point out the key elements of the technique. Correct the students individually and as a group. Some errors are almost universal, and some are idiosyncratic. As the classics say, "it is easy to learn but very difficult to change," so it is particularly important to form correct form at the beginning. If a mistake becomes a habit it will be more difficult to change later.

- The above being said, allow time for the student to examine his or her own movement. Do not constantly correct or correct fine details beyond the level

---

[24] Editor's note: I have collected these teaching suggestions from throughout the original book and placed them all together to avoid repetition and make sure they are noticed. I have also added a few notes taken during teaching sessions, not written in the book. I have not put words into the author's mouth, but I have taken them from his mouth and written them down (with his permission).

## CHAPTER FOUR: THEORY AND TEACHING

of the student. In the old days, the teacher would show something three times, then it was up to you to find the technique yourself – "if you find it yourself you won't forget it".[25]

- Explain and demonstrate the universal principles of Xingyi behind each action, so the students can understand and apply the principles and learn to self correct.

- Demonstrate often to give the students a firm impression of the actions. Demonstrate not only the proper movements as you wish students to perform them, but also lively action with power and rhythm to give students an image of what they seek to achieve.

- When the students are learning they should start out slowly and speed up only when they are comfortable with the action.

- Do not explain too much about rhythm and power at first. Wait until the students are ready to absorb new or advanced information. When a comfort level is reached at a certain level, you can explain more detailed action, power and coordination.

- Use 'part and whole' method for both teaching and training. This establishes a solid understanding of the movement. This method is explained in detail in the following pages.

- Explain and demonstrate the line of power and the expression of both soft and hard power in each action so the student understands the efficiency of the proper movements and has an idea of whole body power for each action.

- Explain and demonstrate fighting and self-defense applications so that students can easily see where a wrong action would not work, and can imagine what they might be doing.

- Once the students have placed the feet and hands essentially in the right place, emphasize the action of the more central segments – shoulders, hips, elbows, and knees. Power and smooth lines come from moving from the centre of the body.

- Beginners must study and practise the basics diligently to master the requirements. They must wholeheartedly work on the finer points of the movements. They must work gradually and in an orderly way, never trying to rush the learning process. Repeated practice will bring gradual improvement. Although the movements are not complex, mastering their essence is not the work of a day.

---

[25] Editor's note: My Chen Taijiquan teacher Huan Dahai used to say this, but the author agreed that he had also heard it from his teachers.

## SAMPLE CLASS ORGANIZATION

1. Post standing.

2. Warm-up.

3. Five minutes of soft techniques.

4. Main class: steady and hard (techniques, forms, applications).

5. Gradual cool down with soft techniques.

6. Cool down relaxing movements.

## PART AND WHOLE METHOD

Techniques should be taught using the 'part and whole' method to help students learn and get a good grasp of the actions and specific requirements of each technique. This methodology has quite good results and helps students learn quickly. Note, however, that the part method should not be continued too long because all actions in Xingyi form an integrated whole.[26]

**PART METHOD: (EXAMPLE) STRAIGHT-LINE ADVANCING FOOTWORK** ACTION 1: Stand in the *santi* stance with the left foot leading. Clench the right fist and place the fist heart on the belly. Grasp the right wrist with the left hand. Tuck the elbows lightly in at the ribs. Hold the head up and look forward. (image: legs only 1)

ACTION 2: Advance the left foot a half-step and follow in with the right to beside the left ankle without touching down (beginners may touch the toes down). Stand firmly on the left leg with the right foot about an inch off the ground and the knees flexed and together. The body should not come up. Stance height should remain the same as the *santi* stance. Press up the head and look forward. (image: legs only 2)

ACTION 3: Take a big step forward with the right foot and follow in a half-step with the left to take a *santi* stance with the right foot leading and the left behind. The hands remain on the belly. Press the head up and look forward. (image: legs only 3)

---

[26] Editor's note: In stepping, for example, the body action is not done. Doing straight-line stepping as a practice is good for learning the drive off the back leg and the raking power of the lead foot, but does not use the body power of, for example, split or drill. Too much stepping alone may lead to students not understanding the difference between the techniques. Both stepping and hand technique part training are useful, however, as a warm-up even for advanced practitioners.

CHAPTER FOUR: THEORY AND TEACHING    239

LEGS ONLY    1    2    3

- Carry on with right and left steps.

**Pointers for Part Method Footwork Practice**

   o   Do not take too big a step forward with the first half-step advance; the back foot should be able to step without great effort. Do not lift the toes up too much when stepping. Lift the foot naturally and keep in mind that you are using the toes to reach forward and grab. This should prevent you from lifting the foot up too high and flipping the sole of the foot upwards. The progression for landing the foot is: first land the heel, then immediately place the whole foot and grab with the toes.

   o   Press the knees together when you follow the right foot in beside the left. The right foot should stop at the inside of the left ankle. Pick up the foot quickly and stop with stability. The sole of the raised foot should be level and about an inch off the ground.

   o   When you stride the right foot forward into the final stance, you should reach out, keeping in mind that the right foot is striking forward. Fully utilize the backward thrust from the left foot – the lead foot charges and the rear foot thrusts. As the right foot lands it should have a forward and downward trampling power. Once you are comfortable with the action of the stepping you can increase the trampling power and pay more attention to the kinesthetic awareness in the knees [the feeling of compressing like a spring, and getting the spring rebound back for the drive forward, and the sharp braking power of the lead knee, neither holding it stiff nor really bending].

   o   The left foot follows in again to take a *santi* stance but the stance length is slightly shorter than a post standing *santishi*. Pay attention to using the lower back to bring the hip up, keeping the hip joint rolled inward, using the hip to bring the knee in, and using the knee to bring the foot in. The follow-in step should be quick.

## 240  THEORY AND TEACHING

    o    You should train the footwork a lot to develop a correct and dependable movement pattern.

**PART METHOD: (EXAMPLE) HANDWORK FOR SPLIT**

Separate hand technique practice is a fixed stance practice. Stand with the feet shoulder width apart and parallel, with the left hand in front and the right hand at the belly. Put the left shoulder forward, so that the hands are in a similar position to *santishi*. (image: arms only 1)

ACTION 1: Clench the left hand and pull the fist in to the belly, then bring it up past the solar plexus to drill forward and up to nose height, twisting the ulnar edge and fist heart up. (image: arms only 2)

ACTION 2: Drill the right fist out to the left elbow and along above the left forearm. As it approaches the left hand rotate both inwardly and unclench the hands. Chop the right hand forward and down to chest height, and pull the left hand back to the belly. Put the right shoulder into the split. Press the head up and look forward. (image: arms only 3)

ARMS ONLY  1                2                3

- Carry on alternating left and right until you get a good grasp of the line and the requirements of the hand technique. This develops the correct pattern that should carry over when the footwork is added.

**WHOLE METHOD**

Once the student has gained a basic command of and becomes comfortable with the movements of the feet and hands separately he is ready for whole movement training.

The foot and hand actions can be put together and practised following a count from the teacher. The command must be cleanly followed, especially in group situations. The command should be given slowly at first then sped up once the students are comfortable with the movements.

CHAPTER FOUR: THEORY AND TEACHING    241

During this process the teacher should continually work to improve the students' understanding of and body awareness towards Xingyiquan's basic requirements.

## USE OF IMAGERY TO TEACH XINGYIQUAN

A teacher needs to demonstrate the correct movement so that the student can imitate the action. But in order for the student to learn more quickly, the teacher needs to explain how to use power, the nature of the specific power, and the coordination between body segments. Otherwise, the student will simply copy the apparent action and not get the full idea, with less than ideal results. The use of power is especially difficult to understand and difficult to teach. Imagery is a good method to use when the student is learning the movements, before he is used to them, before he understands the requirements, and before he understands how to get and use power. At this time the student can use imagination to direct his actions. Using this method enables the student to get a grasp of the power in each movement within a relatively short time.

It is important that the teacher uses the appropriate method, and it is also important that the students are enthusiastic and involved. If the students are mentally engaged in a practice session then they get a grasp on the actions more quickly and have better quality of movement. The method is to borrow some image when explaining movements, usually an action or example that is met with or seen everyday, something the student can personally know from experience. It needs to be something that further illustrates the power of Xingyiquan, which can deepen the understanding of a movement from a variety of angles. When the students are practising, they have a clear example or an image of an action imprinted in their minds, so that they can get the feeling themselves and find the action from their own experience. The things that one learns through imagery leave a deeper imprint, are understood more quickly, and remembered more surely. Using imagery can get twice the results with half the effort.

**A FEW EXAMPLES OF IMAGERY:**

**CANNON:** Introduce the image of how the cannon punch hits out, "It explodes like an artillery cannon, the cannon ball is launched suddenly, and it has the most violent nature. " How can one reflect this violent nature? How can one perform this whole body power, then add in the driving footwork, and get the upper and lower segments to work together? How can one pre-load then launch the punch to hit out quickly with stability and ferocity? When doing slow motion practice you should try to feel the connections between the segments, but when fighting there is no separation between the first to start and the last to arrive. "Once one thing moves there is nothing that does not move," "the eyes arrive, the spirit arrives, and the hands arrive ". Often, students can get the basic movement, but cannot get the power of the back and shoulders.

- Give the students this image – pretend the lead fist is a heavy rock. When you launch your power, forcefully push the rock forward, the farther the better. Do this action in a fixed stance position at first to learn it, and then add the footwork.

**CROSSCUT:** Crosscut is like wringing a rope. The fists and arms must have three types of power – twist, roll in, and drill. The legs should have a scissoring power between them. How can this type of power be put into action? How do you need to do it to be exactly the right kind of power?

- Give the students this image – pretend you are wringing a towel to dry, one arm twists outwardly and one twists inwardly. The leading hand twists and extends outward, while the rear hand twists inward and pulls back, tightening the towel.

This example gives them the idea of twisting the arms, one outwardly and one inwardly, one up and one down, helping each other out. You need to add that when the leading hand hits with the crosscut it should have a drilling power, as if it is an awl boring a hole, driving forward. It should have a pressure forward and a spiraling strength.

- To learn the scissoring power of the legs, pretend you are standing on ice. Rotate the hip joints to prevent your legs from sliding out.

- To learn the bodywork, pretend you are squeezing a rubber ball. Pull back with the leading hip and push forward with the rear hip, compressing the body core.

- The legs as they step are just like scissors cutting – the shins rub against each other as they pass.

You can add up the images of wringing the towel to feel the twisting power of the arms, the awl to feel the drilling power, standing on ice and cutting with scissors to feel the scissoring power of the legs and body. In this way, the various powers of the crosscut can be understood and the students can more quickly come to grips with the technique.

**TIGER POUNCE** [similar to a double split]: When teaching the tiger pounce, four statements can explain the action well:

> "The hands drill as they rise,
> The hands turn over as they drop.
> The hands and feet land together.
> The lower back lengthens and the shoulders extend."

The first three are relatively easy to understand and do, but the last is neither easy to understand nor do. What exactly is lengthening? What exactly is extending? When do you lengthen and extend? The actions of lengthening the lower back and extending the shoulders are key to launching this splitting power. If these

## CHAPTER FOUR: THEORY AND TEACHING   243

questions are not resolved clearly it will be difficult to get power into the tiger pounce. You should emphasize the actions of lengthening the lower back and extending the shoulders. First explain the line of action, then, once the students have mastered the line of action, add the image.

- Give the students this image: pretend you are holding a large rock at your belly. As you drill up, raise the rock to your chest, and then forcefully push the rock forward with both hands. Use power from your belly as you do the turning over action, use your lower back to press forward and up (bring the shoulders back slightly, open the chest, press the head up) – be sure to do the actions at the same time. At the instant that you push forward, release the shoulders, close the chest, and tuck the belly. This action is what extends the shoulders forward.

Performing the action like this fits with both biomechanical and combat principles. Only when it is done this way does it fit with martial theory of using the body's core area to launch power, give a fierce whole body power, and use internal power.

**NOTE:**

- The power of Xingyiquan has this characteristic – if a student can get a feel for the power of one or two techniques then it is relatively easy to get power for the others.
- The use of images must be appropriate and apt, so that the teacher can explain clearly and the students can understand the power of the action. If the power of an action is complicated, then it should be explained from a number of angles.
- You should choose actions or images often seen in daily life. Transform the strange to the commonplace, the complicated to the simple, and the imaginary to the concrete.

There is also a natural progression in the use of this method.

- In the early stages of learning you should emphasize correct static positions and final positions after action.
- In the intermediate stages of learning you can use imagery to speed up the mastery of power use, using the mind to lead, solidify, and put more detail into the movements themselves.
- After the power of the techniques has been gradually mastered you have to practise more – repeat and repeat to solidify the action, so that the action becomes an established pattern and the use of power becomes deeply ingrained. Once the movements become well established then you don't need to use an image when practising. You can think of the combat application, imagining the attachment and power flow to the opponent's body. In this way you can gradually develop from imitation of an action to being the likeness

of the action.

Only with long term, unceasing, and thoughtful repetition can we improve our fundamental skill. Any teaching method is an aid to the student, but in the end, it is up to the student to learn.

APPENDIX

# GLOSSARY

## PINYIN ORDER

### SECTION ONE: BASIC PARTS OF THE BODY

| | | |
|---|---|---|
| bǎng | 膀 | upper arm and shoulder, deltoid area |
| bēi or bī | 臂 | upper arm, or whole arm |
| bèi | 背 | upper and mid back |
| bō | 脖 | neck |
| chǐ gǔ | 尺骨 | ulnar bone; little finger side of forearm |
| dà tuǐ | 大腿 | thigh |
| ěr | 耳 | ear |
| fèi | 肺 | lungs; Lung when referring to the Chinese meaning (see Chapter 4) |
| fù | 腹 | abdomen, belly |
| gān | 肝 | liver; Liver when referring to the Chinese meaning (see Chapter 4) |
| gēn | 跟 | heel |
| hǔ kǒu | 虎口 | thumb to forefinger web, called the 'tiger's mouth,' |
| jiān | 肩 | shoulder, also called jiān bǎng 肩膀 |
| jiǎo | 脚 | foot |
| jiǎo gēn | 脚跟 | heel of the foot |
| jǐng | 颈 | nape of neck |
| kuà | 胯 | hip joint |
| lèi | 肋 | ribs |
| pí | 脾 | spleen; Spleen when referring to the Chinese meaning (see Chapter 4) |
| qián bì | 前臂 | forearm, also pronounced qián bēi |
| quán | 拳 | fist |
| quán bèi | 拳背 | the back of the fist |
| quán fēng | 拳峰 | knuckle edge of the fist |
| quán lún | 拳轮 | the base of the fist |
| quán miàn | 拳面 | face of the fist, the normal punching surface |
| quán xīn | 拳心 | heart of the fist, into which the fingers curl |
| quán yǎn | 拳眼 | eye of the fist, formed by thumb and index finger |
| shèn | 肾 | kidney; Kidney when referring to the Chinese meaning (see Chapter 4) |

| | | |
|---|---|---|
| shǒu | 手 | hand |
| shǒu wàn | 手腕 | wrist |
| shǒu zhǐ | 手指 | fingers |
| tóu | 头 | head |
| tuǐ | 腿 | leg |
| xī | 膝 | knee, often pronounced qī |
| xiǎo tuǐ | 小腿 | lower leg, shank |
| xīn | 心 | heart; Heart when referring to the Chinese meaning (see Chapter 4 |
| xīn wōr | 心窝 | pit of the stomach, solar plexus |
| xiōng | 胸 | chest |
| yāo | 腰 | lower back, small of the back, waist, lumbar area |
| zhǎng | 掌 | palm |
| zhǎng xīn | 掌心 | centre of the palm |
| zhǒu | 肘 | elbow |

## SECTION TWO: XINGYI TERMINOLOGY

| | | |
|---|---|---|
| àn | 按 | press down |
| àn jìn | 暗劲 | hidden power |
| ào bù | 拗步 | stance with the opposite hand and foot forward, commonly called a reverse stance. |
| bā lì | 扒力 | raking power |
| bā zì bù | 八字步 | character eight stance, feet close to and angled towards each other, not touching |
| bā zì gōng | 八字功 | eight skills of Xingyiquan |
| bǎi bù | 摆步 | hook-out step |
| bān | 搬 | remove, move something |
| bàn mǎ bù | 半马步 | half horse stance |
| bào | 抱 | hold in the crook of the arm, usually with both arms, looking like an embrace |
| bēng quán | 崩拳 | drive, crushing punch; a straight punch done with a driving power, one of the five mother fists of Xingyi |
| bīng bù | 并步 | stand upright with feet together |
| bō | 拨 | knock aside |
| cǎi | 踩 | step on, trample |

# APPENDIX 247

| | | | |
|---|---|---|---|
| chǎn shǒu | 缠手 | coil the hand around something, hooking |
| chāo | 抄 | hoist, bend the elbow to lift up with the forearm |
| chè bù | 撤步 | withdraw, step the rear foot back or bring the lead foot back to the rear foot |
| chén qì | 沉气 | settle or sink the *qi* down |
| chēng | 撑 | brace out with one or both hands |
| chōu | 抽 | draw out |
| cuī | 催 | urge, hurry, press |
| cùn jìn | 寸劲 | one inch power |
| cuò | 挫 | check, a short powerful block or strike |
| cuō dì | 蹉地 | land with a rubbing action, stamp with impetus forward and down |
| dǎ | 打 | hit |
| dài | 带 | draw, drag towards the rear |
| dàn | 弹 | a ball, pellet; a bomb |
| dān tián | 丹田 | *dantian*, in martial arts usually means the lower part of the torso; area within the pelvic girdle |
| dáo | 捯 | pull hand over hand |
| dìng bù | 定步 | a fixed stance, not moving the feet |
| dūn | 蹲 | squat, sit on haunches |
| fā jìn | 发劲 | launch power, shoot force, initiate a hit |
| fā lì | 发力 | launch power, shoot force, initiate a hit |
| fú hǔ zhuāng | 伏虎桩 | subdue the tiger post standing |
| fǔ zhǎng | 俯掌 | facing down palm |
| gài | 盖 | cover, a controlling move downwards |
| gāng jìn | 刚劲 | hard power |
| gé | 格 | block across |
| gēn bù | 跟步 | a follow-in step, the rear foot moving up towards the lead foot |
| gōng bù | 弓步 | bow stance |
| guà | 挂 | hooking block or trap |
| guàn | 贯 | inside hook punch |
| guǒ | 裹 | wrap around, enclose in the arms |
| guǒ jìn | 裹劲 | a wrapping power |
| héng | 横 | a horizontal, crossways or transverse movement or placement. |

| | | |
|---|---|---|
| héng quán | 横拳 | crosscut, crossing fist, one of the five mother fists of Xingyi |
| huà jìn | 化劲 | transformed power |
| hún yuán | 浑元 | primordial, or mixed essence, refers to the time when the heaven and earth began. |
| hún yuán zhuāng | 浑元桩 | primordial post standing |
| huǒ | 火 | fire, one of the five elemental elements |
| huó bù | 活步 | moving stance |
| jī xíng bù | 鸡形步 | chicken stepping, raising the non-supporting foot by the supporting foot |
| jiàng lóng zhuāng | 降龙桩 | descend the dragon post standing |
| jiǎo | 绞 | wind around, entangle |
| jié | 截 | intercept, cut across |
| jīn | 金 | metal, one of the five elements |
| jìn | 进 | enter, advance: step the front foot a half-step forward or the back foot forward |
| kāi bù | 开步 | open parallel stance, shoulder width |
| kē | 磕 | knock, bump |
| kòu | 扣 | tuck in, concave shape |
| kòu bù | 扣步 | hook-in step |
| lā | 拉 | pull |
| lán | 拦 | circular block, trap |
| liāo quán | 撩拳 | slice up with a relatively straight arm |
| liàn gōng | 练功 | train skill; work hard to enhance health, develop fitness, develop martial arts internal and external skills. |
| lǐng | 领 | lead along |
| lōu | 搂 | brush aside |
| luò | 落 | to land, to lower |
| mǎ bù | 马步 | horse stance |
| mài bù | 迈步 | stride, a large step |
| míng jìn | 明劲 | obvious power, hard power |
| mù | 木 | wood, one of the five elements |
| ná | 拿 | trap, hold |
| níng jìn | 拧劲 | twisting power |
| pāi | 拍 | slap or control with open palm |

| | | | |
|---|---|---|---|
| pào quán | 炮拳 | | cannon punch, pounding fist, simultaneous block and punch, one of the five mother fists of Xingyiquan |
| pī quán | 劈拳 | | split, chop down, one of the five mother fists of Xingyi |
| pū | 扑 | | pounce |
| qǐ | 起 | | initiate an action, rise |
| qì | 气 | | vital energy, breath; both energy and matter that carries vital energy |
| qiē | 切 | | cut, slice |
| sān cái zhuāng | 三才桩 | | 'three attributes' standing, also referred to as *santi* post standing |
| sān tǐ | 三体 | | the 60/40 to 70/30 weighted stance when the arms are in positions other than *santishi* |
| sān tǐ shì | 三体势 | | three body stance, the stance itself rather than the post standing training |
| sān tǐ shì zhuāng | 三体势桩 | | three body post standing |
| shàng bù | 上步 | | step forward |
| shuǐ | 水 | | water, one of the five elements |
| shùn | 顺 | | smooth, going along with the natural path |
| shùn bù | 顺步 | | aligned stance. In Xingyi, this is usually a *santi* stance with the same hand and foot forward |
| sōng | 松 | | relax and extend, release the tension |
| suō shēn | 缩身 | | contract, draw in or draw back in the body |
| tā wàn | 塌腕 | | sit the wrist, sink the wrist |
| tán | 弹 | | to shoot (as with a catapult); spring; springy, elastic |
| tī | 踢 | | kick |
| tiǎo | 挑 | | scoop |
| tiǎo jìn | 挑劲 | | slicing up power with the arm quite solid and the wrist cocked |
| tǔ | 土 | | earth, one of the five elements |
| tuì bù | 退步 | | retreat: step the back foot a half-step back or step the front foot back |
| tuō | 托 | | carry, hit with the palm fingers usually down |
| wǔ xíng lián huán | 五行连环 | | the short name for the five elemental fists connected form |

| | | | |
|---|---|---|---|
| wǔ xíng lián huán quán | | 五行连环拳 | the most basic Xingyi form, five elemental fists connected form |
| wǔ xíng quán | | 五行拳 | Xingyi's five basic techniques, five training methods to develop five types of power generation |
| wǔ xíng xiāng kè | | 五行相克 | the controlling order of the five elements |
| wǔ xíng xiāng shēng | | 五行相生 | the creating order of the five elements |
| xiē bù | | 歇步 | resting stance, legs crossed and sitting |
| xīn | | 心 | heart, the emotional mind |
| xīn yì liù hé quán | | 心意六合拳 | Xinyi Liuhequan, the style from which Xingyiquan grew |
| xīn yì quán | | 心意拳 | Xinyiquan, 'heart and intent' style, also referred to as Xinyi Liuhequan |
| xíng | | 形 | form, shape, structure; external structure and action |
| xíng yì lián quán | | 形意连拳 | a basic Xingyi form combining the five elemental fists |
| xíng yì mǔ quán | | 形意母拳 | the five fundamental techniques of Xingyi |
| xíng yì quán | | 形意拳 | Xingyiquan, 'external shape combined with internal intent' style |
| yā | | 压 | press down, control |
| yǎn zhǒu | | 掩肘 | a hooking cover, usually rolling in, with an elbow |
| yǎng zhǎng | | 仰掌 | facing up palm |
| yáo shēn | | 摇身 | shaking the body, is often used to mean a technique of dodging with the footwork |
| yì | | 意 | will, the intentional mind |
| yì quán | | 意拳 | Yiquan, also called Dachengquan, a style developed from Xingyiquan |
| zá quán | | 砸拳 | a pounding strike with the fist |
| zá zhuāng | | 砸桩 | pounding post standing |
| zhāi | | 摘 | pluck |
| zhàn zhuāng | | 站桩 | post standing |
| zhèn jiǎo | | 震脚 | stomp, a heavy stamp |
| zhuā | | 抓 | grab |
| zhuàn shēn | | 转身 | turn around |
| zhuāng gōng | | 桩功 | the training of post standing |
| zhuàng | | 撞 | shove, barge into, ram |

| | | |
|---|---|---|
| zǐ wǔ zhuāng | 子午桩 | meridian line post standing, also referred to as *santi* post standing |
| zuān quán | 钻拳 | drill, one of the five mother fists of Xingyi |

## SECTION THREE: XINGYI MOVEMENT NAMES

| | | |
|---|---|---|
| bā zì gōng | 八字功 | Eight Skills |
| bái hè liàng chì | 白鹤亮翅 | White Crane Flashes Its Wings |
| bái shé bō cǎo | 白蛇拨草 | White Snake Slithers through the Grass |
| bái shé chán shēn | 白蛇缠身 | White Snake Coils its Body |
| bái shé tù xìn | 白蛇吐信 | White Snake Spits its Tongue |
| bái yuán xiàn guǒ | 白猿献果 | White Ape Presents Fruit |
| bēng quán | 崩拳 | Crushing Fist, Driving Punch |
| dài | 带 | Draw |
| dān mǎ xíng | 单马形 | Single Horse |
| dān zhǎn chì | 单展翅 | Stretch Out One Wing |
| dīng bù xià chā zhǎng | 丁步下插掌 | T Stance Stab Down |
| dǐng shì | 顶势 | Butt |
| dǐng zhǒu | 顶肘 | Elbow Butt |
| dǐng zì gōng | 顶字功 | Butting Skill |
| fān shēn pào | 翻身炮 | Wheel Around and Pound |
| fēng bǎi hé yè | 风摆荷叶 | Wind Sways the Lotus Leaves |
| gǔn shǒu | 滚手 | Trundle |
| guǒ shǒu | 裹手 | Wrap |
| guǒ zì gōng | 裹字功 | Wrapping Skill |
| hé jiān shì | 合肩势 | Close the Shoulders |
| hēi hǔ chū dòng | 黑虎出洞 | Black Tiger Leaves its Den |
| hēi xióng chū dòng | 黑熊出洞 | Black Bear Leaves its Den |
| héng dēng | 横蹬 | Crossways Heel Kick |
| héng jiāng fān làng | 横江翻浪 | Cross the River by Overturning the Waves |
| héng quán | 横拳 | Crosscut, Crossing Fist |
| hóu dūn | 猴蹲 | Monkey Sits on its Haunches |
| hóu xíng | 猴形 | Monkey Model |
| hǔ bào | 虎抱 | Tiger Embraces |
| hǔ chēng | 虎撑 | Tiger Braces |
| hǔ jié | 虎截 | Tiger Intercepts |

| | | |
|---|---|---|
| hǔ lán | 虎拦 | Tiger Traps |
| hǔ pū | 虎扑 | Tiger Pounces |
| hǔ tuō | 虎托 | Tiger Carries |
| hǔ xíng | 虎形 | Tiger Model |
| jī xíng | 鸡形 | Chicken Model |
| jī xíng sì bǎ dòng zuò | 鸡形四把动作 | Four Techniques Of Chicken |
| jié shì | 截势 | Intercept |
| jié shǒu | 截手 | Interception |
| jié zì gōng | 截字功 | Intercepting Skill |
| jīn jī bào xiǎo | 金鸡报晓 | Golden Rooster Heralds the Dawn |
| jīn jī dēng jiǎo | 金鸡蹬脚 | Golden Rooster Thrusts a Foot |
| jīn jī dǒu líng | 金鸡抖翎 | Golden Rooster Shakes its Feathers |
| jīn jī dú lì | 金鸡独立 | Golden Rooster Stands on One Leg |
| jīn jī shàng jià | 金鸡上架 | Golden Rooster Blocks Up |
| jīn jī shí mǐ | 金鸡食米 | Golden Rooster Pecks a Grain of Rice |
| jīn jī tà xuě | 金鸡踏雪 | Golden Rooster Treads on Snow |
| jīn jī zhǎn chì | 金鸡展翅 | Golden Rooster Spreads its Wings |
| jīn jī zhuó shuǐ | 金鸡啄水 | Golden Rooster Drinks Water |
| kuà hǔ | 跨虎 | Sit Astride the Tiger |
| kuà shì | 跨势 | Bridge |
| kuà zì gōng | 跨字功 | Bridging Skill |
| lā bō dǎ | 拉拨打 | Pull, Knock Aside and Hit |
| lǎn lóng wò dào | 懒龙卧道 | Lazy Dragon Lies in the Road |
| lǎo xióng zhuàng bǎng | 老熊撞膀 | Old Bear Shoves from its Shoulder |
| lēi quán | 勒拳 | Restrain |
| liāo yīn zhǎng | 撩阴掌 | Slice to the Groin |
| lǐng shì | 领势 | Guide |
| lǐng zì gōng | 领字功 | Guiding Skill |
| lóng hǔ xiāng jiāo | 龙虎相交 | Dragon and Tiger Play Together |
| lóng xíng | 龙形 | Dragon Model |
| lōu shǒu gài pī | 搂手盖劈 | Brush Aside, Cover and Chop |
| lǔ dài | 捋带 | Stroking Draw |
| lǔ shǒu | 捋手 | Stroke or Pull |
| lǔ shǒu guàn ér | 捋手贯耳 | Stroke, Hook to Ear |

# APPENDIX 253

| | | |
|---|---|---|
| lǔ shǒu xī zhuàng | 捋手膝撞 | Pull and Knee Butt |
| lūn pī héng zhé | 抡劈横折 | Swinging Chop with Crossing Cut |
| mǎ xíng | 马形 | Horse Model |
| māo xǐ liǎn | 猫洗脸 | Cat Washes its Face |
| měng hǔ tiào jiàn | 猛虎跳涧 | Fierce Tiger Jumps over the Ravine |
| pào quán | 炮拳 | Cannon Punch, Pounding Fist |
| pī quán | 劈拳 | Split, Splitting Fist |
| qǐ shì | 起势 | Opening Move |
| qiē bó | 切脖 | Cut to the Neck |
| sān pán luò dì | 三盘落地 | Three Basins on the Ground |
| sān zhǎng | 三掌 | Triple Palm Strike |
| shé chán shēn | 蛇缠身 | Snake Coils its Body |
| shé xíng | 蛇形 | Snake Model |
| shōu shì | 收势 | Closing Move |
| shuāng guǒ | 双裹 | Double Wrap |
| shuāng jié | 双截 | Double Intercept |
| shuāng mǎ xíng | 双马形 | Double Horse |
| shuāng zhǎn chì | 双展翅 | Spread Both Wings |
| shuāng zhuàng zhǎng | 双撞掌 | Double Shove |
| shùn shǒu qiān yáng | 顺手牵羊 | Lead a sheep along |
| shùn shuǐ tuī zhōu | 顺水推舟 | Push a Boat Downstream |
| sì jiǎo hóu xíng | 四角猴形 | Monkey To Four Corners |
| tà bù lóng xíng | 踏步龙形 | Stomping Dragon Model |
| tà zhǎng | 踏掌 | Tamp |
| tāi xíng | 鸟台形 | Wedge-tailed Hawk Model |
| tiǎo lǔ | 挑捋 | Scoop and Pull |
| tiǎo zhǎng | 挑掌 | Scoop |
| tiǎo zì gōng | 挑字功 | Scooping Skill |
| tōu dǎ | 偷打 | Sneak in a Hit |
| tóu dǐng | 头顶 | Head Butt |
| tuī chuāng wàng yuè | 推窗望月 | Push the Shutter to Gaze at the Moon |
| tuī shǒu | 推手 | Push |
| tuó xíng | 鼍形 | Alligator Model |
| wū lóng dào shuǐ | 乌龙倒水 | Black Dragon Pours Water |

| | | |
|---|---|---|
| wū lóng fān jiāng | 乌龙翻江 | Black Dragon Overturns the Waves |
| xià bēng quán | 下崩拳 | Low Crushing Punch |
| xióng xíng | 熊形 | Bear Model |
| yǎn zhǒu | 掩肘 | Elbow Cover |
| yàn zǐ chāo shuǐ | 燕子抄水 | Swallow Skims the Water |
| yàn zǐ zhǎn chì | 燕子展翅 | Swallow Spreads its Wings |
| yàn zǐ zuān tiān | 燕子钻天 | Swallow Pierces the Sky |
| yào xíng | 鹞形 | Sparrow Hawk Model |
| yào zǐ fān shēn | 鹞子翻身 | Sparrow Hawk Wheels Over |
| yào zǐ rù lín | 鹞子入林 | Sparrow Hawk Enters the Woods |
| yào zǐ shù shēn | 鹞子束身 | Sparrow Hawk Folds its Wings |
| yào zǐ zhǎn chì | 鹞子展翅 | Sparrow Hawk Spreads its Wings |
| yào zǐ zhuā jiān | 鹞子抓肩 | Sparrow Hawk Grasps a Shoulder |
| yào zǐ zhuō què | 鹞子捉雀 | Sparrow Hawk Grasps a Sparrow |
| yào zǐ zuān tiān | 鹞子钻天 | Sparrow Hawk Pierces the Sky |
| yīng xíng | 鹰形 | Eagle Model |
| yīng xióng hé liàn | 鹰熊合练 | Eagle and Bear Combined |
| yīng zhuō | 鹰捉 | Eagle Grasps |
| yuán hóu dào shéng | 猿猴捯绳 | Monkey Pulls at its Leash |
| yuán hóu dēng zhī | 猿猴蹬枝 | Ape Kicks a Branch |
| yuán hóu guà yìn | 白猿挂印 | Monkey Scratches its Mark |
| yuán hóu pá gān | 猿猴爬竿 | Monkey Scrambles up a Pole |
| yuán hóu zhāi táo | 猿猴摘桃 | Ape Plucks a Peach |
| yuán hóu zhuì zhī | 猿猴坠枝 | Ape Drops off a Branch |
| yuè bù lóng xíng | 跃步龙形 | Leaping Dragon |
| yún shì | 云势 | Pass |
| yún zì gōng | 云字功 | Passing Skill |
| zāi dǎ | 栽打 | Plant a Hit |
| zhǎn shì | 展势 | Spread |
| zhǎn zì gōng | 展字功 | Spreading Skill |
| zhé lóng chū xiàn | 蛰龙出现 | Hibernating Dragon Shows Itself |
| zhèn jiǎo | 震脚 | Stamp |
| zhí tàng hóu xíng | 直趟猴形 | Straight Line Monkey Model |
| zhuàng zhǎng | 撞掌 | Shove |

| zuān dǎ | 钻打 | Drilling Hit |
| zuān quán | 钻拳 | Drill, Drilling Fist |
| zuǒ lǐng yòu zāi | 左领右栽 | Lead left and Stick in right |

## SECTION FOUR: TERMS THAT FURTHER DEFINE MOVEMENTS

| ào bù | 拗步 | Reverse Stance |
| chē bù | 撤步 | Withdraw |
| fān shēn | 翻身 | Wheel Around |
| huàn bù | 换步 | Switchover Step |
| huí shēn | 回身 | Step Around, Turn Around |
| jìn bù | 进步 | Advance |
| shàng bù | 上步 | Step Forward |
| shuāng | 双 | Double |
| shuāng shǒu | 双手 | Two-handed |
| shùn bù | 顺步 | Aligned Stance |
| tuì bù | 退步 | Retreat |
| yáo shēn | 摇身 | Dodge |
| yòu | 右 | Right |
| yuán bù, yuán dì | 原地, 原步 | Fixed Step, Stationary |
| zhèn jiǎo | 震脚 | Stamp |
| zhuàn shēn | 转身 | Turn Around |
| zuǒ | 左 | Left |

## SECTION FIVE: XINGYI PEOPLE REFERRED TO IN THE BOOKS

Cao Jiwu (1622-1722) 曹继武. Apprenticed in Xinyi Liuhequan with Ji Longfeng.

Che Yizhai (1883-1914) 车毅斋. Apprenticed in Xingyiquan with Li Luoneng. Also known as Che Yonghong 车永宏.

Dai Longbang (c. 1713-1802) 戴龙帮. Apprenticed in Xinyi Liuhequan with Cao Jiwu.

Di Guoyong (1948- ) 邸国勇. Apprenticed in Shaolinquan and Xingyiquan with Zhao Zhong.

Guo Yunshen (late Qing dynasty) 郭云深. Apprenticed in Xingyiquan with Li Luoneng. Famous for his driving punch. Also known as Guo Yusheng 郭峪生.

Hao En'guang (late Qing dynasty) 郝恩光. Apprenticed in Xingyiquan with Li Cunyi.

Ji Longfeng (1602-1680) 姬龙峰. Thought to have created Xinyi Liuhequan. Also known as Ji Longfeng 姬龙风 and Ji Jike 姬际可.

Li Cunyi (1847-1921) 李存义. Apprenticed in Xingyiquan with Liu Qilan.

Li Luoneng (c. 1808-1890) 李洛能. Apprenticed in Xinyi Liuhequan with Dai Longbang. Thought to have created Xingyiquan. Proper name Li Feiyu 李飞羽.

Liu Huafu (dates unknown) 刘华甫. Apprenticed in Xingyiquan with Shang Yunxiang.

Liu Qilan (late Qing dynasty) 刘奇兰. Apprenticed in Xingyiquan with Li Luoneng.

Shang Yunxiang (1863-1937) 尚云祥. Apprenticed in Xingyiquan with Li Zhihe and Li Cunyi.

Yue Fei (1103-1142) 岳飞. A famous general and hero of the Song dynasty. Legendary creator of Xingyiquan.

Zhao Zhong (1912-1978) 赵忠. Apprenticed in Xingyiquan with Liu Huafu.

## ENGLISH ORDER

## SECTION SIX: BASIC PARTS OF THE BODY

| English | Pinyin | Chinese |
|---|---|---|
| abdomen, belly | fù | 腹 |
| arm, upper or whole arm | bēi or bì | 臂 |
| back of the fist | quán bèi | 拳背 |
| base of the fist | quán lún | 拳轮 |
| chest | xiōng | 胸 |
| deltoid area, upper arm and shoulder | bǎng | 膀 |
| ear | ěr | 耳 |
| elbow | zhǒu | 肘 |
| fingers | shǒu zhǐ | 手指 |
| fist | quán | 拳 |
| fist eye, formed by thumb and index finger | quán yǎn | 拳眼 |
| foot | jiǎo | 脚 |
| forearm | qián bì, or qián bēi | 前臂 |
| hand | shǒu | 手 |
| head | tóu | 头 |
| heart | xīn | 心 |
| heart of the fist, into which the fingers curl | quán xīn | 拳心 |
| heel | gēn, jiǎo gēn | 跟，脚跟 |

| | | |
|---|---|---|
| hip joint | kuà | 胯 |
| kidney | shèn | 肾 |
| knee | xī, often pronounced qī | 膝 |
| knuckles | quán miàn | 拳面 |
| knuckle edge | quán fēng | 拳峰 |
| leg | tuǐ | 腿 |
| liver | gān | 肝 |
| lungs | fèi | 肺 |
| nape of neck | jǐng | 颈 |
| neck | bō | 脖 |
| palm | zhǎng | 掌 |
| palm centre | zhǎng xīn | 掌心 |
| ribs | lèi | 肋 |
| shank, lower leg | xiǎo tuǐ | 小腿 |
| shoulder | jiān, also called jiān bǎng | 肩, 肩膀 |
| small of the back, waist, lumbar area | yāo | 腰 |
| solar plexus, pit of the stomach | xīn wōr | 心窝 |
| spleen | pí | 脾 |
| thigh | dà tuǐ | 大腿 |
| thumb to forefinger web, the 'tiger's mouth' | hǔ kǒu | 虎口 |
| ulnar bone; little finger side of forearm | chǐ gǔ | 尺骨 |
| upper back | bèi | 背 |
| wrist | shǒu wàn | 手腕 |

## SECTION SEVEN: XINGYI TERMINOLOGY

| | | |
|---|---|---|
| advance, enter: step the front foot forward | jìn bù | 进步 |
| aligned stance, same hand and foot forward | shùn bù | 顺步 |
| block across | gé | 格 |
| bow stance | gōng bù | 弓步 |
| brace out | chēng | 撑 |
| brush aside | lōu | 搂 |
| cannon punch, pounding fist | pào quán | 炮拳 |
| carry; to hit or break | tuō | 托 |
| character eight stance | bā zì bù | 八字步 |

# GLOSSARY

| | | |
|---|---|---|
| check | cuò | 挫 |
| chicken stepping, raising the non-supporting foot by the supporting leg at the ankle or higher | jī xíng bù | 鸡形步 |
| circular block, trap | lán | 拦 |
| clear or obvious power, hard power | míng jìn | 明劲 |
| coil the hand | chǎn shǒu | 缠手 |
| contract, draw in or draw back | suō shēn | 缩身 |
| controlling order of the five elements | wǔ xíng xiāng kè | 五行相克 |
| cover; a controlling move downwards | gài | 盖 |
| crosscut, crossing fist | héng quán | 横拳 |
| crossways or transverse movement or placement | héng | 横 |
| cut, slice | qiē | 切 |
| *dantian*, in Xingyiquan, usually means the lower *dantian*, the area within the pelvic girdle. | dān tián | 丹田 |
| draw out | chōu | 抽 |
| draw, drag towards the rear | dài | 带 |
| drill, drilling fist | zuān quán | 钻拳 |
| drive, crushing fist | bēng quán | 崩拳 |
| earth, one of the five elements | tǔ | 土 |
| elbow cover | yǎn zhǒu | 掩肘 |
| embrace, cradle, hold in the crook of the arms | bào | 抱 |
| entangle, wind around | jiǎo | 绞 |
| fire, one of the five elemental elements | huǒ | 火 |
| five basic techniques of Xingyiquan | wǔ xíng quán | 五行拳 |
| five elemental fists connected form | wǔ xíng lián huán (quán) | 五行连环（拳） |
| fixed stance | dìng bù | 定步 |
| follow, smooth, going along with the natural path | shùn | 顺 |
| follow-in step, the rear foot moving up towards the lead foot | gēn bù | 跟步 |
| form, the external structure | xíng | 形 |
| generating order of the five elements | wǔ xíng xiāng shēng | 五行相生 |
| grab | zhuā | 抓 |
| half horse stance | bàn mǎ bù | 半马步 |
| hard power | gāng jìn | 刚劲 |
| heart, the emotional mind | xīn | 心 |

| | | |
|---|---|---|
| hidden power | àn jìn | 暗劲 |
| hit | dǎ | 打 |
| hoist, bend the elbow to lift up with the forearm | chāo | 抄 |
| hook-in step | kòu bù | 扣步 |
| hooking block | guà | 挂 |
| hook-out step | bǎi bù | 摆步 |
| horse stance | mǎ bù | 马步 |
| inside hook punch | guàn | 贯 |
| intercept, cut across | jié | 截 |
| kick | tī | 踢 |
| knock aside | bō | 拨 |
| knock, bump | kē | 磕 |
| land, lower | luò | 落 |
| launch power. release, strength or energy | fā jìn, fā lì | 发劲，发力 |
| lead along | lǐng | 领 |
| lower the dragon post standing | jiàng lóng zhuāng | 降龙桩 |
| meridian post standing | zǐ wǔ zhuāng | 子午桩 |
| metal, one of the five elements | jīn | 金 |
| mother fists | xíng yì mǔ quán | 形意母拳 |
| moving stance | huó bù | 活步 |
| one inch power | cùn jìn | 寸劲 |
| open parallel stance, shoulder width | kāi bù | 开步 |
| palm down | fǔ zhǎng | 俯掌 |
| palm up | yǎng zhǎng | 仰掌 |
| pluck | zhāi | 摘 |
| post standing | zhàn zhuāng | 站桩 |
| post standing training | zhuāng gōng | 桩功 |
| pounce | pū | 扑 |
| pounding post training | zá zhuāng | 砸桩 |
| pounding strike with the fist | zá quán | 砸拳 |
| press down | àn | 按 |
| press down, control | yā | 压 |
| primordial post standing | hún yuán zhuāng | 浑元桩 |
| primordial, or mixed essence | hún yuán | 浑元 |

| | | |
|---|---|---|
| pull | lā | 拉 |
| pull hand over hand | dáo | 捯 |
| raking power | bā lì | 扒力 |
| relax and extend, release the tension | sōng | 松 |
| remove, move something | bān | 搬 |
| resting stance, legs crossed and sitting | xiē bù | 歇步 |
| retreat | tuì bù | 退步 |
| reverse stance | ào bù | 拗步 |
| rise; initiate an action | qǐ | 起 |
| scoop | tiāo | 挑 |
| settle the *qi* down | chén qì | 沉气 |
| shaking the body, dodging | yáo shēn | 摇身 |
| shoot (as with a catapult); springy, elastic | tán | 弹 |
| shove, barge into | zhuàng | 撞 |
| sink the wrist | tā wàn | 塌腕 |
| slap or control with an open palm | pāi | 拍 |
| slice up with a relatively straight arm | liāo | 撩 |
| split, chop down | pī quán | 劈拳 |
| squat | dūn | 蹲 |
| stamp with impetus forward and down | cuō dì | 蹉地 |
| stand with feet together | bìng bù | 并步 |
| step forward | shàng bù | 上步 |
| stomp; a heavy stamp | zhèn jiǎo | 震脚 |
| stride; a large step | mài bù | 迈步 |
| subdue the tiger post standing | fú hǔ zhuāng | 伏虎桩 |
| three attributes standing | sān cái zhuāng | 三才桩 |
| three bodies or trinity stance | sān tǐ shì | 三体式 |
| three bodies or trinity post standing | sān tǐ shì zhuāng | 三体势桩 |
| train skill | liàn gōng | 练功 |
| trample, step on | cǎi | 踩 |
| transformed power | huà jìn | 化劲 |
| trap, hold | ná | 拿 |
| tuck in, concave shape | kòu | 扣 |
| turn around | zhuàn shēn | 转身 |

| | | |
|---|---|---|
| twisting power | níng jìn | 拧劲 |
| urge, hurry, press | cuī | 催 |
| vital energy, breath, life force; air | qì | 气 |
| water, one of the five elements | shuǐ | 水 |
| will, intent, the intentional mind | yì | 意 |
| withdraw | chè bù | 撤步 |
| wood, one of the five elements | mù | 木 |
| wrap around, enclose in the arms | guǒ | 裹 |
| wrapping power | guǒ jìn | 裹劲 |
| Xingyiquan, 'form combined with intent' style | xíng yì quán | 形意拳 |
| Xinyi Liuhe Quan | xīn yì liù hé quán | 心意六合拳 |
| Yiquan, also called Dachengquan | yì quán | 意拳 |

## SECTION EIGHT: XINGYI MOVEMENT NAMES

| | | |
|---|---|---|
| Alligator Model | tuó xíng | 鼍形 |
| Ape Drops off a Branch | yuán hóu zhuì zhī | 猿猴坠枝 |
| Ape Kicks a Branch | yuán hóu dēng zhī | 猿猴蹬枝 |
| Ape Plucks a Peach | yuán hóu zhāi táo | 猿猴摘桃 |
| Bear Model | xióng xíng | 熊形 |
| Black Bear Leaves its Den | hēi xióng chū dòng | 黑熊出洞 |
| Black Dragon Overturns the Waves | wū lóng fān jiāng | 乌龙翻江 |
| Black Dragon Pours Water | wū lóng dào shuǐ | 乌龙倒水 |
| Black Tiger Leaves its Den | hēi hǔ chū dòng | 黑虎出洞 |
| Bridge | kuà shì | 跨势 |
| Bridging Skill | kuà zì gōng | 跨字功 |
| Brush Aside, Cover and Chop | lōu shǒu gài pī | 搂手盖劈 |
| Butt | dǐng shì | 顶势 |
| Butting Skill | dǐng zì gōng | 顶字功 |
| Cannon Punch, Pounding Fist | pào quán | 炮拳 |
| Cat Washes its Face | māo xǐ liǎn | 猫洗脸 |
| Chicken Model | jī xíng | 鸡形 |
| Close the Shoulders | hé jiān shì | 合肩势 |
| Closing Move | shōu shì | 收势 |
| Cross the River by Overturning the Waves | héng jiāng fān làng | 横江翻浪 |

| | | |
|---|---|---|
| Crosscut, Crossing Fist | héng quán | 横拳 |
| Crossways Heel Kick | héng dēng | 横蹬 |
| Crushing Fist, Driving Punch | bēng quán | 崩拳 |
| Cut to the Neck | qiē bō | 切脖 |
| Double Horse | shuāng mǎ xíng | 双马形 |
| Double Intercept | shuāng jié | 双截 |
| Double Wrap | shuāng guǒ | 双裹 |
| Double Shove | shuāng zhuàng zhǎng | 双撞掌 |
| Dragon and Tiger Play Together | lóng hǔ xiāng jiāo | 龙虎相交 |
| Dragon Model | lóng xíng | 龙形 |
| Draw | dài | 带 |
| Drill, Drilling Fist | zuān quán | 钻拳 |
| Drilling Hit | zuān dǎ | 钻打 |
| Driving Punch, Crushing Fist | bēng quán | 崩拳 |
| Eagle and Bear Combined | yīng xióng hé liàn | 鹰熊合练 |
| Eagle Model | yīng xíng | 鹰形 |
| Eagle Grasps | yīng zhuō | 鹰捉 |
| Eight Skills | bā zì gōng | 八字功 |
| Elbow Butt | dǐng zhǒu | 顶肘 |
| Elbow Cover | yǎn zhǒu | 掩肘 |
| Fierce Tiger Jumps over the Ravine | měng hǔ tiào jiàn | 猛虎跳涧 |
| Wheel Around and Pound | fān shēn pào | 翻身炮 |
| Four Techniques Of Chicken | jī xíng sì bǎ dòng zuò | 鸡形四把动作 |
| Golden Rooster Blocks Up | jīn jī shàng jià | 金鸡上架 |
| Golden Rooster Drinks Water | jīn jī zhuó shuǐ | 金鸡啄水 |
| Golden Rooster Heralds the Dawn | jīn jī bào xiǎo | 金鸡报晓 |
| Golden Rooster Pecks a Grain of Rice | jīn jī shí mǐ | 金鸡食米 |
| Golden Rooster Shakes its Feathers | jīn jī dǒu líng | 金鸡抖翎 |
| Golden Rooster Spreads its Wings | jīn jī zhǎn chì | 金鸡展翅 |
| Golden Rooster Stands on One Leg | jīn jī dú lì | 金鸡独立 |
| Golden Rooster Thrusts a Foot | jīn jī dēng jiǎo | 金鸡蹬脚 |
| Golden Rooster Treads on Snow | jīn jī tà xuě | 金鸡踏雪 |
| Guide | lǐng shì | 领势 |
| Guiding Skill | lǐng zì gōng | 领字功 |

| | | |
|---|---|---|
| Head Butt | tóu dǐng | 头顶 |
| Hibernating Dragon Shows Itself | zhé lóng chū xiàn | 蛰龙出现 |
| Horse Model | mǎ xíng | 马形 |
| Intercept | jié shì | 截势 |
| Intercepting Skill | jié zì gōng | 截字功 |
| Interception | jié shǒu | 截手 |
| Lazy Dragon Lies in the Road | lǎn lóng wò dào | 懒龙卧道 |
| Lead a Sheep Along | shùn shǒu qiān yáng | 顺手牵羊 |
| Lead left and Stick in right | zuǒ lǐng yòu zāi | 左领右栽 |
| Leaping Dragon | yuè bù lóng xíng | 跃步龙形 |
| Low Crushing Punch | xià bēng quán | 下崩拳 |
| Monkey To Four Corners | sì jiǎo hóu xíng | 四角猴形 |
| Monkey Model | hóu xíng | 猴形 |
| Monkey Pulls at its Leash | yuán hóu dào shéng | 猿猴捯绳 |
| Monkey Scrambles up a Pole | yuán hóu pá gān | 猿猴爬竿 |
| Monkey Scratches its Mark | yuán hóu guà yìn | 白猿挂印 |
| Monkey Sits on its Haunches | hóu dūn | 猴蹲 |
| Old Bear Shoves from its Shoulder | lǎo xióng zhuàng bǎng | 老熊撞膀 |
| Opening Move | qǐ shì | 起势 |
| Pass | yún shì | 云势 |
| Passing Skill | yún zì gōng | 云字功 |
| Plant a Hit | zāi dǎ | 栽打 |
| Pounding Fist, Cannon Punch | pào quán | 炮拳 |
| Pull and Knee Butt | lǔ shǒu xī zhuàng | 将手膝撞 |
| Pull, Knock Aside and Hit | lā bō dǎ | 拉拨打 |
| Push a Boat Downstream | shùn shuǐ tuī zhōu | 顺水推舟 |
| Push the Shutter to Gaze at the Moon | tuī chuāng wàng yuè | 推窗望月 |
| Push | tuī shǒu | 推手 |
| Restrain | lēi quán | 勒拳 |
| Scoop and Pull | tiāo lǔ | 挑捋 |
| Scoop | tiāo zhǎng | 挑掌 |
| Scooping Skill | tiāo zì gōng | 挑字功 |
| Shove | zhuàng zhǎng | 撞掌 |
| Single Horse | dān mǎ xíng | 单马形 |

| | | |
|---|---|---|
| Sit Astride the Tiger | kuà hǔ | 跨虎 |
| Slice to the Groin | liāo yīn zhǎng | 撩阴掌 |
| Snake Coils its Body | shé chán shēn | 蛇缠身 |
| Snake Model | shé xíng | 蛇形 |
| Sneak in a Hit | tōu dǎ | 偷打 |
| Sparrow Hawk Enters the Woods | yào zǐ rù lín | 鹞子入林 |
| Sparrow Hawk Folds its Wings | yào zǐ shù shēn | 鹞子束身 |
| Sparrow Hawk Model | yào xíng | 鹞形 |
| Sparrow Hawk Grasps a Shoulder | yào zǐ zhuā jiān | 鹞子抓肩 |
| Sparrow Hawk Grasps a Sparrow | yào zǐ zhuō què | 鹞子捉雀 |
| Sparrow Hawk Pierces the Sky | yào zǐ zuān tiān | 鹞子钻天 |
| Sparrow Hawk Spreads its Wings | yào zǐ zhǎn chì | 鹞子展翅 |
| Sparrow Hawk Wheels Over | yào zǐ fān shēn | 鹞子翻身 |
| Split, Splitting Fist | pī quán | 劈拳 |
| Spread Both Wings | shuāng zhǎn chì | 双展翅 |
| Spread | zhǎn shì | 展势 |
| Spreading Skill | zhǎn zì gōng | 展字功 |
| Stamp | zhèn jiǎo | 震脚 |
| Stomping Dragon Model | tà bù lóng xíng | 踏步龙形 |
| Straight Line Monkey Model | zhí tàng hóu xíng | 直趟猴形 |
| Stretch Out One Wing | dān zhǎn chì | 单展翅 |
| Stroke or Pull | lǔ shǒu | 捋手 |
| Stroke, Hook to Ear | lǔ shǒu guàn ér | 捋手贯耳 |
| Stroking Draw | lǔ dài | 捋带 |
| Swallow Pierces the Sky | yàn zǐ zuān tiān | 燕子钻天 |
| Swallow Skims the Water | yàn zǐ chāo shuǐ | 燕子抄水 |
| Swallow Spreads its Wings | yàn zǐ zhǎn chì | 燕子展翅 |
| Swinging Chop with Crossing Cut | lūn pī héng zhé | 抡劈横折 |
| T Stance Stab Down | dīng bù xià chā zhǎng | 丁步下插掌 |
| Tamp | tà zhǎng | 踏掌 |
| Three Basins on the Ground | sān pán luò dì | 三盘落地 |
| Tiger Braces | hǔ chēng | 虎撑 |
| Tiger Carries | hǔ tuō | 虎托 |
| Tiger Embraces | hǔ bào | 虎抱 |

APPENDIX 265

| | | |
|---|---|---|
| Tiger Model | hǔ xíng | 虎形 |
| Tiger Intercepts | hǔ jié | 虎截 |
| Tiger Pounces | hǔ pū | 虎扑 |
| Tiger Traps | hǔ lán | 虎拦 |
| Triple Palm Strike | sān zhǎng | 三掌 |
| Trundle | gǔn shǒu | 滚手 |
| Wedge-tailed Hawk Model | tāi xíng | 鸟台形 |
| White Ape Presents Fruit | bái yuán xiàn guǒ | 白猿献果 |
| White Crane Flashes Its Wings | bái hè liàng chì | 白鹤亮翅 |
| White Snake Coils its Body | bái shé chǎn shēn | 白蛇缠身 |
| White Snake Slithers through the Grass | bái shé bō cǎo | 白蛇拨草 |
| White Snake Spits its Tongue | bái shé tù xìn | 白蛇吐信 |
| Wind Sways the Lotus Leaves | fēng bǎi hē yè | 风摆荷叶 |
| Wrap | guǒ shǒu | 裹手 |
| Wrapping Skill | guǒ zì gōng | 裹字功 |

## SECTION NINE: TERMS THAT FURTHER DEFINE THE MOVEMENT

| | | |
|---|---|---|
| Advance | jìn bù | 进步 |
| Aligned Stance | shùn bù | 顺步 |
| Dodge | yáo shēn | 摇身 |
| Double | shuāng | 双 |
| Fixed Step, Stationary | yuán bù, yuán dì | 原步, 原地 |
| Left | zuǒ | 左 |
| Retreat | tuì bù | 退步 |
| Reverse Stance | ào bù | 拗步 |
| Right | yòu | 右 |
| Stamp | zhèn jiǎo | 震脚 |
| Step Around, Turn Around | huí shēn | 回身 |
| Step Forward | shàng bù | 上步 |
| Switchover Step | huàn bù | 换步 |
| Turn Around | zhuàn shēn | 转身 |
| Two-handed | shuāng shǒu | 双手 |
| Wheel Around | fān shēn | 翻身 |
| Withdraw | chē bù | 撤步 |

# PRONUNCIATION OF PINYIN, THE CHINESE NATIONAL PHONETIC ALPHABET FOR MANDARIN (WITH INTERNATIONAL PHONETIC ALPHABET EQUIVALENTS)

INITIALS (words can start with these consonants, or have a glide or vowel initial)

| PINYIN | IPA | ROUGH PRONUNCIATION GUIDE |
| --- | --- | --- |
| p | $p^h$ | Like English p̱et with a considerable puff of air. |
| b | p | Similar to the *pinyin* "p" but without the puff of air (unvoiced, neither English p̱et nor ḇet). |
| t | $t^h$ | Like English ṯag with a considerable puff of air. |
| d | t | Similar to the *pinyin* "t" but with no puff of air (unvoiced, not d̠og). |
| k | $k^h$ | Like English ḵill with a considerable puff of air. |
| g | k | Similar to the *pinyin* "k" but with no puff of air (unvoiced, not English g̱et). |
| c | $ts^h$ | Like exaggerating English caṯs̱. |
| z | ts | Like the *pinyin* "c" but without the puff of air (unvoiced). |
| ch | $tʂ^h$ | Somewhat similar to English c̱ẖat with a puff of air, but with the tip of the tongue rolled back. |
| zh | tʂ | Like the *pinyin* "ch" but with no puff of air (unvoiced). |
| q | $tɕ^h$ | Somewhat similar to English c̱ẖat with a puff of air, but with the front of the tongue raised and the tip on the lower teeth. |
| j | tɕ | Like the *pinyin* "q" but without the puff of air (unvoiced). |
| m | m | Like English m̱et. |
| n | n | Like English ṉet. |
| f | f | Similar to English f̱at, but with the teeth just touching lightly behind the lower lip. |
| s | s | Similar to English s̱et. |

| | | |
|---|---|---|
| sh | ʂ | Somewhat similar to English <u>sh</u>ow, but with the same tongue placement as the *pinyin* "ch" and "zh." |
| x | þ | Somewhat similar to English <u>sh</u>ine but with the same tongue placement as the *pinyin* "q" and "j." |
| h | χ | Raise the back of the tongue and let the breath come through the obstructed passage without vibrating the vocal cords. |
| l | l | Like English <u>l</u>et. |
| r | ɹ | Like the *pinyin* "sh" but with voicing. |

## FINALS

| | | |
|---|---|---|
| n | n | Like English pi<u>n</u>. |
| ng | ŋ | Like English si<u>ng</u>. |

## VOWELS

| | | |
|---|---|---|
| a | A a ɛ | Usually close to English f<u>a</u>ther (not p<u>a</u>t). Like y<u>e</u>t when written "-ian" or "yan." |
| e | ɤ e ɛ ə | Usually similar to English p<u>e</u>t, can tend towards a mid vowel. |
| i | i ɭ ɪ | Usually similar to English b<u>ee</u>. Similar to w<u>e</u>t when written "ui." After c, z, s, ch, zh, sh, and r it is similar to s<u>ir</u>. |
| o | o u | Usually close to English r<u>o</u>ll. Similar to c<u>ow</u> when written "ao," and <u>owe</u> when in "ou." |
| u | u y | Usually similar t English o b<u>oo</u>t. After the *pinyin* "x", "q", and "j" and in the vowel groups starting with these consonants, it is pronounced "ü". |
| ü | y | Similar to French <u>ü</u>. It is written after "n" or "l," because these are the only positions where both "u" and "ü" are possible |
| y | i | A glide, partially like an English 'y', tending towards i. |
| w | u | A glide, partially like an English 'w', tending towards u. |

## INITIALS

| place of articulation \ manner of articulation | Unaspirated Stops | Aspirated Stops | Unaspirated Affricates | Aspirated Affricates | Nasals | Fricatives | Voiced Continuants |
|---|---|---|---|---|---|---|---|
| bilabials | b | p | | | m | | |
| labio-dentals | | | | | | f | |
| dental-alveolars | d | t | z | c | n | s | l |
| retroflexes | | | zh | ch | | sh | r |
| palatals | | | j | q | | x | |
| velars | g | k | | | | h | |

| TONES IN PINYIN | | | |
|---|---|---|---|
| NUMBER | PINYIN | NAME | RANGE |
| 1 | ¯ | high level | 55 |
| 2 | ´ | high rising | 35 |
| 3 | ˇ | dipping | 214 |
| 4 | ` | high falling | 51 |
| none | ° or blank | neutral | in context |

With tone sandhi, tones may change according to the preceding or following tone.

The tone marking is put over the main vowel when there are two vowels written together (usually involving the pronunciation of y or w).

## ABOUT THE TRANSLATOR

Andrea Falk has practised external and internal Chinese martial arts since 1972, and has concentrated on internal styles since 1981. She started Xingyiquan with Xia Bohua in 1981. In 2001 she met Di Guoyong, and has trained with him ever since.

Andrea honed her skills in Vancouver, Beijing, and Shanghai – with a Bachelor of Arts majoring in Chinese, a Bachelor of Physical Education and later a Master of Physical Education with an emphasis on biomechanics and coaching science from the University of British Columbia. She trained in wushu full time from 1980 to 1983 at the Beijing Physical Culture Institute, earning an advanced studies diploma in Wushu under the tutelage of professor Xia Bohua. There she gained the basics of Yang and Chen style Taijiquan, Baguazhang, Xingyiquan, Chaquan, and modern Wushu (Changquan and weapons). She also spent the summers of 1984 and 1986 at the Beijing Physical Culture Institute. She started learning purely traditionally after 1986, visiting China on extended trips as often as possible. She trains Chen style Taijiquan and Baguazhang as an inside apprentice of Huan Dahai (and with elder martial brothers) in Shanghai, and Xingyiquan and Baguazhang as a close student and friend of Di Guoyong in Beijing. When not in China or traveling to teach, she is usually in Québec city or at a cottage in the Laurentian hills, Canada.

Andrea has worked teaching and translating since 1983. She founded the wushu centre in Montreal in 1984, in Victoria in 1992, and has been based again in Quebec since 2003. She has taught Chen Taijiquan, Baguazhang, and Xingyiquan around North America and Europe, but especially in Canada and England. For years Andrea translated materials for her own students, and in 2000 set up tgl books to try to bring the best Chinese martial arts books to a wider audience.

trois gros lapins traversent le chemin

www.ingramcontent.com/pod-product-compliance
Lightning Source LLC
Chambersburg PA
CBHW071815230426
43670CB00013B/2458